ROONEY

WAYNE'S WORLD

FRANK WORRALL

MAINSTREAM
PUBLISHING
EDINBURGH AND LONDON

This edition 2006
Copyright © Frank Worrall, 2005

First published in Great Britain in 2005 by
MAINSTREAM PUBLISHING COMPANY
(EDINBURGH) LTD
7 Albany Street
Edinburgh EH1 3UG

ISBN 1 84596 144 7

A catalogue record for this book is available
from the British Library

All internal illustrations © Cleva

Typeset in Frutiger and Galliard

Printed in Great Britain by
Cox & Wyman Ltd, Reading

For Angela, Natalie,
Frankie Lennon, Jude Cantona,
Mam and Dad,
Bob and Stephen.

ACKNOWLEDGEMENTS

SPECIAL THANKS: Alex Butler and Colin Forshaw.

THANKS: My publisher Bill Campbell, Graeme Blaikie, Paul Murphy, Sharon Campbell and Ailsa Bathgate at Mainstream; Lee Clayton at the *Daily Mail*; Alan English at the *Sunday Times*; Natasha Harding, John Perry, Jonathan Worsnop, Neil Rowlands, Dave Morgan, Steve Waring, Alan Feltham, Nick Chapman (ICF) and the boys on *Sun Sport*; Derek Whitfield, Adrian Baker, Duncan Craig, Pravina Patel, Andy Bucklow and John Fitzpatrick at the *Mail on Sunday*; Peter Willis at the *Daily Mirror*; Bruce Waddell at the *Daily Record*; Matthew Clark at *The People*; Andy Coulson, Neil Wallis and Nick Jones at the *News of the World*; Craig Tregurtha at the *The Times*; Hugh Sleight, editor of *FourFourTwo*; Nick Louth of MSN for background information on Malcolm Glazer; Piers Morgan, Mike O'Brien, Tom Henderson-Smith, Lee Hassall (Merry Xmas Lee, wherever you are), Roz Hoskinson, David Welch, Paul Collett, Chase, Miles Hedley, Roy Stone, Paul and Karen, and, of course, Wayne and Coleen.

RESPECT: *United We Stand*, *Red Issue*, Cantona, the boys from the K Stand, Patrick McGoohan and Joe Strummer – 'If Adolf Hitler flew in today, they'd send a limousine anyway.'

CONTENTS

1

TRANS-EUROPE EXPRESS

LET'S GET ONE THING STRAIGHT RIGHT NOW. HE WAS NO PELÉ and no Diego Maradona at Euro 2004 – indeed he would have struggled to even get the nod as the tournament's top man. Pelé won the World Cup for Brazil in Sweden in 1958, Maradona did the same for Argentina in Mexico in 1986, and Cristiano Ronaldo and Theo Zagorakis, arguably, had more of an overall, and effective, impact in the last European Championships. The former breathed life into a dormant Portuguese home nation with his wing wizardry, the latter drove on the unfancied Greeks to a miraculous victory with his disciplined midfield holding and inspired captaincy.

No, in a measured assessment of his first international tournament, Wayne Rooney's place lies somewhere just beneath those hallowed gents. A year older than Pelé when he won his first World Cup winner's medal, the 18-year-old Scouser's role was more that of a Gazza. Without the tears, but still the same disappointment at a job not completed: a potential not wholly realised. Yet.

Just as Paul Gascoigne had lit up the 1990 World Cup finals in Italy, so Rooney proved the catalyst for English hopes 14 years later in the Euros. He had certainly come a long way: just the

11

previous season his manager at Everton, David Moyes, had felt it necessary to reprimand him for kicking a ball about in the street with his mates, only hours after he had hit the winner against Arsenal.

Rooney's Euro 2004 odyssey started, as do most good things in life, with a kiss – a good luck one from his mum Jeanette, a former dinner lady at his secondary school, as the squad jetted off – and ended with a bang as his right foot thudded into the Lisbon turf, calling an early halt to his hypnotic tournament contribution. In between, there was enough magic to convince us England at last have a new truly world-class footballer. A powder-keg mix of Gazza's skills, Alan Shearer's determination and Roy Keane's hard-headed refusal to concede any ground to the opposition.

A man-boy who looked like Shrek with the power of a rampaging bull, he was also rapidly becoming a walking, talking football record book. Sixteen months earlier – at the tender age of 17 years and 111 days – he had become his country's youngest ever player in the messy friendly defeat against Australia. Still 17, Rooney then topped that by becoming England's youngest ever scorer in the 2–1 European Championship qualifier win in Macedonia.

He arrived in Portugal with thirteen caps and five goals, including two in the final warm-up match against Iceland. Rooney also arrived as England's number two striker, behind the supposedly irreplaceable Michael Owen. Within three weeks, he would usurp Owen as number one and lay down his marker as an altogether more rounded, complete player.

Manchester United manager Sir Alex Ferguson had already aired the view that Rooney could develop into the sort of intelligent player who could one day operate from an advanced midfield role. For Ferguson, that would mean someone who could play in 'the hole' – that definable space between midfield and attack. For England manager Sven-Göran Eriksson, it would translate into the attacking head of a midfield diamond.

In England's opener against France – dubbed 'Le Crunch' by Fleet Street hacks desperate to crank up the ante – Rooney did indeed move between midfield and the front line, confusing his man-marker Mikael Silvestre into giving away a penalty and aggravating the preening midfielders of Les Bleus who had come to showboat. The arrogant Claude Makele, in particular, suffered as Rooney tailed him non-stop. Rooney later admitted his biting tackles 'on the Frenchman were partly motivated by an urge for revenge after the Chelsea man had tried to wind him up, saying he was a mere pup. Woof! Woof!

The match was made for the boy. He had shown in the real crunch games – the home qualifier with the Turks at Sunderland's Stadium of Light the previous April, and the final qualifier in Turkey in October – that he was made of stern stuff. Taking on the tough-tackling Turks at their own high-pressured game, he had twice given their back four an uncomfortable night at the office. Now here he was, puffing out that barrel chest at the original Stadium of Light in Lisbon, England's number 9 at 18 years old, against the defending European champions. A 64,000 full house in Benfica's magnificent home and a TV audience of millions around the world. This was to be the moment Rooney metamorphosed from local hero into international football's most wanted man.

Yet it had only been 18 months previously that the name Rooney had hit the headlines throughout Britain – with *that* pile-driver free-kick goal for Everton, the one that gave David Seaman no chance and ended Arsenal's unbeaten run. Now for worldwide acclaim, and he was to achieve it without even scoring against the French.

Rooney's early tussle with Zinedine Zidane, arguably the best player on the planet, also rekindled images of Gazza. Just as the Geordie boy had shouted and joked with Lothar Mattheus in the World Cup semi-final in 1990, so the Scouse scally winked and smiled at the undoubted genius of the modern game. The message was clear: you don't scare me.

England boss Eriksson elected to dump his diamond formation, sending out a midfield ripe in attacking prowess but worryingly thin in terms of a defensive shield. The holding role had been earmarked for Nicky Butt, but the Manchester United man was out injured.

To compound fears that Eriksson's men could have a busy night keeping the French at bay, centre-back John Terry was also ruled out. In the absence of Rio Ferdinand – who was still serving a ban from the January of that year for missing a drugs test – Chelsea's Terry had proved a dependable stand-in, a man styled in the 'Thou shalt not pass' manifesto of ex-Arsenal and England stopper Tony Adams. It meant England would face the challenge of the mighty French with Tottenham's Ledley King, who had only made the squad at the 11th hour, starting his first match and with no enforcer in midfield. A true case of no Butt . . . just what ifs . . .

Still, it was England who struck the first blow, Frank Lampard rising to head home a David Beckham free-kick. Zinedine Zidane's brace then ended the challenge of the Three Lions, with that injury-time penalty the ultimate killer. Yet England – and Rooney – did not deserve such a cruel fate. OK, in terms of possession they conceded to the French 46 per cent to 54, but the midfield performed valiantly without Butt, and Rooney was the man of the match, often getting as stuck in as Butt would have done. He won a second-half penalty after Silvestre got sick of his attentions and hauled him down. Unfortunately, Beckham's excuse for a spot-kick was easily saved by bogeyman Fabien Barthez.

Yet the question remains: just why did Eriksson take off Rooney on 76 minutes? He was the focal point for his team and giving the French nightmares. To cap it all, the decision led to France's equaliser when Rooney's replacement Emile Heskey brought down Zidane outside the box, with Zizou punishing him with an immaculate curling free-kick. Later Eriksson would claim, 'Rooney tired, but he had a good run to win the penalty and he always looked dangerous. If we played this game again, I wouldn't change the tactics.'

Very few Englishmen agreed. Even Michael Owen backed the view of the majority who would have left Rooney on – even at his own expense. 'He was fantastic,' said the other-half of the all-Merseyside England attack. As the old adage goes: if it ain't broke, don't fix it, and Rooney was far from broken. Hot from the sun, but it had been gradually cooling after the 7.45 p.m. kick-off, and at the time he was substituted the boy was still full of running.

After the game against France, Eriksson's men had to regroup, lick their wounds and recuperate for three days. For Rooney it meant reassuring chats, golf, swimming and pinball with his England 'minder' and fellow Scouser, Steven Gerrard. Then it was on to Coimbra, two hours from Lisbon, and the potential banana-skin encounter with Switzerland. Supposedly the whipping boys of Group B, they nevertheless had beaten Ireland in topping their qualifying group and had held the Croatians to a 0–0 draw four days before their clash with England.

Debate was raging in the press over Eriksson's team formation – with some pundits calling for a defensive anchorman to be installed. Tony Adams, then manager of Wycombe Wanderers, led the call for a more balanced formation, but put himself out on a limb by insisting the likes of Owen Hargreaves should be accommodated at the expense of Rooney. Clearly, the transition from top player to emerging manager is fraught with mental delusions. Eriksson needed a win and that meant playing his top striker. If Adams's formula were to be realistically applied, it would surely have meant leaving out Owen, whose end-of-season slump for Liverpool had continued against the French. He was in dismal form.

England faced a late afternoon kick-off, and the heat was much fiercer in Coimbra than Lisbon. Temperatures pitchside soared past the 100 degrees Fahrenheit mark, and it was undoubtedly tough for the English players. There again, it was just as tough for the Swiss. The fans from Blighty continued their light-hearted adventure around Portugal – no incidents were reported outside the ground as both sets of supporters mingled. Eriksson resisted the temptation to tinker – sticking with a 4-4-2 formation. Paul Scholes was on the left and John Terry replaced the unfortunate-to-be-dropped Ledley King in the heart of the defence. If the French match was the one that announced Rooney's arrival on the world stage, this one was an emphatic confirmation. He became the youngest-ever European

Championship scorer after 23 minutes when he headed home an inch-perfect cross from Owen. However, the man-boy's early reputation as a volcano waiting to blow preceded him – it is worth recording that five minutes before his record-breaking goal, he was booked for a rash, studs-up challenge on Swiss keeper Joerg Stiel. If you accept the boy, you accept him warts and all.

Ten minutes after his goal, Rooney attempted a hopeful 25-yard blast, but it was comfortably held by Stiel. England went in 1–0 up at the interval. The second half belonged to Rooney after England got a boost when Bernt Hass was red-carded on the hour for picking up a second yellow card. Rooney probed, twisted and tormented his ten-men Swiss interrogators, eventually earning due reward. Three-quarters of the way through the game, Owen Hargreaves picked out Darius Vassell with a sweet cross; Vassell then gently held up the ball for Rooney whose shot hit the post and keeper Stiel before trickling into the net.

Controversy surrounded the goal – was it really an own goal? No. UEFA quite rightly later confirmed that Rooney's original shot was on target and credited it to him. The decision meant Rooney joined Sweden's Henrik Larsson and France's Zidane as joint top scorers on two goals. Eight minutes from time Steven Gerrard fired home to make it 3–0 when he hit Gary Neville's pass beyond the despairing Stiel. Eriksson took the third goal as a cue to withdraw Rooney for the second game in succession, with Kieron Dyer coming on as his replacement. Full time and England celebrated what had turned out to be a comfortable victory. Their Euro 2004 bandwagon was finally on the road after that emotion-draining reversal against the French.

Rooney, inevitably, hogged the headlines. He was bubbling at breaking another record – but just as grateful the second goal had been awarded to him. His self-effacing modesty was touching. He said, 'I hit the second as hard as I could and luckily it went in. For the first one, Michael Owen put it right on my head.' That second goal earned Rooney a further accolade, making him only the third Englishman to score a brace in a

European Championship match. He joined Alan Shearer and Teddy Sheringham, who both scored twice against Holland in Euro 96. No English player has ever netted more than twice in a European Championship fixture.

Boss Eriksson was delighted for Rooney after the match. He said, 'He is a fantastic talent. He played very well against France and scored two this time, one more beautiful than the other. I hope he goes on like that for the rest of the tournament and after it. I think he'll be even better in the future. He can improve still, I'm sure of that.'

Eriksson had to dispel a festering claim that skipper David Beckham was actually picking the team. The Swede insisted there had been no player revolt when it had been suggested he would revert to the midfield diamond formation against the Swiss.

Yet Beckham had *already* told the press he and the players had asked Eriksson to play a flat-four midfield. Eriksson laughed off claims of a blow-up. He said, 'I pick the team, I had meetings with the players of course – I started doing that in 1979 and have always done it with my teams. We tested both formations in training and I decided what to do.'

Rooney then proved he was growing up quickly by also offering his opinions on the general team display. He said, 'It was a big day for us and we came through in the end. It wasn't the best performance but when the Swiss had a man sent off we took advantage. It's a big relief after the France game. We're back on track now, and we've got to go on and win the next match.' That meant a trip back to the Benfica stadium in Lisbon and a make-or-break last group game against the tricky Croats. Lose – and Rooney and Co. would be going home in shame. Win – and a quarter-final against the Greeks or Portuguese loomed.

Rooney-mania was now in full swing. Fans in the Stadium of Light held aloft lifesize cut-outs of the Everton star. Chelsea owner Roman Abramovich had decided he also wanted a slice of the action. The Russian billionaire arrived in Portugal via his private yacht and made his way to the England match with his new coach José Mourinho and chief executive Peter Kenyon.

The young Scouser would not disappoint – adding millions to an already escalating transfer value.

It would later emerge that, for once, Rooney was not the major target. Mourinho had set his sights on Liverpool's Gerrard, although that move would be thwarted by the player's fears for his family's safety on Merseyside if he quit for Stamford Bridge.

The omens before the Croatia contest were good. The weather was milder and more suited to England's fast-flowing style of football – and the kick-off was at the cooler 7.45 p.m. local time. This was the match when even the normally placid Eriksson would go overboard about Rooney, describing the young Liverpudlian as the new Pelé. Eriksson would say, 'I don't remember anyone making such an impact on a tournament since Pelé in the 1958 World Cup in Sweden.'

Rooney sparked off the love-in with a fine performance, grabbing another brace and setting up Paul Scholes for his first England goal in 30 matches as Eriksson's men won 4–2. Yet it didn't start well. England went behind in the sixth minute when Niko Kovac scored off the rebound after keeper David James had punched out a shaky clearance from Ashley Cole. Rooney rallied the troops, sending Scholes through for a one-on-one with Tomislav Butina, the keeper just managing to thwart the Manchester United midfielder. The ginger head made amends six minutes before half time. Steven Gerrard found Frank Lampard, who sent Owen clear with a fine pass. Butina came out to stop Owen and the ball broke to Rooney. The 18 year old showed he possessed a fine footballing brain. Instead of trying to snatch all the glory, he selflessly headed the ball back to Scholes who, in turn, headed England level.

You could sense the relief in Scholes's celebration of his goal. It had been a long time coming – his last international goal was back in June 2001 away to Greece. His drought was all the more baffling when you consider he scored 13 for Manchester United as they clinched the title in 2003. Was he being played out of position – usually on the left – by Eriksson? Was it affecting his game? In the heat of Lisbon that day Scholes felt the lifting of a heavy load, but it was not to be enough to delay his retirement from the England set-up after the tournament.

The 29 year old, still on a high, returned the favour to Rooney. In first-half stoppage time he turned creator, setting up Rooney, who let fly a powerful shot past Butina. Half-time ice packs, and a calm team-talk by Eriksson sent England back out refreshed. The Swede has his critics – chief among them Middlesbrough skipper Gareth Southgate, who scoffed at his 'Captain Mainwaring' team-talk at half time in England's 2–1 World Cup 2002 loss to Brazil – but this time he got it right with a suitably calm appraisal. Keep doing what you did at the end of the first half, and we're through. Now Rooney was simply unstoppable. It was all over bar the shouting on 68 minutes. Rooney took a pass from Owen and blasted the ball home to make it 3–1, claiming his fourth goal of the tournament. Igor Tudor pulled it back to 3–2 with a header, but Lampard ended the contest when he smashed the ball past Butina after a tidy solo run. It was another milestone for Rooney and England – the first time the boys from Blighty had qualified for the knockout stages of the European Championships outside of England. The official stats from UEFA showed that possession was equal, yet England had 19 shots on goal while the Croats had 13.

In the other Group B match, France beat the Swiss 3–1 and would join England in the quarter-finals. As group winners, they would meet Greece, while England had what, on paper at least, looked the tougher task: to beat the host nation.

Of as much significance to Rooney watchers was the fact that his most recent record-breaking feat had been topped. Teenager Johann Vonlathen now became the youngest scorer in the tournament's history after pulling the Swiss level. At eighteen years, four months and twenty days he was more than three months younger than Rooney.

Again, Rooney stole the headlines. Eriksson was quick to elaborate upon his view of the boy: 'I don't really know what to say. He's absolutely fantastic, not only at scoring goals but he plays football – he's a complete footballer. He deserves all the attention and all the front-page headlines. I sometimes feel I shouldn't say too much, but he has been absolutely incredible. I don't need to tell him how to score goals.'

Skipper Beckham backed Eriksson's comparison of Rooney with Pelé. He said, 'I think he's probably right. It's a great compliment, but I think he deserves it because of how he is performing.' And Rooney's closest England pal Steven Gerrard also weighed in with the platitudes. He said, 'On current form, he is the best player in Europe. Everything about his game is spot-on, and he can help us win the tournament.'

Win the tournament? Well . . . amid the euphoria the more seasoned of us England followers certainly had hope in our hearts but also doubt. Certainly, Rooney was playing out of his skin, sometimes carrying out-of-sort superstars like Beckham and Owen, but what if his form dried up? Or worse still, what if he got sent off or injured? What ifs . . . again.

It took grumpy Croatia boss Otto Baric to pour some much-needed cold water on all the hot air. After his team's defeat, he said, 'Rooney is a very good player – although I wouldn't say a phenomenon. There are at least ten players in Europe who may stop him.'

England had just three days to calm down, tone up and prepare for their most important match since that 2002 World Cup quarter-final against Brazil. Now the stakes were at their highest for Eriksson. For all their attacking zeal, his team had continued to often look dozy at the back and to lack a biting edge in midfield. With no Nicky Butt, his options were limited. He could choose Owen Hargreaves as his midfield enforcer/defensive shield. But the Bayern Munich man's form had been indifferent. Or how about employing Ledley King in the Butt role? After all, it was one he had performed many times for Spurs. No, he would not even consider that one – which was a great pity. No, he would gamble all against his old adversary Luis Felipe Scolari, coach of Portugal and formerly, of course, in charge of Brazil: the man who had beaten him hands down when the dice tumbled in Japan.

The stark facts say that Portugal reached the semi-finals of Euro 2004 by beating England 6–5 on penalties, after it had ended 2–2 on 120 minutes. Michael Owen, at last showing glimpses of his old form, had given England a dream start after two minutes twenty-four seconds with a master poacher's goal. David James's massive kick was headed into Owen's path by Costinha and the little man did brilliantly to flick the ball into the net beyond the helpless Ricardo.

Tactically, the early goal presented a problem. It put England on the back foot, under a constant onslaught, as the Portuguese sought an equaliser. It also preyed heavily on Eriksson's mind. Here was a man indoctrinated in the Italian game of cat-and-mouse, where survival was dependent upon maintaining a defensive monopoly. So England defended . . . and defended . . . and defended. Problem was, they could not hold out – how could they, given that the midfield was essentially attack-minded, with Beckham, Lampard, Gerrard and Scholes? Well, they could have also attacked; they could have taken the game to their hosts. But no, that was not within Eriksson's natural remit.

His men made it doubly difficult by giving away possession for long periods. It started to fall apart big-time from the moment Rooney broke his foot while battling Jorge Andrade for the ball. His right leg seemed as if it was glued to the turf in that moment of absolute dread for England fans. When he got help, we all knew it was all over as the boy wonder started crying out in pain.

Replaced by Darius Vassell, the hopes of a nation went with him. The Aston Villa man had proved himself time and again as England's super sub, but now he was required to fill in for most of the match. He was no Rooney: his main magic lay in his speed and ability to finish in tight spots. He could not be expected to also conduct the orchestra, as Rooney had done for the past two weeks.

Now it was as if the Portuguese had been given a second wind. Attack followed attack, and Eriksson finally put up the white flag shortly after the interval, taking off the creative genius of Paul Scholes for the . . . well, the Phil Neville-ishness of Phil Neville. The aim was for the less talented of the Neville brothers to stick close with the attacking midfield genius of Deco. It did not work, as the Brazilian-born maestro frequently left him in his wake.

21

Scolari decided to play a trump card – bringing on the attacking Simao Sabrosa in place of the defensive Costinha. And then, showing Eriksson how it could be done with Beckham if he ever mustered enough guts, took off skipper Luis Figo for Helder Postiga. Figo sulked away to the dressing-room: without him Portugal waltzed towards the semi-final they believed was their destiny.

By now Manchester United's own teenage wonder boy, the 19-year-old Ronaldo, was creating havoc every time he floated into the England half. Luckily for Eriksson, Ashley Cole was having his best game for the national side, and his containment efforts on the Madeira-born genius managed to limit the damage down the right.

It could not last. Ronaldo decided to bypass the courageous Cole, taking his bag of tricks into the centre of midfield and through the very heart of the England defence. The equaliser inevitably arrived. Postiga's headed goal took the match into extra time and England's luck was out. A perfectly legitimate Sol Campbell goal was disallowed by ref Urs Meier on the grounds that John Terry had impeded Ricardo when the three of them went up for Beckham's free-kick. Rui Costa then went on to hammer the ball past a helpless David James to make it 2–1, but Frank Lampard equalised from close range.

The penalty sideshow began with Beckham missing – for the second time in this tournament – for England and ended with Portugal keeper Ricardo firing the winner past James.

In the final analysis, Eriksson bottled it while Scolari got it right, the former trying to hold on to a slender lead by sending on defensive substitutes, the latter deciding that his all-out marauders would eventually win the day. In fairness to the Swede, he had been the manager who, a full 16 months earlier, had been brave enough to give Rooney his international debut at the tender age of 17.

There were other contributing factors in the defeat: Portugal were the host nation – although you might never have guessed from the massed bank of England flags around the Stadium of Light – and were more adept to the steamy night heat; the referee denied England a perfectly acceptable goal; England still cannot take a decent penalty; and Rooney got hurt, leaving England without their talisman.

Can that last sentence really be correct? How can it be that an 18-year-old boy's absence should disrupt the national team's performance to such an extent that they can turn potential victory into irrevocable defeat? Surely the talisman should be the man from Real Madrid or the former European Footballer of the Year from Liverpool? That it *was* Rooney whom the manager, the fans and the team looked to for ultimate inspiration tells us much about him. The looks of a big schoolboy, but the talent of a saviour.

After the match Eriksson was quick to praise Rooney and absolve himself of tactical blame. He said, 'I wouldn't change anything selection-wise. That was our best 11. They were 1–0 down and they gambled. They had a lot of players up front, and if we were fresher we could have scored on the counter attack. We have shown many times we are one of the best teams. We can beat any team. And Wayne Rooney is now a big star not just in England but in European and world football.'

Eriksson was also honest enough to admit that this tournament failure hurt much more than defeat in Japan. He said, 'When we went to the World Cup, I don't know if we said we could win it, or should win it, although during the tournament we started to believe it could be possible. Here, though, I had always been convinced that we were one of the teams that could win it. We didn't, and I am very sorry about that.'

At least for the likes of Rooney and Ashley Cole, the other undoubted success of the England touring party, there would be, fate permitting, many more Euros and World Cups. Big names like Beckham and Gary Neville had under-performed, and, at 29, neither could look to the future as optimistically. Neville contended that England had gone out simply because of a poor surface for penalty-taking. He said, 'It's three times for me now [defeat on penalties]. I suppose the cynics will say it is a mental thing. It was as much down to the penalty spot as anything.

When David Beckham took his penalty the spot just gave way.' And Frank Lampard attempted to reinforce the view England had been cheated by the referee. He said, 'We had a goal at full time that was basically a fair goal taken away. There was nothing wrong with it.'

Beckham reacted angrily to suggestions that he had been off the boil in Portugal but at least found the time to drag himself out of his self-absorption to echo Eriksson's views on Rooney. The skipper's tournament had been bedevilled by his own sense of aggrievement with the press after allegations earlier in the year of his liaisons with Spanish temptress Rebecca Loos and his own incorrectly held belief that he was a better player in central midfield than out on the right wing. Real Madrid coach Carlos Queiroz had pandered to his demands, playing him in the centre at the Bernabéu, but he lacked the pace to cover tackles, and the game would often pass him by. No, he remained the best crosser of a ball from the right wing in the world: that was his forte.

Unfortunately, in Portugal he had tended to move infield at times, as if desperate to prove he should have been there from the start, and his performances backed up the notion that he may have been sulking at being stuck out on the right.

Beckham said of Rooney, 'The biggest positives have been the fans and Wayne Rooney. There was the disappointment of Wayne getting the injury. It was a sad ending to a tournament in which he has been unbelievable.'

But there would be no heroes' welcome on their return to England. Eriksson and his men were ushered through a back-door at Luton airport, with less than 100 flag-waving fans welcoming them home. And most of them had come to greet Rooney. The majority of fans believed Eriksson and his men had under-performed – that they should at least have bettered their quarter-final spot in World Cup 2002. Eriksson is regarded as a lucky manager – it had been his good fortune to stumble upon the England head coach's job when the best batch of youngsters since 1966 was breaking through. Yet his own ingrained cautiousness and negative tactics were now seen to be holding back progress. Apart from Wayne, who seemed to just go out and play his own natural game whatever the opposition.

Rooney had broken a metatarsal bone in his right foot, and would be out of action for at least two months. It was to be the end of the first act for Rooney on the international stage but only the beginning of what would be an extraordinary domestic drama to secure his signature while he recuperated from his injury and post-tournament trauma. Exit boy wonder: enter old man Fergie.

2

BOY TO MAN

IT WAS THE BEST OF TIMES; IT WAS THE WORST OF TIMES. Wayne Rooney limped back to Everton Football Club after his early summer of adventure and sighed heavily. In his heart, he knew things would never be the same again. How could they? Away from his international buddies – like Stevie Gerrard – he suddenly felt a deep loneliness and a realisation that he had reached the end of the line at Goodison.

His mind flitted back to the time when he had shown off a T-shirt – underneath his Everton kit after scoring – with the words, 'Once a blue, always a blue.' He cringed a little: those words would soon come back to haunt him. The problem was he still loved his boyhood club, but his ambition told him it was time to move on. He wanted to test himself in the European Champions League, against the best the Continent had to offer; he wanted to relive those marvellous, if unfulfilled, moments he and his England teammates had experienced in Portugal a month earlier.

Could he do that at Everton? Well, the manager was potentially top-notch, although they had had their disagreements about when Rooney should play or not. David Moyes was from the same stock as Manchester United's Alex Ferguson: a tough Scot who had protected Rooney from press intrusion and introduced him sparingly, just as the great man had with Ryan Giggs. Yet, Moyes was a more approachable autocrat, one who would have frowned at some of Ferguson's fiercer dressing-room rantings. He was a modern version of the man: toned down, more liberal and approachable, yet just as fiercely ambitious. In his early 40s, he had his best years ahead of him. Rooney could work with him. No, Moyes was not a major problem.

But money was. Not just personal wages – although, of course, Rooney could quadruple his £13,000-a-week salary by moving – but hard cash to back up both his ambition and that of Moyes. Everton were in desperate financial trouble – in debt to the tune of £60 million with the club's two major shareholders Bill Kenwright and Paul Gregg at each other's throats as they tried to find a feasible way out of the nightmare. There was no easy way out: no sugar daddy was on the horizon. In fact, there was only ever one realistic solution to it all and that was to sell their biggest asset: Rooney. That way the boy got his transfer and better toys to play with, while Everton bought breathing space and the odd £10 million in the kitty for Moyes to deal with in the transfer market.

Just as the solution was being mooted behind closed doors, and digested, another problem emerged. How would it look to the long-suffering Everton fans if the board were to sell off their hero? Kenwright had been seen as a saviour when he had rescued the club a decade earlier; he did not want to be the scapegoat if Rooney went. This is where the boy came into his own. Many have questioned if he will turn out like Paul Gascoigne and whether he will be able to cope with the demands of fame. Well, let's look at the obstacles he had to overcome to pull on that Manchester United shirt. His strength indicates a mental toughness and durability few have credited him with.

In the first instance, it would mean leaving his boyhood club, the only team he had ever been interested in. His blood ran blue – how could he ever quit? Rooney had first attracted the attention of Goodison at the tender age of nine, when scout Bob Pendleton spotted him playing for Copplehouse Colts in the

Walton and Kirkdale Junior League. Pendleton had no problem persuading Wayne's mother Jeanette and father Wayne snr that their son should sign for Everton – the Rooneys were an Evertonian family.

Ray Hall, director of Everton's youth academy, quickly recognised Pendleton had found a gem when he was introduced to the boy Rooney. Hall told BBC Sport: 'When you get an experienced scout quivering when you talk to the lad, you know he's a special talent.' Rooney netted 99 goals in his last season with Copplehouse – and even made Manchester United sit up when he scored with a scissor kick at the age of ten playing for Everton juniors against the Old Trafford club's juniors.

When he moved up to secondary school, Rooney also moved away from district football, and into Everton's academy full-time. His progress was so swift that he was playing for the Under-19 side when he was 15. Walter Smith was Everton manager at the time. The Scot had won every domestic trophy at Glasgow Rangers and knew a talent when he spotted one. He would later admit his biggest regret at Goodison – and indeed one of his biggest in football – was that he had been unable to give Rooney his first-team debut at 15 because FA rules did not allow schoolboys to play at that level.

Rooney also won early international honours with Everton – four England schools caps and twelve England Under-17 caps – and scored eight goals for the club during their run to the FA Youth Cup final in 2001. When Rooney broke through into the Goodison first team at the age of 16, few people would have predicted he would leave the club within two years: the bond was that deep. He made his debut against Spurs in the 2–2 draw at White Hart Lane in August 2002 and opened his goalscoring account with two goals in the 3–0 Worthington Cup win at Wrexham in October.

The glory continued apace for both player and club. In December, he won the BBC Young Sports Personality of the Year award and on 17 January 2003 signed a new deal to keep him at Goodison until the end of the 2005–06 season. A month later he made his England debut in the humiliating 3–1 defeat to Australia at Upton Park.

Rooney had always been destined to sign for the Toffees – he had even refused to remove his blue Everton top when he had a trial for Liverpool at Anfield. His bedroom at the family's council home in Croxteth was a shrine to the club – adorned with posters and pennants and set off by the Everton car number plate in the window. His dad Wayne was also a big fan and had taken him to his first match. Mum Jeanette and brothers Graham and John also loved the Blues. Surely it was Wayne's fate to remain at the club he and his family idolised? He would need to be tough to walk away – didn't he owe a certain loyalty to Everton and, for that matter, to his family?

It could not have been easy to tell his father that he was going to quit their dream team – especially when it meant he would be joining those much-despised arch-rivals up the other end of the East Lancashire Road. His England pal Stevie Gerrard had been faced with a similar dilemma when Chelsea had come in for him a few weeks earlier. In the end, he had decided to stay at Anfield when, in long-term career terms at least, a move to Stamford Bridge was a wiser option. With Roman Abramovich's millions, a set of superior players and a European champion, José Mourinho, as manager, Gerrard would have been lining up for a club on the brink of potential mega success. At Liverpool, there was also potential but nowhere near as much funding available to strengthen a promising squad.

Yet Gerrard had backed away from London: in no mean part, as he was to admit, because his family had received death threats and members of the Kop had turned sour. Now Rooney – faced with an even worse scenario with the involvement of Manchester United – would ignore similar threats and ugly slogans, such as 'Die Manc Judas' sprayed on walls near his home and Everton's Bellefield training ground. Full credit to him and his family for their strength of mind and unwillingness to give in to the law of yobs.

Decent Everton fans were to accept his decision with regret, if hardly grace. He had served them well and helped saved the club from financial ruin, putting them on a sound footing. Better to have loved and lost, than to have not loved at all, and ask any man in the street if he would not change his job if it meant much-improved prospects and money. Of course, he would.

To join Manchester United, Rooney had to overcome his feelings of nostalgia for Everton, his family's allegiances and the mean-fisted intransigence of some Toffees fans. He also had to ignore his agent's links with Newcastle, the club who had initiated the scramble for his signature.

Paul Stretford was a major player in modern football. The millionaire founder and chief executive of the Proactive Sports Group, he had secured Rooney from his previous agent Peter McIntosh in a move that left the latter gutted. Now Stretford was the man who pulled Rooney's strings, or so it seemed. When it came to the big transfer, everything pointed to Stretford wanting his boy to head further north: up to Newcastle in fact. Stretford was a friend of Newcastle chairman Freddy Shepherd, and his firm even had an office at St James' Park, from where Shepherd's son Kenny worked for Proactive. But Rooney looked at the Geordies and saw a set-up in disarray, from the public fallings-out between manager Sir Bobby Robson and impudent rich kids like Kieron Dyer, to the fact that the club had not won a major honour since 1969. And that was the European Fairs Cup – the league trophy had last made an appearance in Toon in 1927. So wouldn't he simply be swapping one sleeping giant for another if he left Everton for Newcastle? Again, he was his own man and made his own decision – with a little help from Freddy, but more of that later.

Rooney had another problem to overcome – he was a Scouser, and Scousers did not mix with Manchester United. Or did they? Wayne admitted it had crossed his mind that he might not be accepted in Manchester. Traditionally, United's biggest rivalry had been with Liverpool, and the Mancs and the Scallys did not mingle well. But a look at the record books would show Rooney there was little to fear – he was not the first Scouser to sign for United, and no doubt he would not be the last.

When he finally signed, Rooney was the eighth to pull on a

United shirt. Steve Coppell, United and England winger during Tommy Docherty's stewardship in the mid-'70s, is perhaps the best known before the reign of Wayne. Like Rooney, he was born in Croxteth, and he went on to play nearly 400 games for the Red Devils. Full-back John Gidman also made a big impression at Old Trafford – making 115 appearances – after signing from Everton in 1981.

Rooney had weighed up all the potential drawbacks of a move during his summer holiday with fiancée Coleen McLoughlin after Euro 2004. Still, he had refused to buckle – as we have seen there is a little tough nut behind that schoolboyish innocence. So, when he limped back into Goodison at the start of July 2004 nothing had changed, but everything had changed. He wanted out.

It would not be easy. Rooney told Bill Kenwright of his decision that afternoon, but the club's owner was not happy. If he really wanted to go, he would have to put in an official transfer request. Rooney left with the situation at stalemate – and it would be another six weeks before things reached a head.

A week after his meeting with Kenwright, reports filtered through the press that he wanted a move – and that he had told close friends he had set his heart on Manchester United rather than Chelsea because he wanted to stay in the North-west. Meanwhile, Toffees' chief executive Trevor Birch was still saying in public that he was confident of keeping Rooney. Indeed, he planned to sit down with him to thrash out a new contract. A week later, David Moyes appeared in print working hard to reshape public opinion of himself at Goodison. The fans had let it be known they blamed Moyes for Rooney's discontent – he should have picked him more, should have praised him more. Moyes vowed to do everything he could to keep his boy wonder – even saying he would offer him the captain's armband if it would help sway his decision. The same day, the first inkling that the saga might be about to take an unexpected twist came when the *Mail on Sunday* claimed Newcastle United were lining up a £30 million move for Rooney.

Claims and counter-claims continued throughout July and

early August. It was the traditional silly season for the press – and stories abounded about him staying and going. On 3 August, the *Daily Mirror* revealed that Wayne had cancelled his booking for an executive box at Goodison. Traditionally, his family and best pals had enjoyed sumptuous meals and lashings of booze – at £29,000 a season – while he had toiled for the Toffees. Surely the cancellation was only further confirmation that it was all over for Rooney and Everton?

By 22 August, Rooney was running again after an X-ray revealed his broken metatarsal was healing well. Then, there was a new development. Rooney admitted visiting prostitutes when he was 'young and stupid'. He had been forced to come clean after the *Sunday Mirror* offered photographic proof of his trips to massage parlours in Liverpool. With head bowed, he proclaimed: 'Foolish as it now seems I did on occasions visit massage parlours and prostitutes.'

OK, he made a mistake, and he was certainly naive to leave one of the hookers an autographed picture of himself. The doom-mongers were quick to claim it was only the start of a slippery slope. But wasn't it really more of a case of a daft aberration by a mischievous young lad? And consider this if we are talking about morals: in the same week, it was revealed that Home Secretary David Blunkett had been having sex sessions with a married woman. At the time, few criticised him because he was a 'blind man in love'. Yet whose 'crime' was the greater? The teenage footballer just crossing the threshold of adulthood or the supposedly responsible middle-aged Cabinet Minister we looked up to for guidance on matters of morality?

The hooker allegations would not go away. As such, they provided more concrete proof in Rooney's mind that a move was the right decision. According to an insider, his fiancée Coleen was even on the brink of giving him an ultimatum: get us out of Liverpool or we're through. It was their first major bust-up since the previous March – when Coleen's 18th birthday bash had turned into exactly that as drunken relatives from both her, and Wayne's family brawled at a lavish hotel party laid on by the footballer.

Transfer events took another dramatic turn on 24 August when Newcastle officially entered the fray. They were awash with cash after the shock £14 million sale of England centre-back Jonathan Woodgate to Real Madrid. The Toon offered £20 million for Rooney, but Everton immediately dismissed the bid.

Manchester United boss Sir Alex Ferguson was fuming: he had allowed England midfielder Nicky Butt to join the Geordies in the summer for a mere £2 million and had planned on putting the money aside to help buy Rooney at a knockdown price the following January or summer. The last thing he had anticipated was that Newcastle would reward his generosity by forcing his hand over Rooney.

Manchester officially entered the race two days later – matching Newcastle's bid. Of course, it was merely a ploy by Ferguson. He wanted Rooney to know he was still as keen on him as he had ever been. Ferguson hoped that by showing his hand, Rooney would, in turn, show his by making it plain he was going nowhere but Old Trafford.

The tanks were rolling. The same day the Toon upped their offer to £23.5 million, which was also rejected by the Everton board. Then Freddy Shepherd aimed a broadside at Old Trafford: 'We don't know what is going to happen, but we certainly have not given up hope of signing Rooney just because Manchester United have come in. Not everyone wants to sign for them – look at Alan Shearer.' His argument was less than convincing. Big Al went to Newcastle because he was a Geordie boy. However, what had Shearer won with them? Nothing.

Sir Alex broke cover, fired up by Shepherd's jibe and determined that Rooney would not 'do a Shearer.' He believed Manchester United with Rooney would become as strong as his Treble-winning side of 1999. Even his old adversary David Beckham chipped in with a hint for Rooney: 'Ferguson brought me into the team and gave me the chance when others wouldn't have done. We think we helped the club win trophies, but without Alex Ferguson's guidance, we wouldn't have grown up as we have done.'

One day later, on Friday 27 August, Rooney granted the

wishes of Kenwright, Moyes and the Goodison board by slapping in an official transfer request. They were now off the hook with the public, but Rooney remained confident he could handle any aggro; he was a big boy now. He said, 'I feel now is the right time to move forward with my career.' Now he was on the move for sure; how could he stay at Everton with the inevitable death threats on walls and verbal abuse on radio phone-ins?

Transfer deadline day was the following Tuesday. Four more days to go. He had made the key decision that he wanted to join United, but it was not public knowledge. Fans across the country pored over his supposed dilemma: Sir Alex or Sir Bobby? Which to choose? It emerged Ferguson was so keen to get Rooney he had agreed to part with the whole of his £15 million transfer budget for the *next* season.

Both he and Sir Bobby were legends, if both a little cantankerous. Sir Alex had the edge: he was in charge of the bigger club with better players. He was renowned for his 'father figure' handling of younger players and he was busy building what he hoped would be the third, and final, great team of his reign at Old Trafford. He also made it clear young Wayne would be the figurehead around whom his new team would revolve.

The following day, Manchester put in another bid, the £25 million minimum Everton had been demanding. That Saturday the Goodison outfit were at home to West Bromwich Albion and some of their fans turned on Wayne. Bitter and twisted, their gratitude to having witnessed the development of their greatest ever home-grown talent was to sing: 'One fat bastard, there's only one fat bastard.' Forgive them Wayne, they knew not what they did. One clever wag had made a banner telling him to stand by the T-shirt he once unveiled after scoring a goal – yes *that* one: 'Once a blue, always a blue.'

Even the normally unflappable Arsenal boss Arsène Wenger was beginning to get the wobbles about Rooney moving to Manchester. He said, 'If United get Rio Ferdinand back, Rooney in, Gabriel Heinze back, suddenly, they look a lot stronger . . . '

It was now Bank Holiday Monday, but that was no reason for

Newcastle chairman Freddy Shepherd to avoid another spectacular own goal as he sacked manager Sir Bobby Robson. At the start of the season, he had told Robson this would be his last at St James' Park. That, of course, eased the slack still further in a Newcastle dressing-room full of likely lads such as Dyer and Craig Bellamy.

Now Freddy had gone one further – with his own inimitable version of a 'Nightmare on Wor Street'. It provided Rooney with the perfect excuse for snubbing any chance of a move to St James' Park. Why would he want to sign for a club that had no manager, dressing-room problems and underachievers galore? The alternative was lining up with a strike partner like Ruud van Nistelrooy and playing in the Champions League rather than the second-rate UEFA Cup.

Freddy's final act in the saga was to pave the way for Wayne's inevitable move to Manchester and meant there was no need for him to answer any questions about Newcastle, thank you very much. By dismissing the admirable Sir Bob, he had taken away the biggest reason Wayne may have even considered heading up the A1.

So it was, that on the last day of August 2004, Wayne Rooney finally ended the two-month long drama by putting pen to paper for a six-year £50,000-a-week deal which would keep him at Manchester United until 30 July 2010. In the final analysis, he had accepted the same salary offered to him by Everton a few weeks earlier as a sweetener to keep him at Goodison.

The breakdown of the transfer fee was complex. Its bottom line was that Everton would receive a guaranteed £23 million provided Rooney remained a United player until 30 June 2007. They could earn a total of £27 million depending on United's success and Rooney's international appearances over the next five years. The move meant Rooney had become the most expensive teenager in the world, beating the previous record of £20 million that Italian giants Roma paid Bari for Antonio Cassano in 2001.

Rooney grinned like the proverbial Cheshire cat as he was unveiled at Old Trafford. Flanked by Sir Alex and United chief executive David Gill, he once again revealed the mental toughness that had made the deal possible, showing little remorse for quitting Goodison Park.

Talking about his reasons for leaving, Rooney said, 'I made up my mind to leave six weeks ago. Once I knew Manchester United were in for me there was only one place for me. After Euro 2004, I made up my mind that I wanted to play for a bigger club. When you are sitting there and all the players are chatting about their clubs, you want to be part of it and playing at that level. It was frustrating. I couldn't achieve that at Everton.'

After his interrogation by the press, Ferguson illustrated how he would look after Rooney by throwing a protective arm around him and saying, 'Well done, son.' The reassurance wasn't really needed – Rooney looked at home in his new surroundings and he later walked around the ground with a swagger once associated with former United talisman, Eric Cantona.

Even United's current main man, Ruud van Nistelrooy, was keen to put out his own welcome mat. In Rooney, he recognised the chance of a partnership that could go down in history as the most magical of his own career. He said, 'Everyone knows Wayne is an amazing talent and the thought of him pulling on a United shirt is frightening. It really excites me to think he will be playing at United. To play with him will be fantastic.'

United announced that Rooney would wear the number 8 shirt vacated by Nicky Butt. Their megastore was quickly inundated with requests for Rooney number 8 shirts.

By the end of the first week of September, Rooney had yet to kick a ball in anger after Euro 2004. Given the dealings and double-dealings of his move to Manchester, it was maybe just as well he had time on his hands to concentrate 100 per cent on the most difficult decision he may ever have to make.

There remained other matters to be considered before he could get down to his football. Sir Alex had made it clear he could no longer live in Liverpool. Well, that wasn't a problem. Both he and Coleen would be glad to escape the tense atmosphere in Formby, where they had recently moved into a £1 million six-bedroom mansion, and Liverpool itself. More mindless graffiti had been daubed on walls near his home, including the sick, 'DIE W. ROONEY'.

The couple began their search for a new home – Nicky Butt's, in the Cheshire stockbroker belt, interested them. It was on the market for £1.6 million and, surprise, surprise, was near to the homes of Sir Alex and United skipper Roy Keane. It also had high walls, electric gates, video surveillance cameras and a state-of-the-art intruder detection system linked to a police station. That was just the sort of place Sir Alex wanted his precious young charge fortressed within. United were also taking the increasing number of death threats seriously. Within a week, Wayne would be accompanied by two SAS-trained minders watching him at all times, plus a personal bodyguard.

Rooney and Coleen, who was also 18 and from the same Croxteth council estate, had made up after falling out over the revelations about his visits to hookers. Like Wayne, she had had to grow up fast as the media spotlight inevitably began to focus upon her. When Wayne had played against Turkey at Sunderland the previous April, she had been unable to watch him because she was starring in her school play, *Bugsy Malone*. That all changed as his star glowed after the Turkey match. She accompanied him to Portugal and looked a different person: a young woman as opposed to the previously star-struck schoolgirl. Now she dressed in designer clothes to match Victoria Beckham and the rest of them – and revealed she had finished her schooling so she could concentrate upon her ambition to become an actress.

They were not short of readies now. Wayne had signed his deal at United. He also had contracts totalling £5 million with the likes of Nike and Coca-Cola, which would continue despite the companies making public their reservations about his visits to the massage parlours. The couple claimed to prefer life out of the spotlight and simple pleasures – admitting their ideal evening was a night in with a takeaway watching videos of *Only Fools and Horses*.

By the second week of September, the new lease of life being enjoyed by Rooney received another boost with an unexpectedly heart-warming spin-off to his transfer. After the grudges, the threats and the painted slogans, Everton revealed that some of the world's less well-off would benefit directly from Rooney's departure. The club sent £66,000 worth of unwanted shirts bearing his name to young footballers in Africa. They were being donated to CAFOD, the Catholic aid agency, which was helping former child soldiers in Liberia to reintegrate into society. The project was run by CAFOD's partner agency, Don Bosco Homes, and its director Allan Lincoln said, 'The kids are passionate about football here and are huge Rooney fans after the European Championships. Many of them have very little clothing and won't care what colour Rooney shirt they get.'

All that remained now was for Wayne to get back to full fitness and make his United debut. Ferguson had hinted that it could be as early as the 20 September clash at home to Liverpool, but in the event that proved too optimistic. It was also the date of Rio Ferdinand's return after his eight-month ban for failing to take a drugs test. That in itself was enough for most United fans to cope with: bringing back memories of the same fixture in October 1995 when Cantona returned from a nine-month ban for his kung fu kick in the crowd at Crystal Palace to score one goal and make another.

More measured opinion from Old Trafford suggested Rooney's debut would be in the home match against Middlesbrough on 3 October – but, whenever, Rooney was raring to go. He was relishing the challenge of proving he could do what he did to defences in Portugal in the Champions League and week-in, week-out in the Premiership. Before the Liverpool match, Sir Alex had offered a glimpse into his future by suggesting he would indeed try him out in the hole – which meant playing behind van Nistelrooy, Louis Saha or Alan Smith, and in front of a midfield led by Roy Keane.

Rooney also wanted to get going for another reason: to dispel rumours that his future would be wrecked by indiscipline. Some critics had again got on to their high horses after the massage parlours revelations, claiming the boy wonder would go the way of Gazza and Georgie Best. They pointed to his on-field discipline to back up the claim, saying he was a hothead. Fair enough, he was booked in Portugal and he did collect more yellow cards than goals for Everton in his last season with them. Those facts are undeniable. But he also controlled that fragile temper against Croatia in Euro 2004, when another booking would have ruled him out of the quarter-final, and he showed he had matured emotionally with his handling of the transfer to United.

He was no young Gazza. The Geordie boy had lost it in the World Cup semi in 1990, his tears masking the realisation that he would be on the sidelines if England made it to the final. Also, Gazza revelled in the spotlight, like a Rolls-Royce guzzles petrol. Rooney did not, preferring instead to do his talking with his feet. He made it clear he intended to use this first season at United to silence the doubters. Even Gazza was impressed with Wayne's down-to-earth attitude. He said, 'He may have a lot to learn, but he's already got a massive head start on most players. The pressure will be on him, but here is a kid who will relish the opportunity to play against the best. He just needs to detach himself from what's going on around him and focus on putting his boots on and playing football. I love the fact that he will go straight from the training ground for a kickabout with his mates.'

Respected figureheads within the game also rushed to his defence. PFA deputy chief executive Mick McGuire felt dealing with superstardom would not be a problem for the wonder boy. He said, 'Obviously nothing can totally prepare you for the adulation or pressure which accompanies being such a brilliant young player. But he is going to a club which has brought through six or seven major young players who have never been in an ounce of trouble. He has joined a very strong club – the future is looking fantastic for Wayne Rooney.' Couldn't have put it better myself – thanks Mick.

Now, let's dim the lights, draw back the curtain and head to the Theatre (of Dreams) for one of British football's most eagerly awaited curtain calls.

3

TURK IT TO THE LIMIT

A FUNNY THING HAPPENED ON THE WAY TO THE MATCH. I bumped into two Manchester City fans. They were short on smiles and long on warnings. Both were friends, but I could have done without them on this night of all nights. The man continually tapped the index finger of his right hand against his head and solemnly proclaimed, 'He's a nutter. He'll end up like Best, he won't be able to handle it.' The woman seemed to draw energy from his ranting: 'He's not going to last, Ferguson should have bought someone like Shaun Wright-Phillips. At least you know he's not a head case and he won't go off the rails.'

I couldn't help it. After all, this was Rooney's big night, no one else's. 'Well, what about Wright-Phillips' missus saying he had been messing about with a lapdancer and other women – and leaving her with two kids to bring up? And don't forget, he's only 22.' They stonewalled me, changed the subject, looking for a way out. Soon I could continue on my merry way. Point proven, leave the boy Wayne alone, or at least give him a chance to prove he's a good 'un.

There's definitely something special in the air on European nights at Old Trafford. Call it nostalgia if you will, but the very evening breeze itself smells magical, with a powerful sense of

40

expectation you just don't get for league matches. Maybe it stems back to United being Britain's football pioneers in Europe – the first team to play competitive matches on the Continent from 1956 onwards. Certainly it has something to do with the tragedy of 1958: the Munich memories and tears live on. It was as if this night had been specially conjured up for Wayne Rooney's debut – and no doubt the likes of the great Duncan Edwards were looking on with approval from heaven.

It was appropriate also in that Rooney had made his name in Euro 2004. Now his big bow for United would come in European competition against the Turks of Fenerbahçe at Old Trafford. Mark the date down in your diary – it was Tuesday 28 September 2004, a full 96 days since he had last kicked a ball in a competitive match, the one that had ended agonisingly prematurely against the Portuguese. Ninety-six days in which he had sorted out his future and finally returned to full-time training at Old Trafford on 13 September. After the high-octane publicity of his signing, it had all gone surprisingly quiet. The boy had gone to ground – devoting his time to getting totally fit, still determined to silence the knockers who questioned his stability and ability.

He could have played the previous Saturday against Spurs at White Hart Lane. But Sir Alex had decided he needed one more full practice session. It was as simple as that: or was it? Unusually for United, the match against Fenerbahçe was not sold out the Friday before the Spurs match. Tickets were being offered by agencies, on United's website and on general sale at Old Trafford. Had Ferguson been given the nod from on high? Delay Rooney's debut until the Tuesday – that way you guaranteed a sell-out. Ferguson announced late on Friday afternoon that the boy wonder would *not* be starting or even on the bench at Spurs, but he *would* be playing a part on the Tuesday. By Saturday afternoon the Fenerbahçe game was sold out. The boy was already starting to pay back his transfer fee.

The kick-off against the Turks was 7.45 p.m., but the United fans had started to appear in droves two hours beforehand. By 6 p.m., thousands were making their way over the Manchester

Ship Canal and from White City, hitting both ends of Sir Matt Busby Way like two massive demented snakes, all hands aloft, the chant as one: 'Roooooooney, Roooooooney!'

The banners proclaimed his arrival too, many offering the very same sentiment: 'Thank you for Rooney'. It was a pivotal moment – not just in terms of acceptance for the man-boy but also for United as a club. For too long the burning hatred between United fans and those from Liverpool and Everton had been allowed to fester. Now they had a major-name Scouser among their own ranks. Surely the time had come for songs about Bill Shankly dying and that anthem from the days when Tommy Docherty was manager – 'We Hate the Scousers' – to be confined to their rightful place, the dustbin. The club was changing and progressing with the era. Now the fans also had the chance to move forwards. Forget the long-held enmity with the Scousers and Leeds for that matter. Only two months earlier, Alan Smith had trekked across the Pennines to join Manchester from Leeds United. The club was becoming cosmopolitan: an all-encompassing, broad church. It seemed the fans had got the message as they trudged in their thousands for the Scouse boy's debut. Humour and high expectation were the order of the night; those bitter, seething grudges of the past three decades seemed to have evaporated into that magical mid-evening autumnal air.

The stadium started to fill from 6.15 p.m.; by 6.30 p.m. Rooney number 8 shirts were everywhere. The marketing men were enjoying their champers with an extra feeling of satisfaction as they surveyed the scene from the executive suites. The visiting supporters also made their presence felt – about 2,000 of them packed together, noisily shouting their allegiance to the Turkish flag, all in rhythm to a constant boom-boom of drums. They too knew of Rooney, and that this was to be his night. They did their best to vocally swamp the chants from expectant United fans as the clock struck 7.30 p.m. They remembered the damage he had done to their national side in the Euro 2004 qualifying games at Sunderland and in Turkey – he couldn't repeat that tonight. Could he?

Manchester United were competing in a ninth successive Champions League. The season before had been the first they had not made the last eight, although they had successfully negotiated every group phase since the 1996–97 campaign. Fenerbahçe were playing in their third Champions League campaign having never progressed from the group phase.

At 7.41 p.m., Wayne Rooney emerged from the tunnel. Rapturous applause rained out along with the soon to be traditional chant of 'Roooney, Roooney.' The boy chewed gum, looked around and waved. Then he smiled. His neck was thick, red and sweaty. He had ripped his shirt at the top because it was too tight against that bulbous neck. He looked fit and ready; he showed no sign of nerves. He clapped his hands together over his head as the United fans chanted his name, giving him a hero's welcome he could only have dreamed of. He warmed up, smashing the ball at goalkeeper Roy Carroll as if he was still playing at the local recreation ground with some mates in Croxteth.

This was one of the things that made him different from the rest. He had no fear. Off the pitch, he was often tongue-tied and nervous: on it, he was totally at home. This was his stage – tonight was the night he would be making his bow on the theatre boards he had dreamed of, in front of 67,000 fans and a worldwide TV audience. This was why he had left Everton: it was as if he were back in Portugal again. This was the big stage he had craved. This was to be his night of destiny.

Rooney made an immediate impact, taking a pass from Ryan Giggs and putting Ruud van Nistelrooy through for a half chance. Boss Ferguson had made it clear Rooney would not get special treatment, and he sure kept to his promise with the United line-up for Wayne's debut. Rooney could have been forgiven for thinking he was still at Everton as he surveyed some of the men around him. Apart from Giggs and van Nistelrooy, the bullets were to be supplied from Eric Djemba-Djemba, Kleberson and David Bellion. There was no Roy Keane, no Cristiano Ronaldo and no John O'Shea. Their replacements had proved spectacular flops. Kleberson had rarely looked like the

World Cup winner he was with Brazil; Eric 2DJ, as he was known to the fans, appeared only a bit-part player, hardly the new Keane as he had initially been heralded. The Cameroon international's efforts had been singularly summed up by his showing in this competition a fortnight earlier: he had had a stinker in the lucky 2–2 draw at Lyon.

Yet tonight something miraculous happened. These very players who had looked anything but the finished article suddenly seemed just that. Was it merely a coincidence that Rooney would bring the best out of them? I think not. Just as Maradona had carried journeymen at Napoli – and, indeed, within the Argentine national team – to glory, so Rooney's presence lifted the mere mortals at United this night. Kleberson, in particular, looked the part for the first time. In one exhilarating moment, he shot from central midfield across to Ryan Giggs's left-wing territory and sprayed an immaculate pass into the path of Giggs for the opening goal. Even David Bellion managed to beat a man as Rooney set the cogs in motion from his initial role in advanced midfield.

Then the boy was everywhere, linking midfield and attack and stepping upfront to provide an intelligent foil for van Nistelrooy. In his four seasons at United, the Dutchman had failed to find a partner he could play with. Even with Holland he had struggled alone. His natural attacking instincts often failed to register on other players' radars – yet tonight it was as if he had finally come home. He and Rooney linked well; they were on the same high-frequency wavelength. They could have been playing as a partnership for years. Both were intelligent instinct players and both prospered off the other. Some punters called Ruud 'The Horseman' because of his looks – now one wag in the press box came up with another label for the Rooney and Ruud partnership: 'Shrek and his best pal, the Donkey.'

Rooney was the man of the match, grabbing a brilliant hat-trick with goals in the 17th, 28th and 54th minutes in a 6–2 thrashing. Van Nistelrooy also got in on the action, scoring his 31st Champions League goal in just 32 starts. Fabio Luciano had been detailed to mark Rooney wherever he went. Luciano stuck gamely to his task for the first quarter of an hour but then it was all a blur: a nightmare he would not want to relive as Rooney left him for dead, time after time.

Rooney's first goal came as he fired the ball home after a class pass from Van the Man. His second brought back memories of his second goal against Croatia as he beat his man and scored with a pile-driver from 25 yards out. But it was his third goal that epitomised his quality and nerve. Gabriel Heinze, van Nistelrooy and Giggs all loomed as United were awarded a free-kick. Rooney arrived a minute later with the words, 'It's mine', herded the others to one side and promptly lobbed the kick past the desperate Rustu Recber in the visiting goal. Almost like a script from *Roy* (or should that be Boy?) *of the Rovers*, he had scored a hat-trick on his debut. It was also the first hat-trick of his career. Absolutely incredible.

Keeper Recber had been dismissive of United's chances before the game and had claimed Rooney would not pose a problem. He had to eat humble pie several times as the 18 year old continued to torment him. Rooney, clearly tiring as the match took its toll, still had enough wit and energy left to set up Bellion for United's sixth, nine minutes from time. He latched on to Mikael Silvestre's long ball out of defence, flicked it on to Bellion and the former Sunderland winger completed the rout with a shot underneath Recber.

By the time Rooney had completed his hat-trick, the United fans had come up with a new song. Every time he touched the ball, they chanted, tongues firmly in cheeks, 'What a waste of money, what a waste of money!'

Some would argue the visiting Turks were ideal fodder for the predatory Scouser, but you can only deal with what is put in front of you. And, let's not forget, they arrived as champions of Turkey and were still top of their league in the current season. They had also begun their Champions League campaign confidently, seeing off the challenge of the dour Sparta Prague in Istanbul a fortnight earlier. And in veteran Dutchman Pierre van Hooijdonk they possessed a striker still dangerous enough to occasionally cause flutters for Rio Ferdinand and Co. at the back.

The stats showed that United had 20 goal attempts to their visitors' 13. Eight of United's were on target, double that of Fenerbahçe. The visiting goals came from Marcio Nobre, who made it 3–1 from a badly defended corner just two minutes after the interval, and Tuncay Sanli, who brought it back to 4–2 on 78 minutes after more poor defending by United. Ferguson, understandably, was annoyed with the lapses at the back, but his face looked years younger – as if the stress lines had been eliminated – as he watched young Rooney go about his night's work. When the hat-trick was completed, he could just as easily have been any proud parent winking and laughing about his son's exploits in a parks Sunday league fixture.

That was the effect Rooney had on those around him. After an indifferent start to the season, he had lifted the gloom and made all those connected with the club – players, manager, directors and fans – believe again. Believe they could still win a major trophy, that their domination of English football had not ended after all. That they could now really start to give Arsenal and Chelsea a fight for their money.

Rooney also brought to an end a personal low for Sir Alex, one that had hung around for nearly eight years. Wayne had just turned 11 when United lost their unbeaten home record in European competition. Inevitably, the script showed that it was tonight's visitors who had inflicted that wound. For United stats fans, it had been Elvir Bolic who grabbed the winner that night back in 1996. Now revenge was complete against Christoph Daum's modern-day Fenerbahçe.

Rooney notched up another record on the way. His hat-trick was the first on a United debut since 1905, when Charlie Sagar scored in the 5–1 win over Bristol City. He and Rooney are the only players to mark their United debuts with three goals apiece. After the match, Rooney asked a bemused referee if he could have the ball to keep. The ref later admitted he hadn't recognised Rooney when he approached him. The boy was wearing Brazilian star Marco Aurello's shirt inside out. The Fenerbahçe midfielder was delighted to get Rooney's debut shirt as a souvenir and said, 'I will keep it until the day I die.' Little did he know that Wayne already had his original shirt bagged up. He had taken it off at half time to keep among his own growing Aladdin's cave of mementos.

Old Trafford emptied slowly as the fans realised what they had witnessed – a twinkling anticipation of what surely lay ahead gripping them in their bellies. The toast was Rooney from the clanking pint glasses in The Trafford pub to the more delicate crystal holding champers in the Old Trafford boardroom, and the praise was heaped high upon the youngster.

First up was a red-faced Sir Alex, trying his best not to smile. He said, 'I know what you want to talk about. But I'd rather talk about the game in general rather than just one player. I have to remember he's only 18.' But even the Govan general could not contain himself for more than a couple of minutes, eventually giving into the urge. He added, 'I've never seen a debut like that before. He was magnificent. Everyone can see the potential the boy has, and you can't help but be excited by it.

'I think he can only get stronger too. But it was more than just the goals. As a partnership, he and Ruud van Nistelrooy were magnificent together. Considering it was the first time they have played together, it holds great promise for us.' The United boss then appealed for his young charge to be given space from the 'media circus': 'There's nothing I can do to stop it. It was a great start for him and that's why we signed him. The important thing, as his coach, is to allow him to develop naturally without too much press and public attention. We want him to lead as normal a life as possible.'

Ferguson then went on to explain why he had not played regular luminaries like Roy Keane and Ronaldo to ease Rooney's path on his debut. Ferguson said, 'I felt that the number of games Roy has played so far this season made it a good time to give him a break. And I also wanted to see how Kleberson has come on in centre midfield. A lot of the games he has played for us so far have not been in centre. I think the boy is a really good talent, and I think he showed that. In the case of Ronaldo, we all know he needed to be given a rest.'

Then Ruud van Nistelrooy admitted he had enjoyed his first

taste of the partnership that could frighten defences around Europe. He said, 'It was great playing with him. If I was to pick out one thing to praise it would be his attitude. He is only 18, it is his debut and he knows all eyes are on him – yet he just goes out and does his own thing.'

Rio Ferdinand, United's England defender – and skipper-in-waiting at Old Trafford – was also generous in his praise. He said, 'Wayne's debut was fantastic. To get a hat-trick is unbelievable, fairy-tale stuff. I do not think he knows what pressure is.' And Georgie Best added a giggle to proceedings, saying, 'He loves the big stage and the sky's the limit. He's got it all but is he as good as me? Don't be silly!'

Even Fenerbahçe coach Christoph Daum admitted he had seen the future. He said, 'It was an outstanding debut. It is something you dream of as a manager for a player to play in this way and to score in this way in his first game. If he does that, it makes you very happy and you're a very lucky manager. Rooney is still very young and maybe he will become the player of the century. He is at the beginning now though.'

The big question at the end of the night was: where's Wayne? True to form, he had slipped off quietly away from all the fuss, preferring to go home to Coleen and a bit of peace, totally unruffled by it all. When he got back home, he would watch the match over and over again. It had been a blow to those who were hoping the boy would blow up on his debut. For the most part, he had not reacted to the leg-snapping terriers at the heart of the Fenerbahçe midfield and defence. He had simply gone about his own game and created havoc and destruction through his talent, not a fragile temperament. The boy was growing up quickly under the master tutelage of that ultimate defender of precocious youth, Sir Alex Ferguson.

The Scot had already predicted young Wayne would surprise people with his growing maturity. He had been quietly impressed by him in the month since he had joined United. Ferguson knew he had a good, supportive family behind him off the pitch – and enforcers like Roy Keane to back him up on it. Before the game, Keane himself had weighed in with some advice for Rooney, warning him to beware hangers-on and back-stabbers. The United skipper advised him not to trust anybody. He said, 'You learn out of experience to choose your friends carefully. Just when you think someone's not such a bad guy, I guarantee you, they'll ask you for something. I'll meet 100 people in the next two weeks and 99 per cent will ask me for something. Some people think it's good just to be seen with you . . . I could give you some perfect examples of people whom I've looked after and then they've come out with something bad about you.'

Keane was also quick to emphasise he did not doubt Rooney had the natural ability to become a world-beater. He added, 'Paul Gascoigne is one of two players from the last ten or fifteen years I would have paid to watch, one of two who really excited me. Rooney is the other one. I watched him against Bolton a while ago, and he hit the post about six times and destroyed them.'

Yet the name Rooney continued to delight some of the people Keane could have been referring to in his put-down – the marketing men. ITV reported that Wayne's debut had brought in the viewers. Their Champions League coverage had averaged 5.5 million over the previous month – now nearly 7 million had tuned in to see Rooney. BBC bosses were cursing the youngster. His performance had stolen the limelight from their new big-money comedy series, *A Thing Called Love*, starring Paul Nicholls of *EastEnders* fame. The show pulled in 5.2 million against A Thing Called Rooney . . .

Before the match, it had also been revealed that Rooney was now more attractive than David Beckham in the eyes of sponsors. City firm Field Fisher Waterhouse, who provided an annual list of the players deemed most desirable by international corporate companies, said Beckham was now 'over-branded' while Rooney was second in the list of 'most wanted' after Arsenal's Thierry Henry. He was already ahead of Beckham and his Real Madrid teammates Ronaldo and Zinedine Zidane.

Beckham remained the player with the most lucrative sponsorship deals – earning around £20 million a year from the likes of Gillette, adidas, Pepsi and Vodafone. But Rooney was starting to make imprints – he had Nike and Coca-Cola among his own £5 million portfolio, and his exploits against Fenerbahçe could only enhance that success.

Young Rooney received more good news in his personal life the day after the match they would never forget at Old Trafford. He had a driving conviction overturned. Police had pulled him over when he was driving a BMW X5 in Liverpool on 6 May. He was convicted of driving without insurance and failing to produce his licence and documents by Liverpool magistrates. Yet the court now threw out the conviction saying there had been an 'administrative error'.

Life was tasting good for the boy wonder after the eventual anticlimax of Euro 2004 and his dramatic transfer from Goodison to Old Trafford. Thanks to his efforts, United were now top of Group D in the Champions League, he was settling in well at the Theatre of Dreams and his personal life with Coleen was on a solid level footing. They were both excited at the prospect of moving into a new home together.

Currently staying in an £140-a-night Manchester hotel, they had decided not to buy Nicky Butt's old pad. Instead, they were opting for a new £3 million home that was still being built in Halebarns, Cheshire – again not far away from Fergie and Roy Keane. United also signed Rooney's 13-year-old brother John for their school of excellence. Again, poor old Everton were the losers.

Yet there remained one more twist to the first remarkable month. A couple of days after the Fenerbahçe match, Sven-Göran Eriksson predicted Rooney could be among those challenging for the World Player of the Year award. The England head coach was on the panel of experts helping to draw up a longlist of 30 candidates. International team coaches and captains, as well as the international players' union FIFPro (*Fédération Internationale des Associations de Footballeurs Professionnels*), would then vote for their preferred choices, although they could not select anyone from their own side. Eriksson admitted, 'I have had to select a list of 30 players, and

I should be very surprised if Wayne Rooney is not on that list. At Euro 2004, he was one of the best players, if not the best. Is he a genuine candidate? I think so. But suddenly when you talk in those terms, the competition is very high.'

Eriksson had also witnessed Rooney's spectacular return to action for United against the Turks. He added, 'I was very surprised as he hadn't played for so long. I know that he can play at that level, but I don't think anyone expected it in his first Champions League game. That was remarkable.

'He had not played football since 24 June, and, from what I understand, he had just four or five sessions with the ball before that game. Probably when you're 18 and mentally strong with all the qualities he has, you can get through on adrenalin. But if he plays like he did in the first half at Old Trafford, then that's good enough for me. He could have scored four or five goals.'

Sure enough, Rooney *did* make the list of 30 – along with United teammates Ruud van Nistelrooy, Cristiano Ronaldo and Ryan Giggs. A shortlist of three would be produced in November before the winner was unveiled at a ceremony at the Zurich Opera House on 20 December. Inclusion on that final list would certainly be some Christmas present for young Wayne.

But first there remained important work to be done on the domestic football front. No sooner had the celebrations ended in the dressing-room, after the victory over Fenerbahçe, than boss Ferguson was plotting how he could use Rooney to turn around United's stuttering start to the Premiership campaign. Arsenal and Chelsea were already disappearing away into the sunset, and a miracle would be needed to catch them. Maybe an even bigger miracle than winning the World Player of the Year award at such a tender age.

4

THEATRE OF DREAMS
(AND NIGHTMARES)

INEVITABLY, THE HOME PREMIERSHIP DEBUT AGAINST Middlesbrough five days later was an anticlimax: a dour letdown. Rooney was playing only his second competitive match after his injury in the Euros – and it showed. After his mighty exertions against the Turks, fatigue had taken its toll. Ferguson should probably have stuck him on the bench and brought him on as a late sub, but he wanted him to get another 90 minutes under his belt. Plus there was the prickly and, certainly in the presence of the United boss, best left unsaid problem of United's early season Premiership form. They had lost only one game but were stuttering like a blocked exhaust on a motorbike. When questioned about it, Fergie would try his best not to blow up and invariably came out with the same old mantra: wait until we get our best players back, then you'll see the real United.

Well, on paper at least, the team that he selected against Boro was his strongest, apart from the still injured Paul Scholes. Those journeymen battlers – Eric 2DJ and Kleberson – were back on the sidelines, with Roy Keane and big John O'Shea replacing them in the heart of the United midfield. The defence was strong – with Rio Ferdinand continuing his rehabilitation from eight

52

months out after his missed drugs test – and Ruud was partnering Rooney up front. Another plus was the first-time outing for Rooney and Ronaldo, while Giggs would be lining up on the left wing.

It looked a much more powerful, balanced team than the one that had thrashed Fenerbahçe, and Boro turned up at Old Trafford in the middle of the worst injury crisis of Steve McClaren's three-year reign as manager. He was forced to give three 18 year olds – James Morrison, Tony McMahon and Daniel Graham – their Premiership debuts. Among those missing from action were strikers Jimmy Floyd Hasselbaink and Mark Viduka and defensive kingpin Ugo Ehiogu. McClaren, Ferguson's former number two – known as Mike Baldwin at Old Trafford because of his uncanny similarity to the *Coronation Street* star – was faced with trying to contain a rampant Rooney with a team of teenage rookies.

In the event, one of the best two players on the field was a teenager – but it wasn't Rooney. It was Boro's sparkling winger Stewart Downing, whose overall performance and clear ability in the way he snapped up his goal marked him down as one for the future – and a possible answer to England's perennial left-wing problem. Veteran Boro and England centre-back Gareth Southgate was the other star man – a one-man blockade and point of frustration for Rooney, Ruud and Ronaldo. His showing belied the fact he was no longer even an England squad member.

Boro were renowned as being United's bogey team. McClaren was looking for his third win in four visits to the Theatre of Dreams. In fact, he had celebrated his 100th league game in charge of the Teessiders when his team notched victory by the odd goal in five in the corresponding fixture the previous February. Joseph-Desire Job had struck the killer blow ten minutes from time. Ferguson could not even blame the poor showing on his team's fatigue after a European tie – Boro had also been in European competition, two days after United, in their UEFA Cup win over Banik Ostrava.

Rooney huffed and puffed from the start, never really looking up for the job, much to the dismay of the 67,000-plus crowd.

He was shackled superbly by Southgate and man-marker George Boateng. It meant he often drifted into midfield, and, because of his obvious fatigue, he was found wanting. His frustration with himself was best summed up by his constant niggling run-ins with Boateng. The boisterous Dutchman must take some of the blame – clearly upending him on a number of occasions – but the hot temper Rooney had managed to contain after the first game of Euro 2004 and into the Fenerbahçe match suddenly re-emerged as he clattered into Boateng, intent on revenge for the Boro midfielder's permanent unwanted attentions. It should have been Rooney's first booking in a United shirt, but referee Rob Styles was in a lenient mood.

The most dangerous attacker for United was not Rooney but Ronaldo. The Portuguese winger twisted aggressively along the right byline, providing crosses that, on a normal day, Rooney and Ruud would most surely have buried.

Instead, it was Boro who took the lead as their boys grew in confidence. The goal, on 33 minutes, was initially fashioned and ultimately executed by the excellent Downing. The left-winger passed the ball to Morrison on the right. He beat Gabriel Heinze and spun in a top-notch ball which Downing gleefully connected with and hammered beyond Roy Carroll in the United goal. Afterwards, even Ferguson conceded it had been class – 'ten out of ten, a marvellous goal'.

The United boss took a gamble on 69 minutes that would change the outcome of the match. Bravely, he took off the disappointing O'Shea, sending on that lovable Yorkshire terrier Alan Smith in his place. United were now playing with a three-man attack – Rooney, Smith and Ruud – and who would have predicted two of those three names linking up together at the start of the season? It helped as the Red Devils picked up the tempo. Ronaldo was now pinging in a series of accurate crosses and, nine minutes from time, Smith repaid his manager's faith by rising high above the Boro defence to head home the equaliser.

In typical style, Ferguson refused to criticise his team – instead concentrating on Boro's blocking tactics. He said, 'They had everyone behind the ball and made it difficult for us. They had lots of young players, but young players also have the legs to do their duties. They worked really hard to make sure it was a difficult day for us.'

And of his own stalwart – Master Rooney? 'Wayne wasn't quite as sharp as he was on Tuesday, but you have to take into account before that game he hadn't played for 96 days. Adrenalin got him through against Fenerbahçe, whereas he was a bit leaden-legged against Middlesbrough.'

Boro boss McClaren saw the outcome somewhat differently. He said, 'We were in Europe on Thursday, late travelling back, had so many injuries and had three 18 year olds making their Premier League debut. Looking at the team, and the way United played in midweek, no one gave us a prayer. It was an absolutely magnificent performance and I am so proud of my players.'

Rooney was quiet and contemplative in the dressing-room after the match. He slipped forlornly out of Old Trafford and back to Coleen at the hotel they still called home. Ferguson had thrown a consolatory arm around him before he left, telling him to keep his chin up. Both knew they would share much better times again – and soon.

Disappointingly, the single home point meant United remained in fourth spot in the Premiership on thirteen points with Arsenal still a distant nine ahead at the top. It had been the story of their season so far – stop, start, hope, deflation. It had all got off to a poor start in the showpiece FA Community Shield match at Cardiff, when Arsenal – and Spanish sizzler José Reyes in particular – had swamped the men from Manchester. Only Alan Smith's 55th-minute consolation goal had stoked the fires of optimism in the 3–1 setback.

Smith, a £7 million summer signing from Leeds, had been the first to trek the dangerous route to Old Trafford that Rooney would eventually follow. He was a Yorkshire lad born and bred, and as renowned for his kissing of the club badge on his Leeds shirt as Rooney had been for his allegiance to Everton. Just as fans of the Goodison Park outfit would condemn Rooney for moving to Manchester, so the Elland Road brigade breathed venom when news of Smith's transfer emerged.

Previously, the blond, spiky-haired firecracker had been their number one hero. Indeed, they had cheered him off after their final home match before being relegated from the Premiership. In the 3–3 draw with Charlton, Smith scored from the penalty spot and was lifted above the heads of fans as they bade him a final farewell. That, of course, was before they knew he was heading for Manchester. Never in their worst nightmares did they believe home town hero Smith, a life-long Leeds supporter, would end up joining the Whites' bitterest rivals.

From being a hero, he was suddenly damaged goods – and those very same fans turned on him like a spitting snake. Simon Jose, of the Leeds United Independent Fans' Association, summed up their attitude. To him and countless others, Smith was now 'a Judas' – just as Rooney would be when he quit Everton. Jose said, 'It's a stab in the back for all Leeds fans. But it reflects football as it stands today. The people at the highest level are in it for the money. It's about making as much as possible in as short a time as possible.

'There's simply no compassion or empathy with the fans any more. There are very few who seem to have any respect for the club or the badge. You cannot say you're a Leeds fan and then go to Manchester United. No Leeds fan would be seen dead in a Man U shirt, so Smith cannot be a Leeds fan. He will now go down on a long list of people who have betrayed Leeds United, and as for him saying he would one day come back, there's no way that will ever happen.'

Pathetic really, ain't it? But to give the other side of the story – in the sake of fairness – some Leeds fans, if only a minority, could understand Smith's need to better himself in his career. Ray Fell, chairman of the Leeds United Supporters Club, was one of them. He said, 'I remember Gordon McQueen saying he was a Leeds man for life just two weeks before he signed for Manchester United. But in wanting to leave Leeds, it put him [Smith] in a position of being able to join who he wants and that's what has happened.

'There's a certain element of the Leeds fans who will be angry and annoyed at his move, but most of them are mature enough to take this in their stride.' Fair enough, Ray. You're a good fella.

Anyway, on with the story – one man's loss is another's gain. And so it proved for the United of Manchester. Smith's sizzling early-season form would continue: it was the one real highlight of the initial letdown – along with those blond streaks in his hair that earned him the dressing-room moniker, Eminem. Yes, he was an unlikely double for the US rapper.

A week after the Community Shield defeat, United were on the losing side again, although it would be their only Premiership defeat of the first three months. Eidur Gudjohnsen grabbed the winner for Chelsea as United went down 1–0 at Stamford Bridge. The victory meant the world to new Chelsea boss José Mourinho, the heir apparent to Brian Clough. He had won the Champions League with Porto the previous season and certainly had faith in his own ability – perhaps to the point of arrogance. His team's win was not wholly deserved. They had had to batten down the hatches as United attacked them late in the second half. Afterwards, Mourinho made few friends as he said, 'I am a European champion. I expected my team to beat Manchester United.' A month later, after Rooney's signing at United, he would also say he wasn't bothered he had missed out on Rooney. He was quite happy with his own men up front: er, yes, José . . . Mateja Kezman and Adrian Mutu were definitely world beaters like Wayne – and are those pigs I see high above the M25 . . . or did only Mutu see them?

The following Saturday, United chalked up their first Premiership win of the season – a 2–1 victory over Norwich at Old Trafford. Again, Smith was on the score sheet, grabbing a goal on 50 minutes, after David Bellion had put the Red Devils in front. A week later, old Eminem was at it again – earning United a point at Blackburn with an injury-time equaliser after Paul Dickov had put Rovers ahead in the first half. Like Rooney, Smith had a reputation as a hothead. In his time at Leeds, he was often in disciplinary wars with the FA. But, also like Rooney, he seemed to be maturing – and stayed out of the referee's book in his first month, instead letting his dynamic forward play and goals do his talking.

August ended with the 0–0 home draw with Everton, a dull game that only served to prove how United needed someone like Cantona to throw in a few explosive tricks and help them step up another gear. Someone like Rooney, in fact. There had been rumours that the Croxteth terror would sign after the match, but no one in their right minds would have expected an announcement while the Toffees were actually within Old Trafford. Truth is, the deal was discussed and finalised between directors of both clubs after the game in the United executive suite. But they left the formal announcement and rubber stamping until the following day. And, no, there were never any plans for Rooney to be within 30 miles of Manchester on the day of the Bank Holiday Monday match.

September came but United were still not firing on all cylinders. Yet morale was picking up quickly. Rooney signed, and Ronaldo and new £6 million left-back Gabriel Heinze finally returned to Manchester after competing in the Olympics for Portugal and Argentina respectively. Heinze wore a particularly wide smile when he arrived at the Theatre of Dreams for the first time – he had ended up a gold medallist in Athens. He was a class buy: a typical Argentinian defender, moulded from the same obdurate metal as fellow countrymen and winners such as Real Madrid's Walter Samuel and that rough diamond blast from the past, Daniel Passarella. He would give as good as he got and was a brave player – never flinching from a 50:50 challenge and, more often than not, winning the ball.

Ferguson had signed a winner, and Heinze quickly proved it by shoring up a previously suspect defence and scoring on his debut at Bolton. Unfortunately for United, they let it slip and only a late equaliser from Bellion saved their blushes at the Reebok Stadium.

Things could only get better – and they did. Wes Brown was back from injury to bolster the backline and defensive kingpin Rio Ferdinand was gearing up for his return from his eight-month suspension. Ferguson confirmed well in advance that Ferdinand would start in the potentially explosive home match against Liverpool on 20 September. The England defender admitted he could not wait to get back on the park. He had kept himself in top shape, training every day, and had performed admirable behind-the-scenes work for charities and in the local community. But he had missed playing – and how United had missed him. When he started his ban after the match at Wolverhampton on 17 January 2004, United were top of the Premiership. During his absence, they fell to third in the league and their once-solid defence and season collapsed without him. OK, they won the FA Cup, but that is small-fry these days – for those reared on Premiership and Champions League success – and not something any United fan would want to shout about from the rooftops. The only bonus of his ban was that it rammed home how much United needed him, how much they relied on him. 'I'm delighted and had no hesitation in selecting him,' said Ferguson. 'We've missed him, and I am amazed at how good a player he is.' The United boss also admitted he would be ecstatic if Ferdinand repeated the feat of Eric Cantona, who served a nine month ban in 1995 for assaulting a Crystal Palace fan after he was the victim of verbal abuse. Ferguson said, 'Eric scored for us [against Liverpool ironically] and Rio has never scored for us, so that would be quite something.'

Ferguson had to be content with no goals from Ferdinand, but a man-of-the-match show. United dictated the game, and the former West Ham and Leeds star was majestic at the back. His confidence rubbed off on fellow centre-back Mikael Silvestre. The Frenchman had looked ill at ease for much of Ferdinand's eight-month ban, now he was rejuvenated and inspired. He scored both goals as United won 2-1 against their bitter Merseyside rivals. It might have been even closer if Kop skipper Steven Gerrard had not been forced off with an injury. John O'Shea put through his own goal, and Liverpool could take heart from the performance of their £11 million Spaniard Xabi Alonso, who took the dispirited visitors by the scruff of the neck when Gerrard limped off.

For Ferguson and United, it seemed the corner was finally being turned. His top men were back – and Rooney was raring to go after eventually resuming training in mid-September.

Ferguson had pencilled him in to start in the next match away at Spurs, but then pulled him out at the last minute, much to the youngster's chagrin. Still, even without him, United deservedly triumphed at White Hart Lane, Ruud van Nistelrooy converting the penalty that won the points just before half time. It's worth mentioning that this was not the spineless Tottenham of previous seasons. Under the guidance of former France international manager Jacques Santini and director of football Frank Arnesen, they had a new-found toughness in defence, with England keeper Paul Robinson and the excellent Ledley King directing operations, and a spritely attack led by the talented Jermaine Defoe. This was a big result for United – Spurs had gone to Chelsea the previous week and claimed a point, much to the disgust of Stamford Bridge supremo Mourinho, who had accused them of 'parking their team bus in front of the Chelsea goal'.

So all was set for Rooney's Premiership bow against Middlesbrough. It was to be a disappointment, but an understandable one, given the boy's fitness. On a personal front, he was sticking close to Ferguson and his agent Paul Stretford. One-to-one interviews were strictly off limit; the papers had to scavenge on the scraps Ferguson allowed him to throw us occasionally after games. Otherwise we were still having to rely on club insiders and people close to Rooney to keep us informed about what was happening. One told me the boy was happy and enjoying himself, although he did sometimes feel Ferguson could give him a bit more rope to express himself – even to allow him more chances to talk to the press.

If you had the money, you had a chance of talking with him. A tabloid newspaper had paid him a reported £250,000 in the summer for a handful of exclusive interviews, and he had told them about how he had met Coleen and they had fallen in love and were living happily ever after. It was all sugary stuff, much to be expected at the time. I still had the impression that this boy was much more intelligent than people suspected. It showed in his football – he instinctively knew how to control a match, where to put the ball, how to use it and where to position himself. In the same way as Mike Tyson had proved surprisingly eloquent about boxing and its chequered history, I felt Rooney would have views that could have made us sit up: about the beautiful game, growing up in Liverpool and the ups and downs of coping with the incredible transformation into millionaire sports star and internationally recognised face at just 18.

United decided he would talk to their official magazine. That was part of his commitment to the club. The interview did provide some extra useful information. Like the confirmation that he does indeed have an endearing sense of humour. The new darling of Old Trafford recalled how United fans had taunted him when he had turned out for Everton against United. They had chanted, 'Fat boy, what's the score?' as United won 3–2 at the Theatre of Dreams. Rooney said:

> I can remember the stick I got – I just laugh at it. It was the same at most grounds I played at. I know when I go back to Everton I will get the same stuff shouted at me. It happens, that's football. It's just the fans being football fans. I would do the same if I was still in the crowd. But since I've started playing I've matured a lot, especially in the last 18 months.

He was grateful to the United fans for their positive welcome:

> It was nice to see them outside Old Trafford waiting to see me after I'd signed, shouting my name and saying I'd made the right decision. Having the England lads like Scholesy and the Nevilles has helped me settle in, too.

He admitted football had always been his major passion. He said:

> It was all I ever wanted to do. That's all I was ever focused on. I was forever practising with my mates. It's not just natural ability. We used to play around the back of the house by some garages and use one as a goal. We'd all

take a turn in goal and play until it was dark. That definitely helped me a lot.

He first saw United in action when they lost to Everton in the 1995 FA Cup final at Wembley. Rooney was a member of Everton's Under-9s that were provided with a trip to the big event as the Goodison outfit won 1–0. He said, 'The atmosphere was brilliant. I couldn't stop singing because United had been winning everything up to then.' Among a list of favourites, Rooney told *United* magazine that *Grease* was his favourite film; Eminem and Kanye West were his favourite pop stars; Everton's Duncan Ferguson was his favourite player; and spaghetti bolognese was his favourite meal. The three words he would use to describe himself were, 'Funny, romantic and hard!'

The last of those words could possibly be used to describe his agent, Paul Stretford. When I rang to ask if I could have a chat with Rooney, one of Stretford's staff asked me how much I was offering. When I said, 'Nothing, but the truth', the voice at the other end of the phone turned to one of disinterest. 'Put it in writing and we'll see,' I was told condescendingly before the receiver went dead.

Days later, Stretford was accused of misleading a court as charges were dropped against three men accused of blackmailing him. The prosecution at Warrington Crown Court offered no more evidence against John Hyland, 42, and brothers Christopher, 34, and Anthony Bacon, 38. John Hedgecoe, prosecuting, said new information showed Stretford had misled the court – that documents revealed Stretford had poached Rooney earlier than he claimed.

The case had come about following a wrangle between Stretford and Hyland and the Bacon brothers, who were business associates of Rooney's first agent, Peter McIntosh. They believed Stretford had poached Rooney as a client and should pay compensation. Stretford had insisted he had not poached the young striker and had acted entirely honourably. But then it emerged he had been representing Rooney while he was still under contract with McIntosh. The new information proved

Stretford had taken on Rooney in September 2002, not December as he had told the court.

After the case, Rooney's management company Proactive said they would consider whether Stretford should face the sack. A source at the company said they could force out Stretford to protect shareholders. If it happened, it would be a devastating fall from grace for the man who started Proactive in 1987, building it into one of the three most powerful football agencies in the country.

There was another development linked to Rooney as the autumn leaves began to fall off the trees. Again, it was all about money. But this time it concerned one of United's investors across the Atlantic, the American billionaire Malcolm Glazer. The 76-year-old owner of the US American football team the Tampa Bay Buccaneers had also noted from across the Pond the dramatic interest in Rooney and the snowball publicity effect his move had on United worldwide. A spokesman for Glazer admitted, 'Rooney had opened Malcolm's eyes to just how big United were – and how he could use assets like him to make United into an even bigger enterprise.' Glazer already owned 19 per cent of United's shares. Now, like a crafty, stealthy prospector, he saw the chance to grab the whole golden pot.

It emerged that Irish horse-racing millionaires John Magnier and J.P. McManus, whose company Cubic Expression Ltd owned 28.9 per cent of United, could be willing to sell their stake at 310 pence to Glazer. That would value United at £805 million. Florida-based Glazer tried to sweeten his expansion by letting it leak that he would provide Sir Alex Ferguson with a virtually unlimited transfer fund. United fans are canny people when it comes to their club and cash.

Six years earlier – through their defence vehicle Shareholders United – they had held back the push of BSkyB. Now they made plans for another battle. They voiced a growing fear that Glazer did not have enough cash to do the deal – and that a takeover based on borrowing against club assets could load United with excessive debt. Shareholders United's plan was simple: to reach a position whereby its 15,000 members would own or control more than 5 per cent of Manchester United PLC. They could then apply to a court to stop the club being taken into private hands.

Rooney's arrival had brought hope on the terraces – unfortunately, it had also started neon lights flashing with Glazer. He had no interest in 'sakka' and had already indicated he would leave the running of the club to his 36-year-old son, Joel. United fans were worried, and no doubt justifiably, that the Glazers would raise admission prices still further and try to implement their own deals for TV rights. It could price United off the TV as well as out of reach of the man on the street. The club would become the preserve of corporate bodies, erasing the fan base once and for all.

By the middle of October, Rooney had come to epitomise the very essence of what would be a battle royale – he was the jewel in the crown among United's fabulous cast of playing stars. His move had alerted Glazer to the possibilities of owning the lot – and paved the way for what would be a very public war between the fans and the Yank they suspected of being little more than a gems thief.

5

INTERNATIONAL RESCUE

ENGLAND'S AUTUMN WORLD CUP QUALIFIERS COULD NOT have come at a better time for Rooney. After the high-octane publicity of the six weeks since his transfer, return to fitness and debut, he could finally take a breather from Manchester United. He would also leave behind him the escalating row over Malcolm Glazer.

Of course, he couldn't get away totally from United. England's first match in a five-day double header was at home against Wales. With Wembley still being rebuilt, it was Old Trafford the FA turned to for this so-called 'Battle of Britain'. A bit of a liberty that one – the Wales team under Mark Hughes were useful but very much a first-division outfit in comparison to England's undoubted Premier League status. Much was made of the Welsh dragon pumping out fire in the build-up week, but it would take a minor miracle for them to beat the English. In their opening qualifiers they had drawn 1–1 in Azerbaijan and 2–2 at home to Northern Ireland. Hardly statistics to get Sven-Göran Eriksson trembling in those famous high-heeled shoes of his. In comparison, England had drawn 2–2 in Austria in a match they should have walked and beat Poland 2–1 away: a fine result against the team who would be their closest rivals in the group.

Plus England – and Rooney – were at home. For Rooney, it meant training at United's Carrington complex and staying in another luxury hotel in the centre of Manchester.

He was bubbling when the boys walked into the reception. Happy to be with old mates again and now feeling much more comfortable in the England set-up. He was still only 18 but no longer the baby of the squad in terms of big-match experience. The Wales game would present him with his 18th England cap and his first international football since that nightmare against the Portuguese in June at Euro 2004. His presence also gave the other players a lift – he had been their talisman in Portugal and now he was back in business.

Manager Eriksson decided to let them have some freedom – and on the Tuesday night a few of the boys embarked upon a night-time walk around Manchester. The ale did not flow freely: Eriksson had limited them to a couple of glasses of wine apiece. Some of the players also enjoyed a bite to eat at Nando's in the Printworks complex. It got a bit silly as they tried to outdo each other by seeing who could scoff the chicken supper with the hottest sauce. But at least it helped the growing sense of camaraderie that Eriksson was at pains to develop. This was very much the plus side of Eriksson as a manager of footballers. He was renowned for giving them their heads – for accepting them as adults.

It brought about a carefree, happy, almost family-style atmosphere to training for the rest of the week. Eriksson, to his credit, certainly knew how to create 'Club England' – and it lightened the load of expectation for Rooney and Co. The England manager is one of life's greatest survivors: he had waltzed through the Faria Alam sex scandal just a few weeks earlier while his boss at the FA, Mark Palios, had been forced to resign. Alam, a lowly secretary at FA headquarters in Soho, had allegedly entertained both men as lovers. Foolishly, when the storm broke, Palios, it seems, had tried to get one of his henchmen to buy Alam's silence and his own survival by brokering a deal with the *News of the World*. It would have hung Eriksson out to dry but the 'Screws' refused, instead revealing Palios's 'plot' to the public. It had left Eriksson even more secure in his post after Palios walked.

Some members of the FA hierarchy still wanted rid of the Swede and his £4 million-a-year salary. But they would now only achieve that if he messed up in the qualifiers and, given the strength of England's rivals and Eriksson's competence in taking them through qualifying matches, that was an unlikely scenario. Plus, of course, in Rooney he had a new world-class talent in his ranks.

By the Saturday, all the talk was of Rooney and how/where Eriksson would employ him against the Welsh. Eriksson could see that the threat was going to be one essentially limited to fire and bluster – sure, they had some names in Ryan Giggs, Craig Bellamy and John Hartson, but the latter – an effective battering ram in the confines of the Scottish Premier League – was often a let-down in a Wales shirt. Bellamy was quick but was also quick-tempered and a slow-thinker, the sort who would moan and groan himself out of a game. In real terms, Wales's major threat was Giggs and Giggs alone. And Eriksson had the luxury of having Rio Ferdinand back after his drugs-test ban and Gary Neville returning at full-back to take on his clubmate down that left-hand side.

The situation, coupled with the emergence of Jermaine Defoe as an international candidate, encouraged Eriksson to throw off his traditional cloak of cautiousness. He decided to go for broke, starting with Rooney, Defoe and Michael Owen. Eriksson admitted he was delighted with the form of all three in training. He said, 'Rooney looks very good and in great shape and it's amazing to see him knowing he's been out for such a long time.' Some claimed it was a three-man prong up front; in reality, it was Defoe and Owen in attack, with Rooney claiming the role vacated by Paul Scholes's retirement. He was in the hole, linking midfield and the frontline. It was a role made for him, employing his footballing intelligence and skills for a full 90 minutes. Later, he would admit he would like to play the same role all the time for England.

The match turned out to be a one-sided stroll between the

millionaires and the paupers of international football. There had even been rumblings in the Wales dressing-room that they would boycott the game in protest at the paltry £100 bonus per man they had been offered to record the win that would have been the greatest result in their football history. Wales were on a basic £300 per man match fee – the English would take home at least two grand apiece plus an undisclosed, but certainly not £100, bonus.

England had lost the injured Steven Gerrard in midfield, but Nicky Butt was a more than adequate deputy. The Welsh suffered a blow during the warm-up, when experienced centre-back Andy Melville was injured. Manager Mark Hughes shuffled his pack, deploying Simon Davies as an emergency right-back and bringing in Jason Koumas in midfield. This was to be Hughes's penultimate match as Wales boss. The former Manchester United striker had already jumped this sinking ship for what he hoped would be the calmer waters of Ewood Park and Blackburn. He may well have been better off keeping Davies on the right wing, where he could have troubled England with his pace.

Some of the 67,000 fans packed inside Old Trafford spoilt what had been a carnival-like pre-match party atmosphere by disgracing themselves during a one-minute silence for Ken Bigley. The Liverpudlian hostage had been murdered in Iraq only days earlier, and the screeches, whistles and taunts made the old stomach churn.

England dismantled any hopes of a truly competitive contest after just three minutes. Nicky Butt played in a probing pass to Michael Owen, he found Frank Lampard and the Chelsea midfielder hammered the ball towards the Welsh goal. It deflected off Owen's heel and past goalkeeper Paul Jones. One-nil and it was all over already, bar the shouting. There was much of that in the stands as the Welsh urged on their team. But the goal had knocked the stuffing out of them and they were forced to soak up attack after attack.

Rooney was the man of the match in his new role. He was simply everywhere, lapping up his licence to roam. He was

England's engine – at the heart of everything they did. Mark Hughes had decided not to put a man-marker on Rooney: that was his second big mistake of the afternoon. He had yards to work in and he exploited the space as he had done against Fenerbahçe for United. Rooney mixed neat short passes with intelligent longer ones aimed in Owen's direction. And, with better luck, the Manchester United youngster should have added to his England goals tally. On ten minutes, he set off on one of his trademark runs from midfield and, as he advanced on goal, let fire with a powerful low shot that keeper Jones managed to deflect on to the post.

England were strolling and Wales were rolling. Perhaps the best illustration of Rooney being well suited to his new role came three-quarters of the way through the match. He controlled the ball splendidly, earned a yard or two on his defender and slotted Michael Owen in for a scoring chance with a glorious through ball. Unfortunately, Mark Delaney blocked well and the ball sidled out for a corner.

A minute later, skipper David Beckham awoke from his long slumber and scored with one of his trademark Old Trafford specials. It was not as good as the free-kick that secured a 2–2 draw with Greece and sent England to the World Cup 2002, but it was not far off. He stepped inside his marker from Butt's pass and let fly from 25 yards with an effort that soared over Jones and into the top corner. Magnifique.

Then Beckham showed his Mr Hyde side by clattering into Ben Thatcher and earning the yellow card that would rule him out of the match in Azerbaijan the following Wednesday. Rooney, remarkably considering he had only recently returned to top-level action, kept running until he was withdrawn by Eriksson after 87 minutes. The Swede finally gave in to his cautious side and sent on Ledley King to safeguard the 2–0 advantage. Rooney had almost netted five minutes earlier, but his shot deflected off Danny Gabbidon for a corner. When the final whistle blew, it was a case of mission accomplished – and another scintillating show from the young Scouser.

Wales boss Hughes immediately put their defeat down to

Rooney. He said, 'Rooney enjoys that role, dropping into those areas sometimes beyond the midfield players so it is difficult for defenders to pick him up. It's stick or twist whether to follow him or stay in position – it's difficult for defenders to make the right decision.' And Eriksson also praised Rooney for his handling of the new role. He said, 'Rooney played well. We had a good balance in the team, and gave a good professional performance. We kept cool heads and that was important in such a game.'

Rio Ferdinand, who had made a towering return to the international stage, snuffing out any threat from Hartson and Bellamy, suggested England with Rooney could go all the way and win the World Cup in Germany. He said, 'The amount of young talent we have got is unbelievable. There's Shaun Wright-Phillips, Jermaine Defoe, Ledley King, John Terry – oh, and Wayne Rooney, of course. They are all chomping at the bit, so it really bodes well for the future. When you look around, there is no question we have some great young talent. Wayne is a great young player. There aren't many around who can take up the positions he gets into. In fact, only Paul Scholes comes to mind. Wayne put on a show against Wales that not many older players could have matched.' Too true, Rio. But no time for sitting on laurels yet. A few drinks to toast victory on Saturday night, then back to work on the training ground for Wednesday's trip to that bleak, unwelcoming outpost of eastern Europe, Azerbaijan.

Bleak it certainly was, but one ray of sunshine lit up the dark, wet night of the match as gale force winds lashed the 'stadium'. The Azerbaijan coach was none other than Carlos Alberto, the man who captained the greatest Brazilian side of them all to World Cup victory in 1970. Before the game, the veteran spoke with admiration about the emerging talent of Rooney, conceding that he would be the major threat to his team. Still smiling after all these years, Alberto commented, 'Rooney is an excellent player. He will be our big problem and we may need two or three players to look after him.' Alberto had been disappointed with the quality of football on show when Azerbaijan played Northern Ireland and Wales, but added, 'England play much better football. They will probably beat us, but at least we will have the chance to show we can play football.'

A sell-out crowd of 32,000 had been expected to pack inside the Tofik Bakhramov Stadium in Baku. In the event, the weather stole the show and less than half that figure huddled together in the cold. The ground had been named after the Azerbaijan linesman who allowed that Geoff Hurst goal that never crossed the line in the 1966 World Cup final. The locals had come to see Rooney and Beckham, but the latter was out after suffering a hairline fracture of a rib against Wales.

He would have missed the game anyway through suspension after picking up a yellow card on the Saturday. Beckham was back in Madrid as the match kicked off, but, inevitably, the talk was still of the missing skipper. He attracts publicity as light attracts moths. Before the game, he had admitted he had lunged deliberately into Ben Thatcher the previous Saturday and asked to be given a little credit for his intelligence. He claimed he had worked the system for his own benefit, so that he would sit out a suspension when he was injured. Er, pardon, David? Some intelligent thinker, who would deliberately hurt an opponent and expect people to applaud him. And this was the captain of the national team. Controversy raged, with aforementioned England legend Hurst, now Sir Geoff, leading the call for Beckham to be stripped of the captaincy.

In his absence, England focused on the matter in hand – extracting three points from a tricky away match. Beckham's Real Madrid colleague Michael Owen took the skipper's armband – a clever psychological move by Eriksson to boost Owen's suffering confidence. The striker had been having a terrible time at Madrid, spending most matches on the bench and being booed by impatient supporters. His form had taken a hammering, although there had been encouraging signs against the Welsh that he was picking up the tempo again.

Eriksson also stuck with Defoe as Owen's partner and Rooney just behind them in his roving role. The only change was on the right, as Jermaine Jenas came in for Beckham. Shaun Wright-Phillips had expected a game, but Eriksson had made it clear that he could not play the Manchester City winger in the same team as Rooney, Defoe and Owen. That could have left the midfield and defence too stretched. Fair point, Sven.

Rooney's showing was typical of a pattern that had emerged with his comeback. One cracking display, one average – as in Fenerbahçe and Middlesbrough and now Wales and Azerbaijan. While he was the star against the Welsh, he was not as effective against the east Europeans. Tiredness after that injury lay-off played a part – so, no doubt, did the swirling wind that made attractive football impossible. He wasn't the only England player to suffer with the conditions – the only true stars of the night were the back line, who held tight throughout. For everyone, it was a case of backs to the walls: holding out for three points at any cost.

To their credit, the home outfit showed glimpses of good football – clearly influenced by Alberto's thinking. Since a 6–0 thrashing by Israel in his first game in charge, the Brazilian had transformed a team lying 116th in the FIFA rankings into a fairly competitive outfit. Wins over Kazakhstan and Uzbekistan were followed by creditable draws against Latvia, Wales and Northern Ireland. Now came their real yardstick of progress: Alberto did not expect to beat England, but he certainly told his troops he wanted them to know they had been in a match. And so it turned out.

Michael Owen missed a sitter from a loose ball just two yards out after two minutes but he and England settled down, and he seemed to thrive on the captaincy, urging on his men and showing tactical nous by organising a strong defensive wall when the hosts were awarded a free-kick 25 yards out. The decisive goal arrived on 22 minutes. Ashley Cole fired in a superb cross from the left wing and Owen nipped in between two defenders to head the ball home. A treat of a goal.

Another memorable moment came when Azerbaijan worked a complex series of dummies from a corner-kick. It was left by three players in a row before Nadir Nabiev smashed an effort wide. It had Carlos Alberto clapping his hands in delight. Rooney almost scored with a 25-yard free-kick five minutes before half time but keeper Jahangir Hasanzade deflected the shot, which was cleared and led to an Azerbaijan attack. Rooney spurted back and, out of frustration, brought down Rashad Sadygov. He was promptly booked for his indiscretion and that just about summed up his difficult night out in this desolate outpost. Just before half time, he had another bust-up, this time with his man marker Aslan Kerimov. From the bench, Eriksson gestured to him to calm down.

The second half was dull, limited by the gale-force winds and the determination of England to hang on to their lead, and of Azerbaijan to not concede again. Rooney dug in like the rest – tackling as best he could and probing when the wind allowed. He sent a free-kick wide on eighty minutes and was replaced by Joe Cole four minutes later. Not one of the boy's best cuttings for the old scrapbook, but he still emerged a winner as England held on in the swamp. There would be no headlines of 'Sven Azer To Go' in the morning's red-tops.

The win strengthened England's position at the head of Group Six. It had been an exhausting, sobering night, and Rooney was quiet on the charter flight that left a couple of hours after the game, returning the players to Manchester and London. It had been another important part of his learning curve. Sometimes you can't win in style: you just need to win. Full stop. Acting skipper Owen nonetheless made a point of patting him on the back and offering words of encouragement as they left the pitch and on the plane home. Owen, who had done himself a power of good with his solid captaincy and inspired goal, conceded that the result had been the main thing. He said, 'It is always tough away from home. We'd have taken a 1–0 win before the match. We've got six points from two games and we're happy with that.'

Sir Alex wasn't as jovial when Rooney and United's other England players reported back for duty. In particular, he could see that Rooney was jaded. That was a problem. Ferguson had made it clear he would not rest him. He had said, 'People who think that are in for a shock. I think Rooney needs games to be honest. He's only 18 years of age and he's been out for 96 days.

Since then, he has played twice for England and twice for us: that is only four games and if you think about it, you would always like to give a player six pre-season games before the start of the season and Wayne hasn't had that. Saturday's game at Birmingham and Tuesday's in Prague makes it six games before we play Arsenal the following Sunday, and that may be the start of our season.'

But having seen his exhaustion after the return from Azerbaijan, the United boss relented slightly – making him a substitute for the match at Birmingham three days later. It was probably just as well Rooney sat out the first 60 minutes at St Andrews. At least he escaped Ferguson's half-time lashing for a showing that was no more than average. Birmingham were well worth their first ever Premiership point against United – and could have won all three if keeper Roy Carroll had not denied Emile Heskey with his legs either side of the interval.

For United, van Nistelrooy and Alan Smith were the initial strike pairing. They battled hard, but Brum fought even harder on the day, with the exuberant Robbie Savage even coming out on top in his personal war with Roy Keane. Van Nistelrooy had the best chance of the first half when Quinton Fortune found him with a fine cross on thirty-six minutes, but the Dutchman hit the ball straight at keeper Maik Taylor from six yards.

Ferguson eventually brought on Rooney for the ineffective Kleberson. Wayne immediately got stuck in and appeared hurt after a confrontation with Savage. Luckily, it was only a dead leg. United could not escape the Brum shackles in midfield. Ferguson had been having a problem since the start of the campaign with his central midfielders. With Keane often a shadow of his former imperious self, and sometimes rested, the United boss had been juggling his cards like a compulsive gambler. He had tried out John O'Shea, Darren Fletcher, Kleberson, Eric 2DJ and Phil Neville in the problem spots. None had impressed well enough to nail down a regular starting role and it was now becoming a major problem. On 77 minutes, Ferguson went some way to solving that problem when he introduced Paul Scholes who had been rehabilitating from an early season injury. The point was this: it was all very well Ferguson boasting that he had the best four strikers – Rooney, van Nistelrooy, Saha and Smith – of any club side in the world but not very clever forward thinking to have duds delivering them blanks. Sure, Giggs, Keane, Scholes and Ronaldo, if they maintained their fitness, would be automatic choices – but what about when they were injured, lost form or needed a rest? The back-up men were just not up to it. Even Rooney could not elevate them beyond their talents every game. He was only 18 and would have dips himself.

The situation made a mockery of Ferguson's decision to offload Nicky Butt to Newcastle for peanuts in the summer. He was a battler who could have stepped into Keane's shoes early season no problem. He would never have let United down. Butt had provided his worth as a defensive midfield anchorman in England's games against Wales and Azerbaijan. United could certainly have done with his composure and unflappable talents at Brum. Sure, it's easy to talk about things in hindsight, but Ferguson moved him on too early, when so-called worthy replacements were simply not ready to take his place.

After the Brum match, the United boss was grim-faced. His team stood 11 points behind Arsenal in the Premiership. He said, 'Everybody is right to write us off because we're a few points behind, but football is a funny game and things can change. We are capable of winning the league, but we need to show the form that is capable of doing that. We are not doing that at the moment.' The Premiership table showed that Ferguson had a mighty job on if he was going to snatch glory from Arsenal. United were sixth, with fourteen points, and although they had only let in seven goals in nine games, their multi-million-pound attack had scored just nine goals. To put it all in perspective, Everton, who had flogged Rooney, were third in the table, with nineteen points, and, even without Rooney, had scored a goal more than United.

The pressure was piling up on Ferguson to deliver – and quickly. His team were in European competition the following Tuesday at Sparta Prague, and, then, the crunch loomed on the

Sunday – Arsenal at home. In an ideal world, the United boss needed in the region of another £30 million to paper over the cracks in central midfield. That sort of money and a whole lot of persuasive wooing might have enticed Steven Gerrard, Patrick Vieira or Pavel Nedved to Old Trafford. The problem was he had no funds – they had all gone on the Rooney deal.

Rooney was in business from the start when United took on the bottom team in their Champions League group in Prague. It was to be another match of frustration for the young Scouser as United's midfield again failed to provide the bullets for him and van Nistelrooy. Ferguson had gone out on a limb before the game, admitting he had got his team selections wrong this term. He had said, 'Maybe at the moment I am making too many changes. We have got the players, but at the moment I am picking the wrong teams for a variety of reasons.'

'We are not getting any consistency and that is definitely affecting our performances,' added Ferguson, who admitted his decision to play Cristiano Ronaldo in the draw with Birmingham had been a mistake. 'I thought Ronaldo would be fresh enough, but he was not. I made a mistake. And we accept the mistake of the pre-season campaign was calling players back too early. Paul Scholes was one. As can – and did – happen he got an injury.'

After the gaffer's confessional, you would have expected to have seen a settled United team in Prague. But Fergie further enhanced his reputation as the new Tinkerman – in the wake of Claudio Ranieri's departure from Chelsea to Valencia – by making *seven* changes. He gave former Celtic stalwart Liam Miller his first European start in place of Cristiano Ronaldo. Miller formed part of a new-look midfield with Ryan Giggs, Paul Scholes and O'Shea all returning. Rio Ferdinand was also missing, to attend his grandmother's funeral. That meant a return for Wes Brown in the heart of defence as Mikael Silvestre's partner.

They had their work cut out keeping Sparta at bay. The hosts made a mockery of their position at the bottom of the group – although United, once again, lacked that penetrating edge in midfield. Paul Scholes was clearly still short of match fitness after his return from injury, and John O'Shea gave away possession too many times for comfort. The home side were inspired by former United winger Karel Poborsky, who twice brought smart saves from Roy Carroll. United had the first opening when Rooney burst clear down the right with van Nistelrooy free in the middle, but a poor cross from the Liverpudlian allowed Radoslav Kovacs to clear.

The game burst into life before half time with a flurry of chances at either end. First a long-range Rooney effort cannoned off defender Jiri Homola but skimmed just wide of the post with keeper Jaromir Blazek stranded. Soon after, Gabriel Heinze fed Rooney again, having intercepted a poor Blazek clearance, and this time the England striker's effort was even closer, hitting the side netting. He and van Nistelrooy were working their socks off trying to create an opening, but it was to be a frustrating night. United did not manage another effort on goal until the 62nd minute when Rooney cleverly set up O'Shea with a looping cross, but the Irishman's volley ended up on the roof of the net.

Ferguson took off Rooney on 78 minutes, giving a run-out to Louis Saha, the Frenchman who was returning from injury. Rooney had worked hard but maybe had been forced to graft too much because of the United midfield's inability to slow the game down and control it. He had been given a centre-forward's role by Ferguson but had been forced to track back to win possession. By the time of his substitution, he was huffing and puffing, his face tomato red and sweating – he looked knackered. Afterwards, Ferguson conceded he was disappointed by the 0–0 result but predicted that United would come good.

He said, 'I felt that we had goals in us, so it's a bit frustrating not getting anything. It's not a bad result away from home. They played quite well and got a few chances due to a few mistakes at the back that I'm not happy with. But we also played quite well, worked hard and had some good counter attacks. It's always a concern when you don't score, particularly with a team that has such a great striker-rate.'

Rooney and Co. were contemplative on the plane back from Prague. The euphoria that had crowned his debut against

Fenerbahçe earlier in the month now seemed a distant memory. United had scored just once in their three games since he had hit three of the six against the Turks. Still, he had shown in the past that he was *the* big-match player, scoring on his debut and taking everything in his stride. Well, now would be a chance for him to live up to his reputation yet again – for United's biggest match of the season on the following Sunday. Yes, champions Arsenal were coming to town – unbeaten for 49 games, and determined to be the big bad wolf, break United's hearts and ruin their Premiership season by making it 50 without loss.

Defeat would leave United 14 points behind the Gunners – and with little realistic chance of catching them. Victory – and they would be eight behind and back in the chase. Wenger was smiling and confident; Ferguson looked worried. And Rooney? Well, this was the kind of stage that was made for him.

6

NINETEEN WITH A BULLET

WAYNE WAS IN HIS ELEMENT BEFORE, DURING AND AFTER THE biggest match of the season so far. Rooney's family hail from a long line of amateur boxers, and the Arsenal game towards the end of October was made for someone of that ilk. Traditionally, the United fans had looked forward with relish to local rivalry encounters against Leeds, Liverpool or Manchester City. But it had all changed over the last decade. Sure, meeting hicks from the sticks still got the blood pumping, but it was when the Gunners came to town that the Red Devils knew they would be in for a real winner takes all war.

The rivalry between these footballing citadels of the north and south had grown in tandem with their domination of the Premiership over the decade. Between them, they had won all but one of the twelve league titles since the inception of the Premiership – with United on top with eight to Arsenal's three. But Arsenal had won the title at Old Trafford in 2002 when Sylvain Wiltord's second-half goal ensured they would also end the season unbeaten away from Highbury. Now the stakes were just as high. If United won they would be back in the title race, eight points behind their visitors but with a massive psychological boost. If Arsenal won, or drew, they would have gone 50 Premiership games unbeaten – and driven a stake through United's heart and soul, on their very own doorstep.

There was another significance – and a good omen for the Manchester men. It was Wayne Rooney's 19th birthday on the very day of the match. Plus, of course, he had scored the wonder goal that had ended Arsenal's previous 30-game unbeaten record in October two years earlier. If United were the last team they would have chosen to play at this stage of their current unbeaten run, then Rooney was most definitely the bogeyman they would have prayed to avoid.

The build-up was as tense and nerve-racking as the action itself. The previous season, both teams had been punished in what had been just the latest battle of Old Trafford. There had been ugly scenes at the end of that match after Patrick Vieira had been sent off for aiming a kick at Ruud van Nistelrooy. It finished 0–0, but Arsenal's players allowed their frustrations to run high after the Dutchman also missed a last-minute penalty. Still angry at their skipper's dismissal, they shoved and taunted van Nistelrooy for the miss when the final whistle blew. Defenders Lauren and Martin Keown were fined and hit with four- and three-game bans respectively for their part in the chaotic scenes. Ray Parlour and Vieira earned one-match suspensions, Ashley Cole was fined £10,000 and Arsenal were ordered to stump up £175,000 as punishment.

The wounds had healed, but the psychological scars remained – even though Arsenal had since topped the fair-play league. There was also the small matter of that 'invincibles' tag. Ferguson and his boys did not like it – how could they be invincible when United had beaten them in the FA Cup semi-final and Chelsea had knocked them out of the Champions League? It was a fair point and it continued to nag away at Ferguson until he eventually blew up. Exactly one week before the match, he let rip with an ominous blast at his bitter rivals, claiming that the behaviour of Arsenal's players a year previous was, 'the worst thing I've seen in this sport'.

He went on to add, 'Arsenal got off scot-free really, they got away with murder. The disciplinary treatment was ridiculous when you think Eric Cantona got nine months for attacking a fan. All right, that was a serious offence and no one would disagree that something had to be done. But United took their own action in suspending him for four months. I don't think Arsenal would suspend one of their own players for four months no matter what he had done.

'The FA said what Eric did set a terrible example to young people. Given that he did it in a night match that wasn't on television, while United v. Arsenal kicked off at lunchtime with probably about ten million kids watching live on TV, I wonder what was really the worst example.' Brilliant mind games to get Arsenal twitching – or desperate words from a desperate man at a desperate time of United's season? Probably a bit of both. Ferguson loved to play out his verbal sparring with Wenger, but he was also aware that United's season and position, and consequently, his own, was very much under threat. They could not afford to let the Gunners get 14 points ahead with less than a third of the campaign gone. It would have been a disaster, especially given he had blown all his transfer budget and would not be able to buy his way out of the nightmare.

Wenger, for once, tried to defuse the war of words. He knew that on this occasion he had no need to resort to a bare-knuckle fight. His aim was composure – keep cool at all costs. United were essentially a team in transition; they were not as talented a team as the Gunners, whatever the individual merits of the likes of Rooney, Ruud and Ronaldo. Wenger knew that in pure footballing terms, United – for the moment at least – could not compare with his men. They could only win by getting stuck in and mixing it. So, from the ship's helm, he tried to negotiate potentially choppy waters with a firm resolve.

The Arsenal boss told his United counterpart to 'calm down' after learning of his comments. And he added, 'Alex Ferguson has a good sense of humour. Maybe it would have been better to have put us all up against the wall and shot us! We have improved and learnt from last year. We are now contending for the fair-play league, so I hope we don't lower our standards.'

On the day of the match, the form guide told its own story. In

United's last 49 league games, they had won 28, drawn 11 and lost 10. They had scored 79 goals and conceded 44, earning 95 points. Arsenal's 49-game unbeaten run broke down this way: 36 wins, 13 draws, 112 goals scored and 35 conceded. The total points haul was 121. This term, United had made their worst ever start to a Premiership campaign while Arsenal had made the best ever by any team. One minor carrot for a United win would be that they would become the first club to amass exactly 1,000 Premiership points. It was clear who would start as favourites, but since when had that mattered in a match like this – essentially a one-off FA Cup-style encounter? Winner takes all, well almost all, and certainly an advantage into the next phase of the season.

A cliché maybe, but you could have cut the tension with a knife as the players emerged from the bright lights of the tunnel into an emotionally charged Old Trafford. Rio Ferdinand once more led out United, after Roy Keane had cried off with flu. The team was otherwise Ferguson's strongest – with a back four of Gary Neville, Ferdinand, Silvestre and Heinze; Phil Neville, making his 200th Premiership appearance for United, was in for Keane and alongside Ronaldo, Scholes and Giggs in midfield, with Rooney and Ruud up front. Patrick Vieira led out the French national side: sorry, Arsenal. Rooney looked ready for a bruising encounter. He smiled at Vieira and Henry, and chewed his gum like a mini-Ferguson. Unusually, Sir Alex had already unwrapped a few pieces as he left the tunnel, a proud man walking in front of his boys on this do-or-die day. Normally, he would wait until the game kicked off before chewing fiercely on the old Wrigley's.

The United fans were in full voice with the 30-year-old favourite, 'We are the pride of all Europe, the cock of the north, we hate the scousers, the cockneys, of course', rippling around the ground, packed to the rafters. Arsenal had brought about 3,000 followers, and one cheeky banner summed up their pre-match mood of confidence. It read, 'Old Trafford – Champions enclosure'. Wenger looked as comfortable and confident as his fans as he climbed into his seat. He was on the brink of signing a new three-year extension to his contract and felt self-satisfied in the knowledge that he held an advantage over Ferguson in their one-to-one battles. The Frenchman had eleven wins to Sir Alex's eight – and they had, of course, already beaten United in the Community Shield at the start of the season. One other fact made him feel still more secure as the rain sheeted down from the grey Manchester skies: Thierry Henry was the Premiership's top scorer with nine goals in all competitions (including eight in the league itself) – the equal of United's total goals tally in the Premiership.

Wenger had left out Robert Pires for the sublime skills and pace of Spanish signing José Reyes, at 21 a young man with a future expected to be almost as big as Rooney's. Referee for the day was Mike Riley – one of Britain's top officials and a FIFA badge holder – from Leeds. He had been a little surprised to have a visit from the local constabulary before the kick-off. The police had taken it upon themselves to get involved after emotions had run so high on the pitch the previous season. They had warned Mr Riley to stress to the players the importance of staying calm and avoiding trouble in what could be a combustible cauldron.

Little wonder then that he decided to embark upon a softly-softly approach for the first half-hour. He was under pressure from the police and also from his own boss, Keith Hackett, who was sitting in the stands watching his every decision. Unlike Philip Don, the previous man in the job, Hackett was not one for ruling with a big stick. Maybe that helped persuade Riley to initially tread carefully. But he is a decent man and admitted later that he had also taken into account the atrocious wet conditions, which made the pitch a nightmare.

Afterwards, he would be damned for being weak – but would also have been damned if he had been too tough given the prevailing tension among the players and the lottery of a playing surface. Both teams were initially afraid to make a mistake, but the conditions forced errors upon them. And most of them came from Arsenal as United tried to impose themselves. Indeed, it took the Gunners 42 minutes to force an opening, and then Thierry Henry failed to test Roy Carroll in the United goal.

Overall, Arsenal edged possession with 52 per cent, but United had five shots on target to their one.

Rio Ferdinand was lucky to stay on the pitch after 19 minutes when he brushed Freddie Ljungberg off the ball. The speedy Swede had left the United skipper flailing as they both raced for a through ball – and that takes some doing given how fast a defender Ferdinand is. Referee Riley gave him the benefit of the doubt, much to the chagrin of Arsenal skipper Vieira. At times, it appeared that the big midfielder was jointly refereeing the match with Riley. He rarely left his side and seemed to be holding a constant conversation with the official.

Rooney was trying hard to get involved. He spent a lot of time in midfield, hustling and tackling back and trying to get United going forward. It wasn't easy – as in Azerbaijan for England, when the gales and rain made touch football impossible, so the conditions here did not suit his natural game. Alongside him, Phil Neville was quietly having a belter of a match. He shadowed Henry throughout and was so effective that the Frenchman's role was limited to virtual bystander. It made you wonder why Ferguson had not turned to him more during the first three months of the season as United struggled without Nicky Butt and a subdued Keane. The younger Neville brother proved himself a warrior – and worthy of the five-year new deal Ferguson had awarded him in the summer. It was another of those puzzling Fergie moments – why give a man a long-term, improved contract if you are going to dump him in the reserves and play less able men?

Rooney was also a warrior against the Gunners. Often, he can be reminiscent of the great Jimmy Greaves in that he can seem not to be making a major contribution and yet suddenly change the outcome of a game. So it was against Arsenal. With the match still deadlocked after 72 minutes, he picked up the ball and advanced into the penalty area, dragging Sol Campbell with him. Suddenly, he changed direction and Campbell raised his leg high. Rooney fell to the ground and a well-positioned Riley immediately pointed to the spot. Rooney clasped his fists, yelled, 'Yes!' and escaped from a furious Campbell. The big defender had the look of a condemned man – it was as if he had aged years as Rooney rounded him. Pointing desperately at Rooney he could have been a double for the great but elderly movie star Morgan Freeman. I felt sorry for the big guy, the only thing he was missing was a walking stick. It was a moment that emphasised that this is a cruel man's game at times: yes, a young man's game.

Later, the controversy would naturally rage over Rooney's 'dive'. But Campbell remained at fault. He could not cope with the youngster's guile or speed and should not have raised his leg high in the box. He was caught napping: a victim of the ravages of time. Anyone looking at the incident from Riley's position would have pointed to the spot. After the previous season's miss, van Nistelrooy proved he had considerable bottle by dispatching the ball past Jens Lehmann. The story was not over for Rooney – his incredible season was to reach an even greater height as he smashed home United's second, once again proving a pain in the neck for Arsenal.

It was injury time when the boy wonder struck to celebrate his 19th birthday. Substitutes Alan Smith and Louis Saha worked the ball to Rooney and he side-footed home. It was his latest destruction of Arsenal's unbeaten record – two years after he had scored that superb opening Premiership goal of his career, aged sweet sixteen.

As the final whistle blew, Rooney trooped off like a kid who had got every toy on his Christmas wish list. He saluted the crowd and smiled. There were no smiles from Arsenal or their manager – just a long list of complaints, grumbles and grimaces. Their behaviour brought to mind George Foreman's surliness after Muhammad Ali had crushed him in Zaire 30 years previously. But at least Foreman would later admit that he had been wrong to behave like a spoilt child. The reason for Arsenal's behaviour was the same as Foreman's. A few years after the fight, the big man explained it like this: 'For a while I was bitter. I had all sorts of excuses. I should have said the best man won, but I'd never lost before, so I didn't know how to lose.'

Arsenal had also forgotten how to lose – and, more

importantly, had forgotten how to be good losers. Their after-match comments and exploits on the way back to the dressing-room – the so-called 'Battle of the Buffet' – certainly left a bitter taste in the mouth. Thierry Henry walked off the pitch arguing with anyone who passed by, mostly with Roy Carroll, but even with his own players. He was that hyped up. Vieira and Campbell were also loose cannons – nothing new in the skipper's case, but it was unusual for the big defender to get so animated. Maybe his fury had its roots in a past flare-up – ironically also against United in April the previous year. Then, in another rumbustious encounter, Campbell had been sent off for elbowing Ole Gunnar Solskjær.

Campbell had expressed his sense of injustice after that 2–2 draw at Highbury, and now he felt United had cheated him again. If truth be told, he was also at fault in the Solskjær incident. The Norwegian is one of the nicest guys you could ever meet – as well, of course, as being the man who won United their second European Cup in 1999 with his injury-time goal. Campbell was out of order to claim Ole had made a meal of the elbow – and was also to blame for the Rooney penalty this time, after his outstretched leg had reached heights normally only scaled by ice-skaters. Big Sol trudged off sulking and in obvious turmoil.

Nearby, he watched as Sir Alex and Rooney saluted the fans, fists once again clenched in delight. It did not help Campbell's mood. His team had lost their unbeaten record and he had been the fall guy. On the walk up the tunnel Rooney turned to him and flashed a full teenage smile. No matter that just over four months earlier Campbell had treated him as an old pro should treat a fresh-faced newcomer to England's Euro 2004 base camp. He had welcomed him and spent time patiently looking out for him.

Now that goodwill had gone. The Rooney smile and some youthful mickey-taking by the boy about United's win and the penalty award touched a raw nerve and it took Campbell all his inner resolve to keep his cool. The boy wonder was unfazed by the big man and continued his celebrations right up to the dressing-room. A United insider told me, 'Campbell had a face like thunder. I have never seen him so wound up. Rooney's celebrations were the last straw.' The first United players were back in the dressing-room as the likes of the still jubilant van Nistelrooy and Sir Alex brought up the rear. As the duo passed by the Arsenal dressing-room, slices of pizza and some soup came hurling out of the half-shut door. The volley of food missed the Dutchman but splattered all over the United manager's suit – the one in which he would have met the awaiting TV interviewers for post-match comments. The insider added, 'There were scuffles and lots of industrial language. The stadium security staff managed to get the United men out of the corridor and into the dressing-room. It could have been a lot worse – but it looked as if one of the Arsenal contingent got a bit bruised when it all went off.'

Initially, Ashley Cole had been fingered as the food thrower – although he later denied the allegation. The young Spanish midfielder Francesc Fabregas was also seen near the door. And Wenger was alleged to have strode towards Ferguson asking him if 'he wanted some'. But does it really matter? We are not talking about trying to hunt down a murderer here; it was a bit of a blow-up after a tense battle, the sort that often happens and goes unnoticed at countless matches throughout the season. The only real downer was that it again showed Arsenal up as bad sports, while also, surprisingly, casting further doubts on the downward spiralling character of their manager Wenger.

When he arrived at Highbury in 1996, Wenger had come across as a sophisticated Frenchman: the sort of manager uncommon to British football. He was almost professorial in his outlook and appearance. He earned kudos through his calmness and sense of proportion in what, after all, was not as Bill Shankly had once claimed 'more important than life and death', but just a simple, beautiful game. But Wenger changed over the years. He seemed to become more British, more emotional, as each 12 months passed by. His traditional calm and Buddhist outlook on life had certainly disappeared after this defeat.

As a practising Buddhist, one would have expected Wenger to

be a philosopher and a man more interested in promoting good causes. A man of peace. Yet here he was in the Old Trafford tunnel after the match allegedly shouting foul abuse at Ferguson and van Nistelrooy. The great Buddha had lost it. Later he would claim that 'nothing happened in the tunnel'. Perhaps that was a comment from a shamed heart, it was certainly one from a man who had thought carefully about his behaviour some time after the event. In a literal sense, he had not told a lie, but it was only on a legality. The 'buffet' battle had actually taken place away from the main tunnel, in a corridor near the dressing-rooms. Of course, it was good to see the passion both teams had for the game and result – who does not like to see their team fight for the badge? But Wenger and his men had overstepped the line, and should have apologised for their conduct.

Inevitably, the jokers in the press ranks doubled over at their own witticisms on the situation. One had suggested that Ferguson had been hit by soup thrown by one Arsenal man and one United: Campbell and Heinze. Hilarious, hey? Ferguson was not laughing – he had to get changed in the United dressing-room and did his Sky TV interview wearing a United tracksuit, but he did not mention the battle underneath Old Trafford, preferring instead to concentrate on the victory on the pitch.

Ferguson would later defend the penalty decision. He said, 'When I saw it on *Match of the Day* I thought it was soft. But when we analysed it during the week, the view from behind Campbell shows his leg two feet high. The ball was on the ground, so why the hell was his leg up so high? If I was his manager, I'd be asking that question. It was either done to intimidate the player or it was just bad defending.'

Wenger, naturally, laid the blame for the defeat fairly at the feet of referee Riley. He said, 'In a game like that, the referee had to be sure. We got one [a penalty] against us last season and now this. I think you should look at the track record of the referee with Manchester United. We got the usual penalty for Manchester United when they are in a difficult situation. I don't think there was any contact at all. Even Rooney told our players that no one touched him. In a game like that, to see how lightly the referee gave a penalty is difficult to take.' The Arsenal manager also accused van Nistelrooy of stamping on Ashley Cole and claimed Gary and Phil Neville had tried to 'kick José Reyes off the park'.

Reyes would later add to the accusations, describing the defeat as 'the hardest match I have played in England'. He said, 'I have never received so many kicks as in Manchester. The referee should have stopped the violence of the Manchester United players. The penalty should not have been given – but now we all know what a good actor Wayne Rooney is in the penalty area.'

With his last comment, young Reyes fired the opening salvos in a verbal feud that could last for years. He and Rooney, along with Ronaldo, Fabregas and Chelsea's Arjen Robben, were the best young players around – and were likely to be battling for supremacy when van Nistelrooy and Co. had long retired.

Reyes was licking his lips in anticipation of the return bill at Highbury in February. He said, 'I already have a big desire to play the return match in London. We want to give back the defeat to them and by more goals.' Ominous words indeed.

Rooney and the other United heroes celebrated wildly after the win while Arsenal got out of Manchester as quickly as they could that night – angry and licking their wounds. The affair was not over, though. Van Nistelrooy pleaded guilty to a charge of serious foul play for his challenge on Cole. His admission earned him a three-match ban. It was the first time in his career that he had served a club suspension and he said, 'There was no deliberate attempt to harm Ashley Cole, and I would like to apologise to him.' But Wenger was in no mood for conciliations. He rapped, 'What is he doing getting involved in silly things? He always does it like he's innocent. Play football, my friend, and forget about all the rest. Who do you want to impress by doing that?'

Those words would enrage Ferguson. The United manager replied quickly, claiming Wenger had 'a mental problem' with the Dutchman. It was like a tennis grudge match at Wimbledon – serve and volley. No sooner had Ferguson commented, than Wenger responded: 'I can assure you I do not have a mental problem with him.' Ferguson claimed it may have been rooted in Wenger's frustration at missing out on signing van Nistelrooy.

By now it was getting childish, two grown men catapulting insults back and forth, and it all hit rock bottom when Ferguson revealed he was compiling a dossier of Arsenal's misdemeanours in the match to send to the FA.

Much of the United manager's week after the Arsenal bruiser seemed overshadowed by his 'dossier of shame'. He was going to get the FA to look at the moment when Thierry Henry jumped over Gabriel Heinze and the Frenchman's knee hit the Argentine's head and at some indiscretions by Dennis Bergkamp. In the case of the Henry 'attack', it would have taken a brave man to safely confirm he deliberately set out to hurt Heinze. I looked at the video several times and must say that in this case I am a coward.

The gap between the teams was down to eight points as United travelled to Portsmouth on the Saturday and Arsenal hosted Southampton. On paper, both fairly comfortable fixtures. For Rooney and Co., a win was vital, otherwise their sterling efforts the previous Sunday would have been for nothing. Yet the fallout from the Old Trafford bust-up continued to have an impact. Both teams looked washed out and mere shadows of the heavyweight champions they were. Arsenal struggled to a 2–2 draw at Highbury, with Henry grabbing an injury-time saver. But United lost 2–0 at Portsmouth after laying siege to the Pompey goal but failing to convert their many chances.

No doubt Monsieur Wenger would have said it was the forces of karma that led to Pompey's opener. This time, United were on the receiving end of a controversial penalty. Rio Ferdinand was judged to have pulled back Ricardo Fuller, and David Unsworth blasted the spot-kick past Roy Carroll. Cristiano Ronaldo hit the post with a header as United piled forward but Aiyegbeni Yakubu killed them off with a shot that deflected in off Mikael Silvestre. It was Pompey's second successive Premiership triumph over United at Fratton Park – and was a crushing blow to the Reds.

Frustration washed over the visitors – especially Rooney, who had a running battle all afternoon with Pompey's physical midfielder Nigel Quashie. At one stage, Ferguson ran off the bench and gestured to Rooney to calm down. The teenager was in grave danger of being sent off, and Fergie may have served him better by substituting him. It had been a killer result for United after the week had started so brightly at Old Trafford. Ferguson ripped into his men in the dressing-room afterwards and warned Rooney and his misfiring forwards to buck up. He hadn't spent millions to see the ball going wide or over. The boy wonder took his lashing, keeping his head down in a corner of the dressing-room. Ferguson remained a supreme motivator of footballers, knowing when the arm around the shoulder or a sharp, swift piece of that infamous Glasgow temper was required. Rooney was a tough nut, but he wisely kept his mouth shut. He had only respect for the manager who had gambled so heavily on his skills.

Yet he, like Ferguson, was bewildered by United's inconsistency. One match they looked like world beaters; the next they were all over the place. The situation caused Roy Keane to also speak out a few days after the Portsmouth defeat. Like Ferguson, he was alarmed at the way half-chances were being spurned by men who should have buried them. But at least he was honest enough to take some of the blame himself. He said, 'You can have all the individual talent you want, but it counts for nothing if the team are not performing properly. What matters more than anything is the way the team are playing. The onus is on midfield players like myself to create more chances for our strikers. I'm sure that when we do the goals will start flowing.'

Meanwhile, on the far horizon, there was another problem that needed some attention. While the two heavyweights of United and Arsenal continued to slug it out and knock each other over, the super confident José Mourinho and his Chelsea were zipping up on the inside like a lean, mean boxing machine. They had reached the summit of the Premiership with a 4–1 win at West Bromwich on the same day United had lost at Portsmouth and Arsenal had drawn with Saints. How ironic it would be if Ferguson and Wenger continued to batter each other into submission – only to see the new boy on the block take their place as the leader of the gang.

7

BEAUTY AND THE BEASTS

AS SIR ALEX MIGHT SAY: LET'S TAKE A WEE BREATHER FROM THE relentless pace of the football and have a closer peek behind the scenes as Rooney settled in at Manchester United during October, November and December 2004. First, we'll jet off to America, Florida to be precise, and set up camp at Tampa, the sporting home of Malcolm Glazer, the irritant who would not disappear. No doubt *Pop Idol* Mr Nasty, Simon Cowell, would have been proud of him: well, of his peculiar dress sense, at least. Trousers hitched high above his waist, almost hugging his breasts, old ginger-beard Malcolm was not your traditional flashy billionaire.

He was more in the style of a recluse like Howard Hughes. When he did appear in public – and those showings were becoming less and less frequent – the all-laughing, all-smiling, all-joking Mr Glazer tried to effect the persona of your small-time man done good. He was one of you; he felt your joys and despair as your team triumphed and floundered. Or at least that was the impression he liked to foster among the public – *his* public – in Florida.

The reality was somewhat different. After a love-in with the fans, which culminated in the team winning the Super Bowl, relations with their owner, the 244th richest man in America, had become more strained. The way he operated at Tampa after taking over in 1995 – softly-softly, then tough guy with the big stick – would have been enough to make most United fans shudder. What's that about a leopard and its spots?

Glazer snapped up the Buccaneers for about £125 million after they had notched up a long string of losses both financial and on the pitch. His first act was to fire the manager, and he did eventually bring success. In 2003, the club won the Super Bowl. But he also embarked upon some very unpopular measures. As part of his purchase in '95, he had promised the Tampa authorities he would go halves on a new stadium with them. Then, after gaining control, he quickly backed out of the deal and told the city of Tampa they had two years to build it, or he would relocate the team. Local taxpayers were still footing the bill for the ground via a municipal levy years later.

The Buccaneer players also had to travel 80 miles to a training ground each day because their existing Tampa training facilities, which Glazer had yet to update and improve despite promises, were infested with rats. Given these background factors and the hostile way in which the man known to Tampa fans as 'the leprechaun' had been targeting United, it was hardly surprising that a groundswell of opposition was building steadily against him across the Pond. His opponents had disrupted United's reserve-team matches to get their anti-Glazer banners on TV, and Shareholders United had made it eminently clear they did not want Glazer in command.

The American admitted he had been sparked into action by Wayne Rooney's arrival at Old Trafford. He had been amazed by the worldwide publicity and clamour for a piece of the boy wonder generated by the £27 million transfer. Inevitably, he now wanted his slice of the action – but he wanted the whole of the cake for himself. Rumours that he would sell Old Trafford and lease it back, set up an expensive, exclusive TV and Internet facility, and raise entrance prices did not help his case. Neither did his arrogance. He refused to talk to the press and his public relations team was non-existent. When I attempted to talk to him – or at least get to talk to him – via the Buccaneers general phone number, I was fobbed off by an operator who had been briefed to give short shrift to enquiries from the press. He would not talk to me, but I could order a Buccaneers replica shirt if I would be so good as to hold the line. On yer bike, Malcolm.

So just who is the leprechaun, and what makes him tick? He was born in Rochester, New York state, in 1928. His father Abraham died in 1943, when Malcolm was 15, and he took over the family watch-parts shop in the city. At that time, he had just $300 to his name. One of the few quotations attributed to Glazer concerns this time of his life. He said his father's death was, 'probably the most tragic thing in my life. But it was good in one way. It made me a man'.

He and his family were orthodox Jewish immigrants from the Baltic republic of Lithuania. His father was said to have arrived in America after deserting from the Russian Army. Glazer was nothing if not hard working – after his father's death, he expanded into other businesses and the readies rolled in. He made a fortune from his interests in banking, nursing homes and real estate, mainly in the Florida area. Allied Corporation, the family property firm, now owned shopping centres in 15 US states. Glazer's first attempt at a takeover was in 1984 when he tried to buy the bankrupt US Conrail system. United fans would not be enamoured by the fact that he offered $7.6 billion, when he actually had only $100 million of his own. Rang a bell, didn't it . . . Attempts to raise the difference eventually failed. In 1989, he also failed in a bid to buy the motorcycle company Harley-Davidson, and, in 2003, the serial bidder was also snubbed as he tried to get his hands on the baseball team, the LA Dodgers.

Worse news was to follow for Glazer and his takeover attempts. The US Securities and Exchange Commission was said to be investigating allegations that Glazer's family had artificially boosted the market values of two family-controlled companies which may have been used as collateral for bid finance.

Glazer was also taken to court by tenants at one of the residential caravan parks that he owned in New York after he started charging each household an extra £2 a month per child and £3.50 per dog. And, in his personal life, a bitter row broke out through the courts between him and his five sisters over the contents of his mother Hannah's will. He is alleged to have refused to allow his sisters a share of a reported $1 million legacy after revealing a secret document Hannah had signed, which made him the sole beneficiary.

Ruthless? Certainly. Determined to have his own way at any cost? The evidence above suggests so, as, indeed, did his stalking of United. It was also suggested Glazer wanted a new toy to play with, that he was growing bored of the Buccaneers. Closer to the truth was that he wanted to leave a toy for his two soccer-fanatic sons Avram and Joel, who were heading up the bid for United. There was nothing to suggest Glazer himself had any interest in the game – apart from a financial one.

Glazer made a major move on 15 October, when he raised his stake in United to 25.3 per cent. His earlier talks with Irish race horse owners John Magnier and J.P. McManus – owners of 28.9 per cent of the club – had broken down and Glazer's swoop late on that Friday was seen as a shot across the bows for those who had claimed he was a defeated man. Glazer almost gleefully confirmed he had purchased 15.4 million shares at 285 pence apiece.

All the earlier speculation had centred around the belief that Glazer had offered 300 pence a share to buy the Irish pair's stake. The United fans were now in the rather ironic situation of relying on the goodwill of Magnier and McManus to keep Glazer at bay. Just ten months earlier they had battled against a possible takeover by the Irish duo as their very public row with Sir Alex Ferguson over the racehorse Rock Of Gibraltar escalated. Now they desperately needed their support – and prayed they would not sell out to Glazer. The mysterious Irishmen refused Glazer's approach but stayed silent over their reasons, although it was suggested their rebuffal was not altruistic. Some commentators claimed it was more to do with them wanting closer to 320 pence a share than the 300 pence offered by the American. Yet the duo also had no urgent desire to be remembered as the men who had betrayed United by selling out.

The anti-Glazer camp received a further boost when United's

board officially ended talks with the American over a possible takeover, claiming the proposed move was 'not in the best interests' of the club because it relied too much on borrowed money. By now, Glazer had increased his stake to 28.1 per cent – if it reached 30 per cent he would be forced to make a formal takeover offer. By the middle of November, more good news followed for the anti-takeover campaigners when Glazer's banker, JP Morgan – who had been lined up to finance the deal – dropped him as a client. Earlier the same day, the American had cast his stake against the re-elections of three United directors. Legal adviser Maurice Watkins, new commercial director Andy Anson and non-executive director Philip Yea were all booted out, but JP Morgan were unhappy at Glazer's boardroom coup and the antagonism directed at them because of their links with him.

By the end of November, the Glazer bid seemed to be running out of fuel. And when United manager Sir Alex Ferguson stepped into the row, just a couple of days before his 1,000th game in charge at the club, few people would have bet on Glazer winning the battle. Ferguson waded into the takeover debate by stating that he did not want United to be in the hands of an outside investor like Glazer. Ferguson said the all-important thing was the relationship between United and its fans, and his words were a body blow to Glazer, who would certainly have benefited from his support in any takeover.

Ferguson told United's official website, manutd.com:

> When the PLC started, there were grave doubts about it – I had them myself. But there is definitely a better balance to it now. I think the supporters have come round to that. There is a stronger rapport between the club and the fans than there has ever been. I have always tried to be the bridge between the club and the fans and I have tried to support the fans in a lot of their pleas and causes. Sometimes we can get too emotional as a club with things that are happening but we are both of a common denominator; we don't want the club to be in anyone else's hands. That is the way that the club stands with that. I support that.

It was a masterful piece of oration by the United boss and seriously dented Glazer's hopes. He had counted on bringing Ferguson on side but had miscalculated. How could he get the financial backing he needed without the board's recommendation or Ferguson's support? Anyone willing to lend would ideally not want to get involved in a hostile takeover and the club's asset base covered barely a quarter of what Glazer intended to pay.

Yet United fans were not convinced it was the last they would see of the American. They had done a magnificent job in repelling him but remained wary and ready for more battles. As Shareholders United spokesman Oliver Houston warned: 'Most wild animals are at their most dangerous when they are cornered and we should treat Malcolm Glazer in exactly the same way. What he did at the Annual General Meeting was declare war on the club. Now we have to end it and put him down once and for all.'

For the moment at least, the likes of Rooney, Ronaldo and Ruud had escaped the clutches of the American and any wild publicity campaigns he had dreamt up for them if he had won the fight. But Rooney had a problem closer to home to contend with: his increasingly questionable relationship with Paul Stretford. The agent had acted quickly to take the spotlight off himself and the boy wonder following the collapse of the Rooney contract blackmail trial. Stretford had quit the board of the Formation Group, the Wilmslow-based sports management and marketing business he had formed as Proactive Sports Group.

In a stock market statement, Formation said 'As a result of the recent High Court case and consequent media coverage and speculation, Paul Stretford, executive director, has resigned from the board with immediate effect, as he believes that this is in the best interests of the group.' Of course, there was a rub: he retained a substantial stake in the company – and remained head of the company's player representation division as a director of the subsidiary Proactive Sports Management.

Stretford received more good news when Cheshire police announced he would not be charged for misleading the court over his signing of Rooney. A police spokesman confirmed:

'Following the collapse of the trial at Warrington Crown Court in October, we have decided in consultation with the Crown Prosecution Service that there will be no action taken against any individuals.' However, there still remained the FA's investigation into the affair, which could lead to questions about his right to continue as a licensed agent.

On an altogether brighter note, Wayne and Coleen were enjoying their new life together in Manchester. They had now moved into a rented house on a 12-month lease while they waited for the completion of their newly built £3 million home. Their rented gaff was just half a mile from the home of Sir Alex Ferguson in Wilmslow. At £3,000 a month, the mock Tudor house would provide them with some stability on the home front. Plans for the new house had been lodged with Macclesfield borough council at the end of November – and they inevitably led to comparisons with the Beckhams and their pad, the so-called Beckingham Palace. Rooney's mansion also seemed to take its inspiration from Southfork, the ranch of the Ewing family in the '80s TV series, *Dallas*. The new property included six en suite bedrooms, a gymnasium, a cinema, an indoor swimming pool with a whirlpool bath and a games room.

Wayne and Coleen were now closer than ever – and it hadn't been just Mike Riley who had handed out the birthday presents most wanted by Wayne. The ref had given him the controversial penalty against Arsenal on his 19th birthday and lucky Wayne had also grabbed another with his excellent goal. Coleen kept the gifts coming with a £15,000 designer watch from herself and a framed boxing glove from her family. No ordinary boxing glove but the one worn by Muhammad Ali in his fight against 'Smokin'' Joe Frazier in 1971.

Coleen's spending was fast becoming the talk of the tabloids, and she made major headlines when Customs men stopped her at Manchester airport after a £13,000 shopping spree in Manhattan. She was questioned for a couple of hours and had to fork out an extra £3,000 in VAT. Travellers are only allowed £145 of items without paying duty. Wayne's girl had been unaware of that. When you throw in an extra £10,000 for flights and hotel rooms for Coleen and two pals, it was easy to see why the tabloids were calling her the new 'Patron Saint of Shopping'. As soon as the boy wonder earned the readies, she was happy to spend some of them. Not that he minded.

Her spending brought a flood of comments in the papers, on websites and on the TV. The country was agog about Coleen, a girl who had been an unknown a year previously. It was quite incredible that the population was so engrossed with her. Some people were witty, others congratulatory, others simply envious – like this typical mixed bag of Internet message board writers:

> Does this girl have a purpose in life, or was she just put on the earth to spend his earnings at the shops? Saw all that stuff in the papers about her designer outfits the other day and felt sorry for her – a total fashion victim and there was nothing that looked good on her. Seems obscene that there are so may families struggling, yet you get these overpaid teenagers going to NY and squandering thousands – it's like money and possessions are Gods that they worship, and their lives just seem so shallow and irresponsible. – Maggie5

> Sorry, but if I suddenly had loads of money to spend, I'd bloody well spend it on whatever I wanted, too! She's a kid, probably hasn't had much money to play with before Wayne hit the headlines, and she's making the most of it. Can anyone honestly say that they wouldn't spend anything on clothes, shoes, or whatever floats their boat if they were suddenly really rich???? Obscene is spending money on funding military coups, subsidising drugs deals and paying for kiddie porn on your computer. Buying a few designer outfits, whether they suit you or not, is not in the same league. – Topwoman

> Agree with Topwoman. The girl is suddenly rich, is only 18, wow, I'd be out every day shopping!!! Leave her alone. – Petal

Who says he's overpaid? Erm when you've got all that money coming into a club like Man Utd for instance, sold out every home game 67,000 people paying to watch the players, plus other monies coming to the club from Sky etc, money from the shop. Why shouldn't the players get the money? Who should get it – the shareholders? People are paying to watch the players like Rooney who are top in their field. I don't understand it when people say overpaid. If they weren't paid that they would go abroad where they would get even more. – JasonL

Some women columnists in Fleet Street also took a keen interest in Coleen. They attacked her for staying with a man who had visited massage parlours and claimed she was only in it for the money. Some also launched vicious personal attacks on her looks and lack of a career. They were surely out of order wading in with the subtlety of the mob when the girl was just 18?

Coleen seemed much like any sweet, pretty girl of that age. Sure, a bit dizzy with the cash cascade and emotionally insecure, but who wouldn't be – who isn't – at that age? Certainly not some of the ever-paranoid, vain writers in the Street. Apart from not leaving Wayne, they said Coleen's other major transgressions were that she had the choice of two motors – a £50,000 17-ft Cadillac Escalade and a £25,000 Chrysler 300C V8 – and, sin of sins, she wore a £20,000 Rolex watch and had her own 'personal shopper' at Harvey Nicks in Manchester.

By December, some of the comments in the papers had become simply spiteful. One day when Coleen was spotted taking her Chow Chow dog Fizz for a walk near the rented house, it was claimed she could be pregnant. It was a particularly cheap shot: a sideways swipe basically saying she had heaped on the pounds – ha, bloody ha. A survey for *Clotheshow Live* also put the boot in – Coleen was voted the worst dressed 'celebrity' by 1,200 women. Worse than Cherie Blair, Jade Goody and Nancy Dell'Olio? Do me a favour . . . even Tony Blair, that 'regular kind of guy' would struggle to say that his wife was more fashionable than our Coleen.

Then there were the TV trendsetters and commentators keen to put Rooney and his girl at the top of a new movement – the so-called Chavs. Just as Beckham and Posh had been elevated to celebrity icons five years previously, now it was Wayne and Coleen's turn to get the treatment. No doubt about it, they were the new faces of football superstardom, the ready-made replacements for the Beckhams now they were in exile in Madrid. They were everywhere you looked – on the front and the back pages. But were they Chavs? This is the definition of a Chav from the Oxford Advanced Learners' Dictionary:

> A young person, often without a high level of education, who follows a particular fashion. Chavs usually wear designer labels, and if they're girls, very short skirts and stilettos. Chavs still see branded baseball caps as a status symbol and wear them at every opportunity. Chavs usually wear designer labels including the Chav favourite 'Burberry'.

Sure, Coleen loved to wear her Ugg boots – or Uggies as she called them – but so what? She did not wear short skirts or stilettos – she was a Liverpool lass, not your typical Essex girl. What it all amounted to was a campaign by certain sections of the press to foster the idea that they were both airheads, and, as I have said before, that is simply not true. Rooney and Coleen are two tough cookies: feisty, determined, ambitious people.

The constant criticism was a prime example of professional envy and jealousy from some writers who should have known better – and who wished they had the advantages of Rooney's talent and wages . . . and his fame and international appeal.

No, Wayne and Coleen were doing just fine, thank you. But clouds were gathering on the horizon for him and United as games with Manchester City and Newcastle loomed. Now he would have the chance to prove he was worth every penny of his money. And then he could enjoy himself in England's 'luxury' friendly in Spain three days after the Toon assignment – well, at least that was how the script was supposed to play out.

8

THE PAIN IN SPAIN

THAT WAS THE WEEK AND A HALF, THAT WAS. TEN DAYS
Wayne Rooney will certainly not forget in a hurry. It started on
7 November with United's rough 'n' tumble 0–0 derby against
Manchester City at Old Trafford, took in the superb 3–1 win at
Newcastle seven days later and concluded with England's
'friendly' disaster in Spain. Inevitably, Rooney ended the ten days
where he had started them: as headline news.

He had travelled with the England squad for what Sven-Göran
Eriksson termed 'a luxury friendly' in Spain at Real Madrid's
Bernabéu stadium. It turned out to be far from that as England
lost 1–0. It could easily have been four or five, and Eriksson
hauled Rooney off just four minutes before the interval 'to teach
him a lesson'. Rooney had become increasingly frustrated by the
inability of England's midfield – which struggled without the
injured Steven Gerrard and off-key shows from Frank Lampard
and Nicky Butt – to supply him and Michael Owen with a single
chance on goal. He was also annoyed by the constant racist jibes
from the Spanish crowd at his pal Ashley Cole.

When Rooney chased a rare through ball with goalkeeper Iker
Casillas, he lost his head, pushing the Spanish number 1 into the
railings behind the pitch. He was booked but that did not deter

him. Soon after, he brought down defender Carlos Marchena, and Eriksson took him off. There were no arguments in Rooney's defence – save youth and frustration – but did Eriksson need to make an example of him? Couldn't he have waited another five minutes and left him in the dressing-room after the interval? You either view it as fine man-management or a crass gesture that fed a 19-year-old boy to the press wolves. And ask yourselves this: would Eriksson have taken off Beckham immediately for a similar transgression? And would Sir Alex have hung one of his boys out to dry in that fashion?

Eriksson and his assistant Steve McClaren gave Rooney a major bollocking in the dressing-room at half time. They were disappointed he had thrown his black armband (a tribute to the recently departed Emlyn Hughes and Keith Weller) on to the ground but also because he had refused to shake Alan Smith's hand as old Eminem replaced him. Eriksson admitted, 'I did not like that. I think it is bad for England, and it is bad for the group as well. You are a professional, and you have to remember that.' He added, 'The game was too competitive, especially for a friendly game. In the first half, I'm sorry to say, we lost our heads, and when you do that it's difficult to come back. We came here to play football, and it was not good from our side in the first half. It was better in the second. Rooney's behaviour was not the best in the world. But I think he learned – he's young.'

The Spanish players had not helped Rooney's black mood. Before the game, Michel Salgado had described Rooney as 'a perfect removal man' because of his physique, and Ivan Helguera claimed he was overrated. Helguera said, 'He is a player with potential. He is now playing for a great club in Manchester United and the media is over-promoting him. But I ask myself, "What trophy has Rooney won?"'

Spain coach Luis Aragones had been blamed for igniting the racist chants. A month earlier he had called Thierry Henry 'a black shit' and would not apologise to the player. After the England match, he turned down another chance to right his wrong, refusing to comment on the racial taunting of the England players in the Bernabéu. He would only say, 'My conscience is clear. I'm only interested in football and in this victory.'

At least Real Madrid keeper Casillas proved himself to be more of a man when asked about Rooney's push on him. He said, 'He has got a bad temper, but he's a very good player. David [Beckham] came over and advised me to concentrate on the game because it was best to leave Rooney in peace. But something like that due to a loss of temper can injure you. I was not expecting a push, and it is not like being kicked when the ball is still in play. I told Rooney a few things that should remain on the pitch.'

It is impossible to talk about England without a mention of Beckham. Like a temperamental child in a nursery, he demands attention, even when your concentration is elsewhere. Throughout the match he was giving it the 'statesman' act – he was playing in his naturalised home and many of the Spanish team were teammates at Madrid. But to act the statesman you need to be respected, and Beckham had not earned that for many a moon. He had a stinker of a match, yet swanned around with that anguished face he has so perfected since his talent started to wane.

What really grated on this occasion was his attitude towards Rooney. The arm around the shoulder, the hands pleading for the boy to calm down, the words of 'constructive criticism' as Rooney made the lonely journey to the dressing-room. You could almost sympathise as he mouthed 'Fuck off' to Beckham as he marched down the tunnel.

Given his own hot temper, just who is Beckham to lecture the young lad who has twice his natural ability? Do the words 'Sent off for England against Argentina in '98' and 'pot, kettle and black' ring any bells, David? No, I don't think Beckham was the man to be taking better players than himself aside and handing out patronising platitudes in his adopted home town.

A couple of days later, when Rooney was tucked up safely back at Old Trafford, Sir Alex Ferguson would make the valid point that England needed to give Wayne some breathing space and asked why a lad of 19 was under so much pressure to make

England tick. 'We'll sort him out. We'll look after him,' he said, before pointing to Paul Scholes and, perhaps not as obviously, Roy Keane, as the men to teach Rooney how to curb his temper. They would be his United bodyguards on the pitch.

The United boss also provided a top-class quote to sum up just how much Eriksson and McClaren had exaggerated the affair. With tongue firmly in cheek, he said, 'But what 19 year old has got maturity? What were you like at 19? What was I like at 19? Jesus Christ, I was trying to start a workers' revolution in bloody Glasgow. My mother thought I was a communist. She was down on her knees praying every night. Then I got the ultimate threat – my granny spoke to me. She said, "Mammy thinks you're a bloody communist."

'I'll be shocked if I don't do the business with that boy. I'll be totally amazed because I think the ingredients are there. He's a smashing boy who's no problem.'

I was told that Rooney *had* said sorry before leaving the England set-up, apologising to Eriksson and the team for storming off and hurling the Emlyn Hughes tribute armband to the ground. Michael Owen, one of Rooney's closest friends in the camp, explained, 'It was sheer frustration. I'm sure he has got a lot of respect for Emlyn Hughes. He was just frustrated and that's understandable.'

One final point . . . Rooney once again proved he has a mischievous sense of humour. After his early bath, he arrived in the England dugout to watch the second half swigging from a green bottle that looked for all the world as if it was a bottle of Stella Artois. It was actually a posh bottle of water. An England insider said, 'Wayne knew he would get a going over in the morning's papers – and just could not resist a wind-up with the bottle in the dugout.'

Ten days earlier, he had faced another problem – one that had again tested his temperament, before the 131st Manchester derby league match, the first of his short United career. It was, naturally enough, drizzling as the United faithful trudged up Sir Matt Busby Way, many of them singing a new little ditty designed to infuriate the City fans on the other side of the street.

It went like this – to the tune of 'Blue Moon', with due apologies to that much more auspicious original little number:

> Red Roon we saw you standing alone
> Without a ball at your feet
> Without a club of your own
> Red Roon we knew just what you were there for
> We heard you saying a prayer for
> A team you really could care for
> Then suddenly appeared before you
> The only place to come and play
> You came along the Trafford Road
> United you're here to stay
> Red Roon now you're no longer alone
> You get the ball to your feet
> You've got a place to call home
> Red Roon (Red Roon) Red Roon (Red Roon)

The irony was not lost on the mass of good-natured away fans as they belted out their own anthem, 'Blue Moon'. The debate continues to rage over which club has the bigger fan base in Manchester itself – we'll avoid that minefield for now – but what I would say is that City supporters, on the whole, do not tend to take themselves as seriously as their United counterparts. How could they? They had grown a hard shell after the financial mismanagements of the previous decade had left their beloved club in the old Division Three at one stage and on the brink of administration another time. No, they were a battle-weary lot who could take a lot of flak and laugh it off – but they didn't take too kindly to 'Blue Moon' being snatched and bastardised by the red army.

United's followers were preoccupied with more serious affairs of the heart. The derby came the day after Sir Alex Ferguson's 18th anniversary in charge at Old Trafford, and many fans could not let go of the idea that the great man might perhaps be losing it at the age of 62. He had dropped Rooney to the bench, claiming that the boy had a dose of the flu virus that had previously sidelined Mikael Silvestre. Well, just what was Rooney doing at Old Trafford at all then? Shouldn't he have been tucked up in his bed – with Coleen administering Lemsip and tender loving care? No, that wouldn't do as an excuse. Old Trafford insiders claimed Ferguson had simply dropped him – to try to 'buck him up'. Ferguson had given a hint of his anger at United's continued spurning of goal chances before the match. He had said, 'The disappointment last week was that we had 18 chances at Portsmouth and didn't score. We cannot accept that because the players are better than that. We need more concentration in our finishing.'

It still did not make sense to leave out Rooney. United were without van Nistelrooy, who was serving the final game of his three-match domestic suspension, and that itself was a major blow. The Dutchman had scored all the United goals in the 4–1 triumph over Sparta Prague in the Champions League group stage a few days before the City match. Yet Rooney had himself grabbed four goals in six starts since joining United and had also become the creative fulcrum of the team. Ferguson had claimed before the Birmingham match that what Rooney needed most was games to build him up after his lay-off. So the change in that policy was as baffling as the decision to let Nicky Butt go. It just made no sense. Rooney was a big-game player – he could have set the stadium alight. Instead, his role was that of a bit player, emerging late in the game. And, if he had the flu, what in the Lord's name was he doing on the pitch at all after 77 minutes?

The word from inside Old Trafford was that Rooney had not taken the axe well. The day before the game, it was claimed he had sulked and pleaded with the United manager to change his mind and give him his full derby debut. But Ferguson stuck to his guns. It was to be their first disagreement, and Rooney was seen skulking off into the night – hardly appeased it seems when Ferguson apparently told him he would put it around that he was out because of the virus.

Perhaps Ferguson had been swayed by the growing groans of some United figures. George Best, for one, had rapped Rooney, telling BBC Radio Five Live, 'For that sort of money you would want Rooney to be performing every week, and he is not. But he is still very young. He came onto the big stage with a bang, scored three terrific goals, but that does not happen every week. He has found out very quickly how life can be tough at the top.'

Old Georgie boy might have been better advised to stay away from the demon drink again – it was clearly affecting his mindset. Rooney hardly needed the advice of the beleaguered hero who had been struggling with his own demons for many years.

Perhaps Ferguson was just over-confident. It had, after all, been 30 years since they had last lost to City at home – when Denis Law's goal backheeled them into the old Second Division in April 1974.

Another rumour about one of United's biggest names refused to go away – and it was another big one, another worrying one. Since the very start of the season, the whisper doing the rounds at Old Trafford was that one key player had been keen to quit the game completely. He was disillusioned with football and wanted to spend more time with his family. The word on the street was that the player was Paul Scholes – and the jigsaw pieces certainly fitted together. He had experienced a poor Euro 2004, constantly played out of position on the left by Sven-Göran Eriksson, and had retired from the international game. His season with United had also been disappointing, although, to be fair, he was returning after injury. That traditional drive and ability to be in the right place at the right time had been missing, and he was fluffing goal chances he would normally have buried.

Time was catching up with him, as it was also with Keane and Ryan Giggs. Giggs was the latest to feel the cold wind of Ferguson's mystifying decisions. Like Rooney, he would be dropped for the Manchester derby, the tidy Liam Miller taking his place in a more compact line-up with Ronaldo switching from right to left wing. Tidy? Whoever would have imagined that would be the best we could come up with for a Manchester United player? But that just about summed up the Irishman. He had been snapped up from Celtic on a free transfer amid much complaining from Parkhead, but his displays had not marked him out as an exceptional talent. Maybe he would go on to prove us wrong, but for now, in the heat of the Manchester derby, his inclusion did not set the fires of hope burning brightly.

Giggs had not been at his best, but surely he presented an altogether better option than the tidy Miller in a beast of a match like this? Not according to Tinkerman Ferguson. To be fair, United did not play as badly as the 0–0 final scoreline suggested – although the result was all the more disappointing given that City are not known for keeping clean sheets in this fixture. United were all over City for three-quarters of the match but could not find the net. It was hardly a typical performance from a team marshalled by Kevin Keegan. The much-derided former England coach was renowned for his cavalier approach to football – attack and be damned if you lose by the odd goal in seven. No, this was a different showtime from Keegan as his team dug in and refused to be battered into submission. It was highlighted by the man of the match, City centre-half Richard Dunne, who was outstanding in keeping United at bay.

The result meant United had been shut out for the second successive Premiership game. It did not justify Ferguson's decision to keep Rooney on the bench until 13 minutes from time. The United manager's problems mounted when Alan Smith was sent off for a second bookable offence. There had been suggestions that playing Smith in midfield could be the answer to two problems for United: it would give him a regular berth, which he was not guaranteed with United's strength in attack, and help solve the problems created by the loss of Nicky Butt and the loss of form by Scholes and Keane. As Smith clambered recklessly into Dunne to earn himself an early bath, it became clear why, for the moment at least, even the new Tinkerman would not gamble on Smith in midfield. Would he ever finish a match? His tackling was currently worse than that of Scholes – and that was saying something.

One other thing: just what were the United fans doing applauding Smith when he was red-carded? Why clap a man down the tunnel when he had just let down his teammates, his manager and the fans who pay his wages? Surely, stunned silence would have been more appropriate? As it was, Smith responded by applauding back to the Stretford End. Again, another perplexing aspect of an overall frustrating afternoon.

United's central midfield of Scholes and Keane also suffered ups and downs. Scholes had his best game for a good while, although he still looked as though he needed to beef up after losing weight during his injury lay-off. Keane was a disappointment. He tried once again to pretend he was Peter Schmeichel, bollocking the youngsters throughout the match and then sending his own passes astray. The great Dane had the advantage of being able to back up his bollockings of his defence thanks to a series of fabulous displays. Now, Keane, often a mere shadow of his former self, was out of order. His frustration probably said more about his anger with himself – how he knew he could no longer cut it in every match he played. As the therapy saying goes, 'hurt people hurt people' – don't they, Roy?

Rooney could not get into the game and saw about as much action as the unemployed Nicolas Anelka, City's lone, lonely, attacker. United's best two attempts came when David James fumbled the ball to Saha, but the Frenchman shot straight at him, and when Steve McManaman cleared Smith's acrobatic bicycle-kick effort off the line. Keane and Rio Ferdinand led United off at the end of the match; it had been a poor present for Rio on his 26th birthday. Ferguson was bristling as he faced the press, admitting that performances like this would not lead to United catching Arsenal and Chelsea at the top of the Premiership. He said, 'We are not good enough to win the title on that display – we have dropped another two points. One win in our last five games is not championship form and I cannot excuse anyone in the club for that.' United now trailed new leaders Chelsea by eleven points and defending champions Arsenal by nine.

Not unusually when things went wrong, the United boss stoked the fires of a conspiracy theory, claiming this time that his team paid the price for the penalty they were awarded against Arsenal a week earlier. He felt the Reds should have had two spot-kicks early in the game when Silvestre and Louis Saha went down to City challenges in the box. And he felt they also had a legitimate claim when substitute Giggs appeared to be tripped by the tough-tackling Paul Bosvelt after the interval. Ferguson said, 'After what happened against Arsenal, we're going to be penalised for that. No way was the referee going to give us a penalty today; somebody would have needed to have been hit with an axe for us to get one. But the rules are there to be applied and they should be regardless if players are pulled or pushed in the penalty area.'

Of course, City boss Keegan saw it all much differently. He was proud of his players for keeping United out and said, 'People will know there's another club in this city; for years they've thought there's only one. The players did the club proud, the supporters can enjoy it, and they can go round the city knowing they haven't lost. Given our resources, it was the best system for us to play, and why should we make it easy for them? We weren't going to lie down for them. They've got to earn the points, and despite a tremendous effort from them they didn't get the three points.'

It meant United *did* need to get three points from their next crunch match – another monster of a game, this time away at Newcastle. A couple of days before the trip to St James' Park, Rooney had been in the news again, on the front pages of the tabloids after he was involved in a road accident. The news flashed around the world and United fans breathed a sigh of relief that the teenager was unhurt. *The Sun*, in typical style, raised a laugh with the headline, 'Rooney in crash with 23-ton truck' and the subhead, 'But the truck survived'. The 19 year old had been on his way to United's training ground at Carrington in his 4x4 when it collided with a fully loaded builder's lorry. The accident crushed the right-hand side of the car, but Rooney was able to walk uninjured from the crash because his American imported Cadillac Escalade was a left-hand drive. The driver's side was untouched but the passenger side was caved in, causing thousands of pounds' worth of damage.

After the accident, the England striker was able to drive on to United's training ground, where he left the car with a repair firm. It left his fiancée Coleen in tears and Rooney shaken – but ready to take out his frustrations about the City match, and smashing up his motor, on the Toon on the Sunday. If the truck could not stop his progress, what chance the Geordies? Little, as it turned out. Rooney was the star man, tearing an already fragile Newcastle defence to bits and heaping more trouble on to new Toon boss Graeme Souness. The passionate Scot had a triple heart bypass in 1992 and his early-evening rage at his side's 3–1 loss prompted renewed fears about his health. Crimson and angry, a walking, talking body of stress, he could have done with asking himself: is it all really worth it? Well, is it Graeme? You have money, a lovely family – do you really need all this aggro when you have already walked a health tightrope?

Rooney did Souness's heart no good at all. He was everywhere, prompting United, scoring two goals and creating the other, proving to Ferguson once and for all that he was indispensable. Don't dare leave me out again was his clear message. Every United game had now taken on the appearance of a mini cup final – because they needed to win their games and hope Chelsea and Arsenal slipped – and this was a minor classic. It had everything except a sending-off, and that factor was only missing because of the leniency of ref Mike Dean towards Newcastle's verbal abuse over the penalty that always was a penalty. The Toon men blamed Dean for their third successive defeat after he failed to punish Rooney's apparent foul on Andy O'Brien in the second half, just before the boy wonder went on to help win a penalty for Manchester.

Television replays later favoured Dean and Rooney in the 74th -minute incident. It appeared O'Brien had collapsed to the ground hoping for a free-kick. Contact, if any, was certainly minimal. Rooney advanced, chipped the ball into the box, and Shay Given smashed into Scholes. Ruud van Nistelrooy stepped up and slammed the ball past the impotent Given. Dean was showered with abuse when he left the field – and the Toon army were just as unforgiving to Rooney, still mindful that he had chosen Manchester instead of Newcastle.

Rooney had played a game of cat-and-mouse with the home crowd all afternoon, saluting the Gallowgate End with clenched fists after his two goals and raising his right hand to his right ear after scoring the first. Underneath the abuse, the Geordie faithful liked him; he was moulded like many of them, out of steel, grit and a fiery determination to do something with their lives. They called him names but admired him for his balls.

Van Nistelrooy's return from a three-match ban also helped, putting more fire in the Manchester bellies. For a while, he linked well with Rooney, then with Scholes, as Wayne headed into central midfield, taking up the Scholes role. By the end of the match, Rooney had also played as a left-winger and a left-back. He would have been a tremendous acquisition for the Ajax total football squads of the '80s, with the emphasis on players who can literally play anywhere.

Manchester ended with 55 per cent of the possession and seven shots on target to Newcastle's two, and Roy Keane did well to out-tackle the tenacious Nicky Butt in midfield. United had a 64 per cent success in their tackles to Newcastle's 49 per cent in theirs. The Toon knew they had a battle on their hands when United went one-up. It had been seventy-eight Premiership games – and three years – since Manchester had lost a lead. Butt had certainly been up for a war in this match, his first against United since transferring in the summer, and he was lucky not to be booked for one particularly tough challenge on the impressive Scholes. Ferguson had again left out Giggs, replacing him with the highly effective Darren Fletcher. The Scotland international played on the right, in the role Liam Miller had tried out against City, with Ronaldo again on the left. Fletcher added balance to the midfield foursome, his gangly legs often proving resolute in the tackle and his passing ability never in doubt. Indeed, one lovely pass set up Rooney for the opening goal.

The result highlighted the awesome ability of Rooney as a free spirit and his imaginative and intelligent play. It also proved that when Scholes and Keane were on form in the engine room, United could motor. But how long before the car would break down again?

Alan Shearer's opportunism pulled a goal back for the Toon,

when he cleverly beat Silvestre and fired home from 12 yards. But the van Nistelrooy penalty and Rooney's second in second-half stoppage time put the result beyond doubt. He scored from the rebound after Shay Given could only parry a shot by van Nistelrooy.

The 3,000-plus contingent from Manchester had enjoyed the free-flowing game and had proved they also have a sense of humour – like neighbours City – when the mood takes them. They had sung heartily, 'Shearer for England' when big dull Al had blasted wide with only the keeper to beat after a slip by Rio Ferdinand.

More good news arrived. A grateful Ferguson allowed Rooney to talk to the press after he was voted man of the match. Rooney said he believed United could still win the title despite trailing Chelsea by 11 points. He said, 'We are still a good enough team to do it, but obviously it will be a very difficult job. We all believe in ourselves, especially after today as coming to Newcastle is always difficult. With Chelsea and Arsenal winning we needed the victory here to keep ourselves in the race.' Rooney also admitted he and his family had not found the move from Everton to United easy. He had initially struggled to settle down, and he and his family had suffered from the hate campaign waged against him. He confirmed, 'I'm settling in fine now, but there was a bit of trouble when I first moved.'

Someone who was experiencing a bit of trouble was Ryan Giggs. The United winger, who surely one day could also be awarded the term legend, was not a happy bunny. He had lost his regular first-team spot and had been peeved to be offered only a one-year extension to his contract, which would finish in summer 2006. The 30 year old had played in more than 600 games for United and had won all the major domestic honours. He said, 'I have been offered a one-year extension to my current deal, but I turned it down. I hope that they come back with a longer deal. I'll just have to wait and see.'

Giggs had the feeling he might be a scapegoat as United tried to bring in 'modern-era' deals for their players. Even the biggest club in the world was having to come to terms with the realities of an economic downturn. The days of wine and roses – and bumper pay deals for flops such as Juan Sebastián Verón – appeared to be over. The tough new world would include players working on appearance- and success-based contracts, with possible pay cuts following their implementation. Chief executive David Gill said deals offered to new or younger players would see wages go down if they failed to reach, for example, the Champions League quarter-finals. He said, 'Part of their remuneration would be dependent on that. If we don't get in, our income goes down.'

Gill also made it clear that United would need to cut their wage bill and sell if Ferguson's wish of bringing in new players in the January transfer window was to be realised. Gill confirmed that Rooney's earlier than expected arrival at the club had depleted the coffers. He added, 'We intended to get Wayne Rooney next summer, but we've bought him now. So that is next year's budget gone. You have now got to assess where we are as a team at the end of the season – what we have achieved, where the weaknesses are and try to work it out.

'Currently, in terms of the first-team squad, we've got 25 players. The manager has to give his views on those players and decide where the squad needs strengthening or where it doesn't need strengthening. Bodies will have to leave before we invest further. But bodies will have to leave anyway because of the numbers. If Sir Alex wanted to invest more, we would have to lose someone. And all our players are high profile.'

Two other United stars joined Giggs in the glum club during the week – and both were goalkeepers. Tim Howard spoke out in public to reveal that he believed he had unfairly taken the blame for United's poor start to the season. The American had lost his place after a series of early-season mistakes and a particularly bad night in the Champions League clash in Lyon. Howard said, 'A goalkeeper is a very convenient scapegoat. I understand that. I'm always going to own up to my mistakes but did I lose us games? No. Did I contribute to it? Yes. But it takes 11 of us to win and 11 of us to lose.'

It was no wonder Fergie was rumoured to be looking for

another new number 1, with Middlesbrough's Mark Schwarzer saying in public that he would love the job. Directly after Howard's moans and groans, Roy Carroll, the man in current possession turned down a new contract. That saddened Ferguson. He said, 'We hope there will be a change of mind and that he will stay. Roy is the first choice because he has never let us down.' Goalkeepers like Howard and Carroll reminded me of the 'stars' who quit soap operas – like Brian Tilsley in *Coronation Street* – believing they can go on to better things. Invariably, their careers nosedived. Howard and Carroll should have thought more about how lucky they were to be at United – they were no Gordon Banks or Peter Schmeichel – but being at the biggest club in the land appeared to have gone to their heads.

Roy Keane had better news to end the week when it was confirmed he would be inducted into the National Football Museum's Hall of Fame. The United skipper joined the likes of Alan Shearer, Wilf Mannion, Billy Bremner and Geoff Hurst. What price Rooney joining him there one of these days?

9

A GRAND (DON'T COME FOR FREE)

TUESDAY 23 NOVEMBER. THE DAY HE FINALLY MADE IT – against the odds. Not even his staunchest admirers over an 18-year reign at Old Trafford would have realistically expected Alex Ferguson to still be United manager in 2004. Not when you recall the dark days of 1989 when he seemed certain to be sacked. That year, the late Emlyn Hughes famously penned a piece in the *Daily Mirror* under the headline, 'Fergie OBE – Out Before Easter'. Not for the first time, he was to be proved wrong – a great footballer, a not so great columnist and analyst.

Just a year later, United won the first of an avalanche of trophies when they lifted the FA Cup. A Mark Robins winner in the tie at Nottingham Forest had earned the big man breathing space – and Ferguson certainly used his reprieve well. In his 1,000 games as United manager he guided them to Champions League glory in 1999 and a Cup-Winners' Cup title in 1991. The Scot had left Aberdeen in 1986 having broken the stranglehold of the Old Firm of Rangers and Celtic. His first match at United was a 2–0 defeat at Oxford United in the old First Division on 8 November 1986. After winning the FA Cup in 1990, his team had also collected eight Premiership titles, four more FA Cups and one League Cup, as well as those two European crowns.

In total, he had won 563, drawn 188 and lost 248 of his 999 previous games in charge of United. He was particularly proud to be following in the footsteps of legendary predecessor, Sir Matt Busby, in reaching the 1,000 game milestone at Old Trafford. The 1,000th match, appropriately really, was a European one – the Champions League group stage clash at home to French champions Lyon. Ferguson had always conceded that his prime ambition at United was European glory and that he enjoyed European nights at United more than any others. And Lyon would be sure to provide a competitive test – they were a top-notch outfit and, despite the eventual 2–2 scoreline, should have comprehensively beaten United in the earlier group match in France.

The tributes poured in before kick-off. 'Sir Alex can feel very proud, not just of the time he has spent here but with what he has achieved in it,' said Carlos Queiroz, Ferguson's right-hand man. 'For one man to spend 18 years at a single club is very unusual. Sometimes in Portugal, where coaches can lose their jobs before the season even starts, 18 days can be considered a good achievement.' Even his biggest adversary, Arsène Wenger, chipped in. The Arsenal boss said, 'Of course, it's fantastic – to reach 1,000 games means you have suffered a lot and worked hard. I congratulate him.'

Rooney played a key role in providing his boss with the win he wanted on his big night. He hit the woodwork and worked his socks off, darting from midfield into attack. United won 2–1 with a rare goal from Gary Neville and, inevitably, a winner from Ruud van Nistelrooy. The Dutchman notched his 34th goal in 35 Champions League matches for United with a close-range header. In between, keeper Roy Carroll had gifted Lyon an equaliser six minutes before the interval when he fumbled Mahamadou Diarra's 30-yard shot. No matter: Fergie was delighted with the result and the reception he received for his 1,000 not out.

He said, 'It was an excellent performance. The confidence and rhythm is coming back now. I was ecstatic with the second half. There was a lot of composure and of course Ruud scored another for us. Lyon are a very good side, undefeated this season, and it always takes a lot to beat a side like that. All day I was a bit nervy. I suppose, you think that it could fall flat, that you could lose the game, but I kept saying to myself, "Look, there's the 999 before it, and in games of football you can lose them." The fans' reaction was terrific, and I'm proud of them.'

Typical of the man that just a day earlier he had not been so warm with the BBC. Niall Sloane, the Corporation's head of football, had thought it might be a good time to make up with the United boss, what with the inevitable backslapping and laughter that would accompany his 1,000th game. Surely he could get on his good side in such a convivial atmosphere? Sloane contacted Ferguson and asked him if he would reconsider his refusal to speak to the Corporation – a boycott imposed for the full season in protest at a documentary that turned an unpleasant spotlight on his football agent son Jason. Of course I will reconsider, Sir Alex told Sloane. As from now, it's a lifetime ban.

Ferguson still harboured one final major ambition at United: he wanted to win the Champions League once more. He would have to do it soon – at the end of the season he would lose his job security as he moved on to a 12-month rolling contract at United, and just how much more stress and punishment could his body take? He was already operating with a pacemaker, and the bulging red veins in his face at the end of each match did not augur well health-wise.

At least the team was taking shape – at last – for this season. Rooney was playing a star man's role and consistently supplying United's penetrative edge. Keane and Scholes were staying fit in that worrying central midfield area – still worrying in the sense of able deputies for the first-choice duo. It was rumoured that Ferguson had set his sights on two other journeymen: Owen Hargreaves of Bayern Munich and Thomas Gravesen of Everton. Hargreaves's main talent was that he could run and would cover every blade of grass. Gravesen would be a cult figure with his crunching tackles and bald head. A sort of Danish Vinnie Jones. Neither were true United players in terms of class.

As November turned into December, United's followers did not need to worry themselves about either man arriving at Old Trafford. Keane was playing well, albeit it in a more disciplined – not running around all over the pitch – role. He had learned to park himself in front of the defence and control operations from a holding position. And Scholes looked like, well, the Scholes of old. United had a run of distinctly dull-looking fixtures directly before and after the Lyon game. It was as if the good Lord was trying to tease Scholes back into form by providing easy skittles for him to bowl over. Charlton had arrived at Old Trafford as suitable fodder for Ferguson's 999th game. They lay down and thought of London as United rolled them over 2–0, with goals from Giggs and Scholes. The latter's superb volley past Dean Kiely was his first appearance on the score sheet in seven months.

Then it was off to the Hawthorns and a reunion with United legend Bryan Robson, just installed as new boss at West Brom after the baffling sacking of Gary Megson. Unequalled as a player, Robbo had a more chequered career in management, taking down Middlesbrough and Bradford while also reaching two cup finals with Boro. Ferguson applauded his return to the Baggies and questioned why other Premiership clubs had not been falling over themselves for his services. Maybe the result helped him understand a little better as United sauntered to a 3–0 victory. Scholes grabbed a brace to help his own personal rehabilitation and van Nistelrooy completed the rout.

Sandwiched in between that stroll and the next at home to Southampton, Ferguson let United's second 11 – which, naturally enough, meant no Rooney – loose on Arsenal in the Carling Cup quarter-final. United, skippered by Phil Neville, won 1–0 with an 18-second goal from David Bellion. It had been labelled 'Battle of the Buffet 2' by the press, but it turned out to be a much more drab affair as United's reserves added another scalp to the Crewe team they had steamrolled 3–0 at Gresty Road in the previous round.

Rooney was back in business as the Saints arrived at Old Trafford for a Premiership showdown early in December.

Showdown? Hardly, just another routine affair: another opportunity for United to make ground on Chelsea and Arsenal at the top of the table. Which they did, winning comfortably 3–0. For the record, it was the first time that season that United had kicked off a home match at 3 p.m. on a Saturday. It was also their seventh consecutive win and their ninth match unbeaten. And, yes, Rooney's goal was the pick of the three. Giggs set Wayne free in the middle of the park and he rampaged forward, meeting the ball with a dynamite shot that exploded into the roof of the net. Scholes added another to his rejuvenated tally of late – his fourth in three Premiership matches – and Ronaldo also got in on the act.

Ferguson, lifted by the winning sequence, warned Chelsea and the Gunners that his team now meant business. He said, 'We're in a good period now where the team is playing well and we don't have injury worries. If we keep the wins going, the confidence will rise and we will get even better.' On paper, the easy run would continue until 15 January – when United were due at Anfield.

It was all getting a bit predictable – what we needed was a distraction to make things a bit more interesting. On cue, a clown appeared to loud cheers – none other than our old pal, Freddy Shepherd, the Newcastle chairman. Yes, the man who had handed Rooney to United on a plate. His own team were doing so well – with the 3–1 defeat at home to United and a subsequent 4–0 loss at Chelsea – that he deemed it time to spread his manifesto for success further afield. To Manchester United, in fact. Freddy said United had lost some of their glitter of late. He said, 'First they lost the captain of the ship in Martin Edwards, then they suffered from losing David Beckham. They lost two characters there.' Would that be the same Edwards who once tried to sell out to that other ball-juggling comic Michael Knighton? And the same Beckham who was struggling in Madrid?

Shepherd's on-field skipper at St James' Park, Alan Shearer, brought some perspective to it all when he turned the spotlight on to Rooney, declaring that he could be the best player ever in the Premiership. Shearer, the Premiership's record goalscorer, now with 273, said, 'In terms of ability, I am not in Wayne's bracket.'

United boss Ferguson then decided to wade in and make a few headlines of his own. United were drawn out of the hat to face Chelsea in the semi-finals of the Carling Cup in January, and the United boss felt it was time to put that upstart Mourinho in his place. The two men had traded verbal blows the previous season when the Portuguese's unfancied Porto saw off United's challenge on their march to winning the European Cup. Now Fergie attempted to psyche him out as the Championship race intensified. He said, 'Chelsea will have a blip, they will lose games. It's then a case of how their players react. Arsenal and ourselves have got that experience. Chelsea don't have the experience of winning when it really matters.'

Ferguson was speaking on the eve of United's early December game in Istanbul – the final match of their Champions League qualifying-group campaign against Fenerbahçe. He decided to rest Rooney, van Nistelrooy, Ferdinand, Heinze and Scholes, safe in the knowledge that United were already through to the knockout stage. It gave him a chance to 'showcase' his other buys – men like Djemba-Djemba, Miller and Bellion. Once again they let him down as United flopped to a 3–0 loss against opposition they had thrashed 6–2 on Rooney's debut. In the case of Miller, United might have been better advised to have gone instead for Aiden McGeady, another midfielder at Celtic who was progressing at a much faster rate than his over-hyped former teammate. At 18, he was already keeping the Brazilian Juninho out of the Hoops' first team.

It also made me think: Ferguson could have used the readies from the cost of his three journeymen (transfer fees and wages) to have snapped up Arjen Robben, the Dutch boy winger who was now playing fantastic football for Chelsea after an injury-hit start to his career in England. Robben would have been the perfect replacement for Giggs, but United had balked at paying an extra couple of million and had let in Abramovich.

It was the second major transfer blunder of the last two seasons, the other, of course, being to allow Ronaldinho to slip the net. For Beckham's transfer fee, United could have brought in the best player on the planet. Ronaldinho's position at the top was confirmed in December as he won the FIFA 2004 World Player of the Year award. Rooney was the highest-ranked English player at number 11 – just imagine them linking up together . . .

Enough of the dreams, back to the nightmare in Istanbul. After Umit Ozat completed his hat-trick, Ferguson refused to criticise his nearly men, instead claiming that United, as runners-up, were still in as good a position to progress as were group winners Lyon. Such was the quality of the teams in the last 16, he said, that you could find yourself up against Barcelona if you won the group, or AC Milan if you finished second. When the draw was made, Ferguson gave a wry smile as Chelsea, who had strolled through their group as winners, landed Barca, while United found themselves up against Milan. The smile dipped a little as Lyon drew Werder Bremen, one of the two weakest teams left in the competition.

It had been a tough night in Istanbul, and the next week proved equally as arduous. United travelled to Fulham five days later and could only take home a point in a 1–1 draw. Before the match it had been announced that Rooney had won the Golden Boy of Europe award. He received the prize – the young players' equivalent of the European Footballer of the Year award – from Italian newspaper *Tuttosport* after topping a journalists' poll to find the Continent's outstanding footballer under 21. He finished ahead of teammate Cristiano Ronaldo, Fernando Torres, Arjen Robben and Obafemi Martins. Rooney was 'made up' with the honour, adding, 'This is the first international trophy I have won.'

His joy was short lived as United struggled to make their territorial superiority count against the Londoners. Van Nistelrooy missed the match with an Achilles' tendon injury – it emerged that he would be out for at least two months and the news was a major setback to United's season. In his absence, Smith and Giggs led the line, with Rooney and Ronaldo swapping wings throughout. That's right: Rooney was now operating all over the place as Ferguson took advantage of his versatility. He had scored seven times for United but had never hit the back of the net against Fulham. Former United striker Andy Cole was skipper for the hosts on a bitterly cold night in west London. Smith put United ahead on 32 minutes, beating Edwin van der Saar from a tight angle with a perfectly placed shot.

This was certainly a game United needed to win to keep the pressure on Chelsea and Arsenal. The London giants had fought out a 2–2 draw at Highbury the previous day in an enthralling end-to-end high-tempo contest laced with skill and artistry. Along with United's win over Arsenal, it was undoubtedly the match of the season thus far. Afterwards, Chelsea skipper John Terry, surprisingly a self-confessed lifelong Manchester United fan, had stuck the knife into the Red Devils by failing to mention them when asked who he thought would be the Blues' main contenders for the title. 'Arsenal and Everton,' he had replied.

That comment got under Ferguson's skin, and he wanted to ram it back down Terry's throat with an emphatic win at Craven Cottage. But for all United's huffing and puffing they could not blow Mohamed Al Fayed's men down. A thunderbolt from Papa Bouba Diop three minutes from time earned Fulham a point, leaving United trailing Chelsea by nine points, surprise package Everton by five and Arsenal by four. Ferguson said, 'Our main rivals both dropped points yesterday, and that's what makes this result so bad. It was a fantastic strike by Diop, but we should have been over the horizon by then.' When asked about Rooney's former club Everton's hopes of winning the title, Fergie grinned, 'No chance.'

The United boss also revealed that he had told Cristiano Ronaldo to take a two-week break at his home in Madeira to recharge his batteries. It could not have come at a better time. In the dressing-room after the Fulham game, Alan Smith had shouted at him for being too greedy and not passing when he was in a free scoring position. Gary Neville had also had a go in the previous match against Southampton, claiming the Portuguese winger was missing easy chances.

More aggro arrived when Malcolm Glazer once again raised his head over the parapet just before Christmas. With rumours rife that he would launch a hostile takeover before the end of the season, his new public relations man tried to smooth over relations with United but achieved the exact opposite. Bob Leffler said, 'The only reason they hate Malcolm – if they hate him – is xenophobia and fear of the unknown. It's not logic and our job is to change that, to show this is a true sportsman who will run your franchise like it should be run and win you championships.' Leffler also made it clear Glazer had not given up with his bid of taking control of United.

In one foul swoop, Glazer's new man had managed to infuriate United's fan base – who clearly, given the vast swathe of different populations across the globe who followed the team, were far from xenophobic – and brought renewed fears with his use of the word 'franchise'. Was this what it had come to – the legend that Busby and Ferguson had committed their lives to building – a franchise? Like a McDonald's or a KFC?

More worrying news emerged with an unexpected shares sale. Well, you wouldn't really anticipate that United chief executive, David Gill, the man who had denounced Glazer, would be the seller, would you? Gill made a £530,000 profit on his share options in United after selling 481,237 to new board director Jim O'Neill. O'Neill, head of global economic research at Goldman Sachs, paid £1.3 million. It led some supporters to claim that Gill was cashing in on the price rise caused by Glazer's takeover speculation. Gill claimed O'Neill was 'a friendly' buyer. At least Gill then issued a statement about Glazer that went some way to easing the trepidation among United fans. It said, 'The board does not intend to open discussions on this matter unless it receives a definitive proposal from Glazer.' In other words, put up or shut up, Mr Leprechaun.

Christmas was coming – and so were another mass of stories in the tabloids about Rooney and Coleen. *The Sun* and the *Daily Mail* reported how Coleen had enjoyed a festive night out with some girlfriends at the Baby Blue nightclub in Liverpool while Rooney earned his wages for United at Fulham. The lasses knocked back bottles of Cristal champagne at £200 a bottle. Or was it? The actual price of the champers caught the eye of the usually austere *Guardian*'s media correspondent Roy Greenslade. Yes, Coleen had even made the pages of the broadsheets. With a big picture of Coleen and the headline, 'Bubble and Squeak Over Coleen's Tipple', Greenslade rambled, 'According to the *Daily Mail* [it was] £200 a bottle. Over at *The Sun*, it was the same brand, but at £275 a bottle. This simple factual detail was easily checkable by simply asking the club. So I did, and a spokesman told me that Cristal sells for £195. And that's a fact.'

Coleen had even managed to get the *Guardian*'s knickers in a twist: her and Rooney's fame was now threatening Beckham and Posh's previously unchallenged supremacy as king and queen of the headlines. And, for the record, Mr 'Speaking from the Broadsheet Moral High Ground' Greenslade, was once features editor of *The Sun* and editor of the *Daily Mirror*. And that's a fact.

The Sun also suggested Coleen was planning to use up some of her spare time by attempting to become a pop star. It claimed she had been having singing lessons with vocal coach Jennifer John, who trained pop group Atomic Kitten. Apparently the sessions had been taking place at the Sense of Sound studio in Liverpool for the last two months. *The Sun* had a close friend saying, 'Jennifer says Coleen is a natural. She loves singing and has recorded some tracks. She has a lot of time and money on her hands.' Coleen would not deny the rumour to me, but I don't think there was much in it.

The festive fun continued as Arsène Wenger failed to turn up for the personal hearing he had requested after the FA hit him with an improper conduct charge over his comments that Ruud van Nistelrooy was 'a cheat'. He denied the charge but was fined £15,000 in his absence – a record for a manager. Wenger decided not to appeal, but the outcome left Alex Ferguson in fits of giggles. He laughed, 'I bet the FA were tickled pink he didn't turn up after asking for a personal hearing.'

Rooney's first United Christmas party bash (appropriate word as we shall see shortly) was also on the horizon, but first there was the small matter of getting the title juggernaut back on track with the home match against Crystal Palace, the Saturday before Christmas. A 5–2 walkover and the sight of Cantona in the main stand helped fend off the seasonal cold snap. King Eric turned up as guest of honour and made some headlines after admitting that he would one day like to be United manager. Getting sidetracked slightly: how is it that even Cantona, the one man whose word you would surely trust as his bond, can leave you feeling confused? Remember when he walked out of Old Trafford for good, grumbling about being depressed by the sales and marketing machine United had become? How he felt uneasy in that atmosphere, as if he himself were a mere marketing tool? All fine talk – yet taking a walk in the club's megastore before the match brought a bit of a shock to the old system. One wall was piled high with sweatshirts, T-shirts, fleeces, caps and hats – all bearing the words, 'Cantona: The Spirit Within', and endorsed by the great man himself. Just how do you square that with all those worthy words of yours when you quit then, Eric?

Back to the match: Scholes continued his fine form with another brace and Keane and Giggs also played a major part in United's dominance. It was not Rooney's best match in a United shirt – in fact, it was his worst. Gabor Kiraly saved his penalty shot on nine minutes and some of his passes went astray. Even boy wonders have off days. Alan Smith grabbed another of United's goals, as did substitute John O'Shea. An own goal from Emmerson Boyce completed the United scoring. Danny Granville and Joonas Kolkka replied with goals for Palace.

Afterwards, Roy Keane revealed that he would like to play on at Old Trafford when his contract expired in 2006. He would be 34 at the time – but surely United could hardly give him a deal and refuse one for Giggs? True, both had given fine service, but Keane had been running on memory at times this season. His legs had almost gone. If he stayed at United, it might be best for him to be given a coaching role? Purely as a player, he certainly had no more right to an extension deal than did Giggs.

Ferguson was buoyant after the win. It had set him up for a

good Christmas. He told the boys to go away and enjoy themselves – but to take it easy on Christmas Day with the Boxing Day clash against Bolton in mind. His mood would have darkened on the Monday. A tabloid newspaper claimed there had been a punch-up at the lads' Christmas bash, directly after the Palace game. In their headline, the paper proclaimed, 'Rio and Rooney in Party Brawl'. From that, you would deduct they had been at the centre of the trouble. In actual fact, Rooney's only crime was to be in attendance. He was headline material purely because he was the biggest name at the club.

The dust-up was said to have involved Darren Fletcher, who was allegedly punched by another guest at the Prohibition Bar in Manchester. It was claimed that later on Rio was also punched, although he denied any altercation. A couple of days later, United's youth players enjoyed a bit of fun at Rooney's expense at their Christmas do at Carrington. One lad put on a Shrek mask, two others dressed as Page 3 girls and another pretended to be a hooker. In a *Blind Date* sketch, Shrek chose the hooker. It all bore a remarkable similarity to Rooney's alleged encounter with a prostitute during one of his massage parlour visits. Rooney and boss Ferguson were in stitches. It was certainly doubtful Coleen would have seen the funny side to it.

Match! magazine had Rooney on their cover just the same week and a few exclusive comments from him. As per usual, they were not earth shattering, but some are worth mentioning. Rooney told the magazine:

> I don't think we have ever been out of the title race. Obviously there's a gap that will be difficult to catch up, but we will always be knocking on the door and if Arsenal or Chelsea do slip up, then hopefully we can take our chances and shorten the gap. [This season] I just want to do the best that I can and for the club to do the best they can. I've still got a bit more to prove on my fitness and on my game as well.

Wayne continued to dominate the front and back pages of the tabloids right up to Christmas Day. He had taken Coleen for a get away from it all trip to Paris – get away from it, that is, apart from a dozen reporters and photographers. Even Beckham, at the very height of his popularity, had not had this sort of attention from the British press. At 19 and 18, Rooney and Coleen were having to cope with a ball game that few celebrities had experienced at such tender ages. And there's the rub: our most talented young player since Gazza had quickly become a celebrity as much as a football genius. No wonder he sometimes exploded. Still, he could enjoy Christmas with Coleen and his family back in Liverpool and then it would be back to business on Boxing Day. A brisk outing to wipe away the cobwebs against Bolton at Old Trafford would be just what he needed. A local derby played in a friendly holiday atmosphere was hardly the sort of fixture that would be likely to present Rooney or United with any problems. Or at least it appeared that way on paper.

10

RED RAGE

MY HEART ALMOST BURST WITH PRIDE OUT OF THE DUFFEL
coat I had thrown on to keep out the snow, hail and a biting
cross-Pennines wind. Sitting in the second tier of the East Stand
– still known as K stand to many United fans of the Tommy
Docherty/Dave Sexton/Ron Atkinson eras – I surveyed the
scene with a lump in my thoat, just as Ferguson had probably
eyed his magnificent Treble-winning United squad of 1999. Old
Trafford, packed to the rafters as usual with a 67,000-plus
crowd, looked magnificent. This is what Boxing Day should
always be about – a welcome livener after the excesses of
Christmas Day. Scanning the crowd – including a boisterous,
good-spirited 2,000-plus from the day's opponents Bolton – I
felt a wee bit nostalgic.

Memories flooded back of my first visit to United, when as a
wild-eyed boy I had sat on my dad's shoulders to catch a fleeting
glimpse of Georgie Best and Co. I could have sworn that
everything was black and white that exciting night, I don't
remember any colour, just being sardine-packed in the
Scoreboard Paddock, my whole little body shaking with nerves
and a pumping heart. Just as I felt today as Roy Keane led out
United. For today I was making my own little piece of family

history. Sitting beside me was my son, six-year-old Frankie, my brother Bob and his two small children, Lucy, eight, and Alex, six.

Frankie jnr had unzipped the two coats his mum Angela had wrapped him in so everyone could see his United replica shirt, his most prized Christmas present along with his United ball and, of course, his Gameboy Advance. I knew what he was up to and winked at him. Given the chance he would have had both coats off and would have shivered in the big freeze that had hit Manchester a few days earlier just so people would see the name and number on the back of his shirt: the name and number that had also ensured my brother had to fork out for two extra tickets for his kids. Yes, Rooney, number 8.

The boy from Merseyside had captured the imagination of the press, the American Glazer and even my boy. It was akin to being in a car on a day trip to the seaside: the inevitable, 'Are we there yet?' replaced by, 'That's Rooney there, isn't it, Dad?' The magic continued as United roared into a 1–0 half-time lead thanks to a high-class tenth minute goal from born-again winger Ryan Giggs. Roy Keane was also superb in his holding role, and Rooney was everywhere, like a busy bee.

My boy and I were living the dream, he busily waving his flag in the faces of those sitting in the row in front, me enjoying the quick-fire passing game United were playing with perfection. Then the dream kind of died, not forever, but certainly for the remainder of this special day. Rooney, who had also been lapping up the precise football and good-natured spirit of the players and crowd, suddenly burst into 'Jekyll and Hyde' mode. It happened just after the United fans had started singing, 'Feed the Scousers, let them know it's Christmas time'. He had looked up at the Stretford End and shaken his head with pursed lips that soon broke into a smile. No, that wasn't the catalyst for what followed: it was pure and simple an almighty rush of blood to the head.

He had been tangling with Israeli centre-back Tai Ben Haim for much of the first half, and when the big defender shouted something at him, after one tangle too many, Rooney reacted by pushing his hand in Haim's face. Haim reacted by falling as if hit by a sledgehammer. My little boy was tugging at my duffel coat, 'Why has Rooney done that, Dad? Why did he punch that man?' I looked at my son's face – a sort of anguish had covered it and his big eyes were watery. I could not speak, instead the big mouth behind me did the shouting, 'It's a man's game for fuck's sake, you big Jessie! Get up off the fuckin' ground!' The referee was consulting his linesman after being confronted by the Bolton players. I tried to find the words I could use to explain to my son as to why Rooney would be taking no further part in the match – a match he had come to see purely because of the Scouse genius.

Incredibly, referee Dermot Gallagher waved play on and the boy survived, rushing in all sheepish at half time. OK, I know Ferguson gave him a bollocking at the interval, telling him he 'was a lucky fucker' to have not been sent off, but the United manager's comments after the game and, indeed, for the next few days, defied belief. It was Ferguson at his absolute worst: a supposed ambassador of the beautiful game temporarily out of touch with reality. He said after the match, 'It's embarrassing, the Bolton player – dear, oh dear – should be ashamed about what he did.'

Really? No, I don't think so, Alex. Sure, no one is denying that Haim made a meal of it, but that is a separate issue. The issue Ferguson should have addressed in public was the behaviour of his own player, Rooney. The boy seemed to be getting out of hand of late – what with the pain in Spain and now this – and the best message Ferguson could have sent him would have been a tough public one, not an ill-thought-out smokescreen designed to make sure he would not be another striker short at a time when van Nistelrooy and Saha were still out injured.

In the event, the FA raced to the rescue, forcing Rooney to sit out the next three games. Even then Ferguson waded in for a fight, claiming there was an FA witch-hunt against United. He said, 'All I hear about is what Wayne Rooney did. Did he punch the lad? No, he didn't. The biggest concern should be what the other player did. He was down on the ground for two minutes, and he is the one who should be up before the FA, not Rooney.' What absolute bollocks. It reminded me of the final days of Brian Clough at Nottingham Forest when all you would see was an angry purple face defying the truth, believing he and Forest were too good to go down. The truth here was simple – Rooney had raised his hands to an opponent's face, and that is a sending-off offence. End of story.

It also made me think that when we look back on United's season, and how Rooney fared, this could well go down as a pivotal moment. His dismissal, and subsequent three-match ban, meant he would miss the Premiership games against Middlesbrough and Spurs, and the FA Cup tie against Exeter. Without him, United would lose two valuable points against Tottenham – moving eleven points further adrift of the rampaging Chelsea – and be forced to play an FA Cup replay at Exeter during a week that had been previously marked down for a rest period away in the foreign sun.

Paul Scholes, on the scoresheet again with his seventh goal in seven games, wrapped up the festive points against Bolton with a typical slide-rule finish in the 89th minute. After the whistle, I tried to explain to my lad what had happened and why Rooney should have been dismissed. He nodded and said, 'I know, Dad, he was a bad man today, wasn't he? But I still like him.'

I guess it was the grumpiness I felt from the match that affected me as I took Frankie for a treat around the megastore. The words from Glazer's PR buffoon came to mind as I observed some of the corporate flock buying goods galore – like converts to Madonna's Kabbalah cult, each trying to prove they were truly of the highest faith. 'Franchise': that's what the Glazer guy had talked about. Well, from what I witnessed after the Bolton match, United were already heading that way. A United ball and shoulder bag left no change out of 40 notes, and the staff on the tills were just not interested in you. They didn't even raise a smile; it was just a case of, give us the readies and make room for some more gullible punters.

Later, as we walked back to the car, I saw two young lads from a bygone era shivering in the snow with books and pens in their hands. A massive black number – probably a top-of-the-range Audi or BMW – stopped at traffic lights and one of the boys knocked on the driver's window. The lads had not been able to afford to get into the match; they had just waited around outside the ground all day for autographs of their heroes, like poor kids glancing hopefully in Hamley's shop window. Eventually, seemingly realising the lights were not going to change that quickly, the owner of the big black number wound down his window, and a hand emerged to sign both autograph books. Judging by the apparent wealth of the owner, the lads must have copped Rio, Ruud or maybe Rooney. They both ran towards us, excited breath steaming in the cold early evening air. 'That was Liam Miller, we both made him sign his autograph,' the lads shouted, almost in unison, shaking their fists above their heads as if they had won the lottery. Jesus, what has it come to: even bit-parters played the big star in the modern world of United. Can you imagine the likes of, say, Gerry Daly – a '70s model, albeit superior to Miller – acting the big I am? No way: he would have just been grateful for the acknowledgement. It served to highlight the distance nowadays between the fans and the men whose wages they pay – a dark hole lit, for the most part, at the edges by mediocre performers like the former Celtic player.

Excuse the cynicism: I guess all us football lovers suffer it at times. Rooney had lost another chunk of the innocence that had so endeared him to us and had popped a small balloon from my son's dreamy vision of how magical the game of football should be.

There were more disturbing comments coming out of Old Trafford as the New Year loomed. Apparently, United were grooming Ferguson's assistant Carlos Queiroz as the next manager at the club. It instantly brought to mind the situation when Sir Matt Busby finally moved upstairs, and the hapless Wilf McGuinness took command. Don't get me wrong here: Queiroz is a reasonably good coach, and the club could do worse than secure his services long-term in that role. However, I don't see him as the manager of the biggest club in the world. The job is too big for him or, to put it another way, he is not big enough for the job. You need a man such as Carlo Ancelotti or Fabio Capello in the hot seat at Old Trafford. The ideal man would probably be José Mourinho, a big-headed, big-mouthed extrovert, who can back up his words with trophies already won. Look how he had turned Chelsea around so quickly. Queiroz seemed a nice enough guy, but was he ruthless enough? Not if his stint at Real Madrid was anything to go by. He pandered to Beckham, allowing him to play central midfield, and was sacked after a season that ended trophy-less.

There was also the fear that he would be Ferguson's puppet – with the old man in an executive capacity at Old Trafford pulling all the strings. And even if Queiroz did manage to become his own man, he would be permanently in Ferguson's shadow. No, when the new manager arrived, it should not be someone shoehorned in by Ferguson. A new broom was needed if United were to continue to progress.

United's festive season continued apace with a trip to Villa Park on the 28th of the month. Just before the match, it was announced that the Spanish FA had been fined a paltry £44,750 for the abuse directed at England's black players in November. Another disgraceful decision by FIFA, who had spurned the chance to make Spain play behind closed doors. If England had been in the dock, you can be sure the punishment would have been much harsher. It highlighted the extraordinarily poor decision-making and management at the very top of the football tree; no wonder the game at lower levels was facing a crisis and a lack of direction as 2005 nudged ever closer.

The Villa game ended in more aggravation for Rooney – this time from injury. He was taken off on the hour with a gashed right thigh after a rough studs-up challenge from rookie defender Liam Ridgewell. Rooney sat in the dugout for the remainder of the match, looking suitably sorry for himself as strapping and ice were applied to his leg. In the event, it was not a serious as it looked, and he had three matches to recover as his ban kicked in at the full time whistle.

United came away with a useful 1–0 win – their seventh in eight Premiership games – thanks to another goal from Ryan

Giggs. The veteran was the man of the match, his 41st minute strike merely icing the cake of another fine showing. Rooney had started the match prowling the left wing, then moved to the right, leaving Giggs space to attack down the centre with Alan Smith as his partner. Ronaldo was on the bench, along with skipper Keane. Rooney played well enough before his enforced departure, causing all sorts of problems for Villa's overworked defence. He might have got on the scoresheet with a powerful first-half shot, but keeper Thomas Sorensen was his equal.

The win was encouraging. United moved up to third in the table, now nine points behind leaders Chelsea. Ferguson said, 'This was the hardest away game of the season, and Villa could have got something out of it. This is a difficult place to come. Arsenal and Chelsea have still to play here, and they are in for a real fight because Villa are a real handful.' Another sign of Fergie sometimes losing the plot? Chelsea had already visited Villa Park in September and had come away with a 0–0 draw.

Another worrying matter was Ferguson's refusal to allow the Rooney 'punch' business to die down. What's that about stopping digging when you are in a hole, Alex? He chose to stir the hornet's nest a little further on New Year's Eve, the day of his 63rd birthday. It all started off sensibly enough with Ferguson explaining that Rooney's volatility, along with a sublime talent, was what helped him stand out as potentially the best player of the next generation. Ferguson said, 'We've got to get him to act like a 30 year old at the age of 19. But if you take the devil out of them, if you take the heart out of them, you don't have the same player.'

That's all well and good, but Ferguson then compounded his previous error of refusing to call a spade a spade when he defended Rooney's actions against Haim. He also called the FA's decision to ban Rooney for three games as 'unfair and immoral'. He added, 'He may have been a bit of a silly boy to put his hand in his face, but he never swung a fist at the boy. I've spoken to him about raising his hands and he knows, but young boys have an adventure about them that older players don't have.

Experience teaches them many things, and, unfortunately, you can't put the clock forward for a boy of 19.

'He's going to have to accept the responsibility of being the most talked-about player in Britain. He can't do anything without it being focused on. This is a definite lesson for him.' And maybe one for Sir Alex too, if he can somehow learn to take contemplative time out to consider his words and actions over the season as a whole. Would it not benefit the club if Ferguson adopted a more mature, worldly-wise attitude with the FA and even the BBC as he now embarked on his 19th year in charge? Why continue to play the bully and the baby who has thrown his dummy out of the pram?

An interesting post-Christmas appointment at FA headquarters provided Fergie with the perfect chance to show another side to himself over the next 12 months. Brian Barwick, the former controller of sport at ITV, and a die-hard Liverpool fan, was appointed the new chief executive. The bookies were already taking bets on when the first blow-up between the two would take place and when Sir Alex would accuse him of Scouse bias.

Meanwhile, the United roadshow headed for the Riverside on New Year's Day and a particularly tricky-looking fixture with Steve McClaren's Middlesbrough. Without the now banned Rooney, United did tremendously well, coming away with a fine 2–0 victory. Ferguson had sent out Alan Smith as United's lone central attacker in the absence of the still-injured van Nistelrooy and Saha and had praised the former Leeds man to the skies, saying, 'Alan Smith: what form he's hit. He's been fantastic. I have to say it was a great bit of business.'

Indeed it was: at £20 million less than he had paid for Rooney, Ferguson had hit the jackpot with old Eminem, who was United's second top scorer with nine goals. It wasn't just his ability to convert chances that made him joint favourite (with Gabriel Heinze) to win United's Player of the Season award at that stage of the season; he was such a committed, passionate soul, who would never accept a lost cause. In a similar vein to Roy Keane, he epitomised Ferguson's vision of a real player. It was sometimes easy to forget Smith was only 24 – as Ferguson said, he seemed to have been around forever. He had made his debut for Leeds against Liverpool as a 17 year old and had never looked back.

A goal in the first half from Darren Fletcher and in the second from Ryan Giggs earned United the points at Boro. It was Fletcher's first senior goal for the club and Giggs's third in as many matches. Afterwards, Smith spoke about the great team spirit now in evidence in the dressing-room. He said, 'We're confident in ourselves. We know we've got to keep winning as long as everyone else is. Whether we've got people injured or not we've got a big enough, and a good enough, squad to keep challenging. But we're not feeling the pressure – we've got experienced players in our dressing-room who have done it before. We'll be there until the end.'

The next two games – at home to Spurs and little Exeter – would throw a massive question mark over Smith's claims about the quality of the squad. Two wins were vital; however, as it turned out, United were lucky to get two draws. England boss Sven-Göran Eriksson waded in with a lovely compliment for Rooney before the Spurs game. He described Rooney's hat-trick debut at United as the best individual performance of the year and hailed him as one of the best players in the world. Eriksson said, 'Of course he can be better, and I'm sure he will be better. That says a lot about him. He's already one of the best in Europe – one of the best in the world.

'The great thing about him is that he can play first striker, second striker and, with United, he is sometimes also playing to the left now and doing extremely well. So he can play in a lot of roles which is very good. Maybe he's better when he drops off a little bit or goes out a little bit but the quality he has he could also be a target player if Sir Alex Ferguson or I wanted that. It's very rare to see a young man with that vision of play because it's normally something you learn with the years, but he seems to be born with it.'

It was a remarkable tribute from the national coach, and the plaudits for Rooney didn't stop there. United great Ole Solskjær, still out with a recurring knee injury that was now threatening his career, admitted that it was the thought of linking up with the boy wonder in a United shirt that kept him going in the dark days of recovery. He told MUTV, 'I want to play with Wayne. He is a world-class player and he will learn so much by being here. He is made for Manchester United. His arrival has given everyone a boost, and I just hope I get a few opportunities to play with him.'

Rooney was in the stands serving the second match of his ban when United lined up against a resurgent Spurs, but, inevitably, he was still making the headlines. It emerged that he had 'bought' Coleen an elephant as an extra Christmas gift, under an adoption scheme to help endangered species in Africa. It cost him 20 quid for the one-off gesture. It was also reported that bookies Ladbrokes had Wayne and Coleen down as the most likely celebrity couple to get married in 2005, at odds of 3–1. By now, their fame was such that even those in the lavish world of movies were using their names as a reference point. For example, in public, Jude Law's former wife Sadie Frost had wished Law and new fiancée Sienna Miller 'all the best for the future'. In private, she was said to have described Sienna's engagement ring as 'something Wayne might buy for Coleen'.

Spurs arrived a much-changed outfit from the one that had gone down 1–0 to a Ruud van Nistelrooy goal in September's Premiership clash at White Hart Lane. Gone was the defensively clinical, if dour, Frenchman, Jacques Santini, and in his place sat the likeable, jovial Dutchman Martin Jol. After an opening sequence of defeats, Jol had started to mould Spurs into a force to be reckoned with – hard to beat, but unlike Santini's side, pretty on the eye. In other words, the sort of team Tottenham fans had longed for – the sort that they had been brought up on during the glory days of the '60s and '70s.

On paper, it looked like a cracking encounter. United were unchanged in the Premiership for the first time that term – they had used more players than any other top-flight team – and had climbed to third in the table after a run of eight wins in nine games. Another fact to delight the anorak in us: United had conceded just eight goals in sixteen Premiership games since Rio Ferdinand's return from his ban in September. The Reds were without the suspended Rooney, but, to balance things out, Spurs were without Fredi Kanoute and the supremely talented Jermaine Defoe. The visitors were also in form – they had won six out of their last seven games, including a 5–2 thrashing of Everton in their last match.

So, the stage was set for a pulsating contest, as Roy Keane led out United to the traditional backdrop of Iggy Pop's 'Lust For Life' anthem from the tannoys. Indeed it was pulsating but rather unpleasantly so for United's massed army of followers. Things started to go wrong from 37 minutes in, when Ryan Giggs limped off with a strain, and David Bellion emerged from the sidelines. Along with Eric Djemba-Djemba and Liam Miller, he had been United's biggest disappointment of the season – a triumvirate of mediocrity and hardly a glowing endorsement for Ferguson's midfield transfer dealings. As the excellent fanzine *Red Issue* pointed out, Ferguson had continued to try to mould the three of them and fellow flop Kleberson into one, in the hope that they would somehow come out of the mix as a Roy Keane.

The sighs reverberated around the Theatre of Dreams as Bellion skipped on, but, with hindsight, that was merely a light-hearted interlude for what was to follow. Of course, the Roy Carroll 'goal' blunder crowned it all, but let's rewind slowly so we don't miss any other mystifying acts.

One: with 14 minutes to go, Ferguson took off Fletcher, the most talented of United's wannabe midfielders and replaced him with Miller. United were down to the bare bones and this was the moment when Ferguson's transfer folly came home to roost. OK, I know he also had Djemba-Djemba on the bench, but we won't even go there . . .

Two: with no Rooney, Giggs, Saha or van Nistelrooy, United were struggling to break through the well-drilled Spurs defence. So what does Ferguson do? He takes off the lively Ronaldo, who had at least provided a threat along with the terrier-like Alan Smith, and brings on young defender Jonathan Spector.

Three: to cap it all, Fergie signals for Rio Ferdinand to play up front, with Spector slipping into his role at the back. Just be grateful that Peter Schmeichel wasn't on the pitch that night. Ferguson had finally demonstrated that his second string were just not up to it.

Surely Manchester United, the biggest and greatest club in world football, did not need to resort to playing their centre-half in attack? Disdain would follow from the Old Trafford faithful. The sight of Ferdinand battling like a confused giraffe for the cause evoked pity; the sight of Bellion not bothering to chase a one-on-one ball with keeper Paul Robinson brought a huge round of boos. Talking of Robinson, what a bargain at £2.5 million. While United continued to bemoan a dearth of quality reserves in central midfield, and worry about the talent of keepers Roy Carroll and Tim Howard, Spurs had solved their goalkeeping problem by signing the former Leeds man. By now also the established England keeper, Robinson would have been a snip – and a fine buy – at that price for Ferguson.

He proved his quality with a series of stops and his special talent was only underlined by *that* late howler by Roy Carroll. Here was a man who had told United he was unhappy with the offer of an £18,000-a-week contract – that's £936,000 a year – and whose future remained in limbo. Well, as far as bargaining tools go, Roy, this was certainly not one of your best, old bean. To add insult to injury, in the programme notes for the match, Carroll had said, 'You might not have to do anything for 89 minutes but then be called upon to make a save in the last minute, so you have to be ready.' It all began when Spurs midfielder Pedro Mendes noticed Carroll was showboating out of his goal. He decided to try to catch him out with an effort from the halfway line. Accurate it was, but it should not have presented a problem for the keeper. Yet Carroll fumbled the ball into the net before hastily pushing it back out. It was a goal, and United should have lost 1–0.

It would have been Tottenham's first league win at Old Trafford since 1989 but it was not to be. Linesman Rob Lewis was also caught out by the offbeat effort. He was out of position and did not see it cross the line. As he later admitted, 'The Spurs player shot from distance, and I was doing my primary job which was to stand in line with the last defender and watch for an offside. There was nothing I could have done differently apart from run faster than Linford Christie. When the ball landed, I was still 25 yards from goal, and it was impossible to judge if it had crossed the line.'

Martin Jol was surprisingly fair-handed considering his team had lost two points – it would surely have not been the case with Sir Alex had United been the victims. Jol said, 'We feel robbed but it's difficult for the linesman and referee to see it.'

Inevitably, the incident brought renewed calls for a video referee to be installed at matches. Jol added, 'The referee is already wearing an earpiece, so why can't we just stop the game and get the decision right? We are not talking about the ball being a couple of centimetres or an inch or two over the line, it was a metre inside the goal.' Sir Alex admitted sympathy for Spurs and backed the call for technology to be brought in. He said, 'I think it hammers home what a lot of people have been asking for and that's that technology should play a part in the game. What I was against originally was the time factor in video replays, but I read an article the other day which suggested that if a referee can't make up his mind after 30 seconds of watching a video replay then the game should carry on. Thirty seconds is about the same amount of time it takes to organise a free-kick or take a corner or a goal-kick. So you wouldn't be wasting a lot of time. How both the referee and his assistant missed it beats me, surely video replay must be introduced in this game. I think you could start off by using it for goal-line decisions. I think that would be an opening into a new area of football.'

Somehow, Arsenal boss Arsène Wenger also got in on the Old Trafford act. He said, 'When the whole world apart from the referee has seen there should be a goal at Old Trafford, that just reinforces what I feel – there should be video evidence. It's a great example of where the referee could have asked to see a replay and would have seen in five seconds that it was a goal.'

My feeling is that video evidence should be used in the case of whether the ball crossed the line, but not for any other reason. It would slow the match up too much, and human error is part and parcel of the excitement of football.

United had escaped, but the future was looking a lot less rosy than it had before the match. Chelsea had not dropped a single point over the Christmas period, and, all of a sudden, the unpalatable fact for United was this: they would need to win, more or less, every Premiership game until the end of the season, and hope Chelsea lost 12 points from their remaining 16 games. It would take more than the 'blip' Ferguson predicted for the Blues if United were to end up champions, and that is without taking into account the claims of second-placed Arsenal.

A friend tried to convince me again that Rooney would have to shoulder the brunt of the blame if United did not overhaul Chelsea. That his suspension at such a key time had left Ferguson bereft of vital quality firepower. Mmmm. My own feeling is that the lack of quality back-up on the bench and Fergie's tinkering was United's main undoing. It had always threatened to be that way and now it was proving to be so. The next outing, a supposed walk-in-the-park FA Cup tie against Conference minnows Exeter, would go a long way to convincing me that I was correct.

11

CAPTAIN BLACK
AND THE MYSTERY ONES

THE BRIEF FROM MY PUBLISHER HAD BEEN SIMPLE ENOUGH back in September 2004. Produce a book on Rooney's first year at Manchester United: how he developed from the highs of Euro 2004 on the pitch and how he settled off it in a new environment. By the end of January/beginning of February 2005, it was clear that, while hopefully fulfilling that mission, we were also, at the same time, caught up in something altogether more dramatic concerning the bigger picture at Manchester United. Had Rooney's debut season come at a time of transition and mere tuning up at the good ship United, or was it a part of a much more wide-ranging, all-encompassing end of an era? In other words, was it the true beginning of the end of the Ferguson glory days? The inevitable sands of time running out on the man who had single-handedly moulded United back into something wonderful after 20-odd years of relative mediocrity.

The Scot had breathed life back into the tired old giant, just as Busby had once done. His presence was everywhere at the Theatre of Dreams; United were now a PLC but still very much in awe of the man who had created the whole damned pleasure dome through his bellicose ambition and vision. Yet January

GOLD TRAFFORD
Wayne and fiancée Coleen are full of smiles, as Sir Alex Ferguson shows them around the Theatre of Dreams. Rooney had signed for £27 million, a deal that would see his wages soar from the £13,000 a week he was on at Everton to £50,000.

THAT'S MY BOY
Ferguson displays a father-like pride, as he welcomes Wayne to Old Trafford and admits he had been a long-time admirer. The duo hold up a United shirt inscribed with Rooney's name and the number 8 he had inherited from Nicky Butt.

ROON AT THE TOP

Wayne has a laugh during the Carling Cup semi-final first leg
0–0 draw with Chelsea at Stamford Bridge. But the joke would
ultimately be on him and United, as José Mourinho's men won
the tie 2–1 in the return leg at Old Trafford.

ARE YOU SIMON COWELL IN DISGUISE?
The American Malcolm Glazer, who likes to wear his trousers
high like the *Pop Idol* judge. Glazer would ultimately win
control of United.

YOUNG, GIFTED AND SLACK
Rooney collects the BBC Young Sports Personality of the Year
award in December 2002. The then Everton stalwart
was criticised, in the newspapers the following day,
for nervously chewing gum and having his tie undone.

THE WIZARD
United fans had come up with the affectionate nickname, after
Sir Alex had led the club to 15 years of success. But the passionate
manager would come under fire from them
during Rooney's first season for some baffling tactical
and selection decisions.

THREE AND EASY
Rooney coolly slots home England's third goal past Croatia keeper
Tomislav Butina. It was Wayne's second of the game and helped
Sven-Göran Eriksson's men to a 4–2 win and a quarter-final match
with host nation Portugal.

LEADER OF THE PACK
At just 18, Rooney emerged as England's key player in Euro 2004
and one of the stars of the tournament. Here, David Beckham and
Paul Scholes pay homage to the man-boy who brought a nation
joy and hope, until he injured his foot.

CURSE OF A GENIUS

Like Maradona and Gazza, Rooney had to work hard to control a hot temper that often landed him in trouble with referees. Here, he gets a yellow card from Valentin Ivanov for a rash challenge in the Euro 2004 3–0 win over Switzerland.

WELCOME TO HELL

The boot is on the other foot for the Turks of Fenerbahçe, whose fans often greet visiting teams from England with the nightmare slogan. Rooney ran them ragged, here scoring United's second goal and the first of his hat-trick.

RED-DY STEADY GO
Gary 'Red Nev' Neville leads the celebrations, hugging Rooney after the Liverpudlian grabbed his first goal for the club against Fenerbahçe. Rooney opened his account with a left-foot curler that soared high into the net.

HATS OFF TO THE WONDER BOY
Wayne Rooney completes his hat-trick on his United debut against the Turks. He had pushed senior players away and demanded he take the free-kick that led to the goal, a 20-yard effort that left keeper Rustu Recber stranded.

2005 felt uncomfortable: as if Ferguson had finally accepted that old age waited for no one. For the first time I can personally remember, the big man sounded tired and resigned to failure. It started with the disgraceful 0–0 FA Cup draw at home to Exeter – when his second string once again proved their lack of talent – and ended with a gut-wrenching defeat by the new kid, or maybe that should be new king, on the block.

Yes, the one and only Mr Mourinho. The Captain Black in the chapter's title – so-called by my kids and wife, who never miss the evil baddie in the animated children's show *Captain Scarlet and the Mysterons*. The Mystery Ones? The guys Ferguson continued to stand by: like the shower who drew with the Conference side in the cup. A true mystery was why the big man believed the likes of Djemba-Djemba would ever make the grade as United players. At times it appeared he stuck with them out of stubbornness – the sort of perverse streak that used to make him pick Juan Sebastián Verón instead of David Beckham. He had splashed out a small fortune on men like these and was determined that they would one day come good, essentially to justify his decision to buy them. Or maybe it was the decision of his foreign scout: none other than his brother Martin.

Mourinho the evil Captain Black? Well, maybe he had his looks, but he was hardly evil. Clever, certainly. Arrogant, yes. Talented, magnificently so. As we have said before, the ideal man to take over from Ferguson, and, ironically enough, the man whose very success was bringing into sharp focus the idea that we were seeing history being made. Maybe United's era of domination was indeed coming to an end – both on and off the pitch – as Malcolm Glazer continued to circle above Old Trafford like a vulture.

By the end of January, Ferguson would have wearily accepted that Mourinho's Chelsea were untouchable at the top of the Premiership and, even more surprisingly, also have conceded Mourinho was the new top man: that the Portuguese was a younger version of himself. Seeing Ferguson wave the white flag brought a lump to my throat and a tear to my eye: it was like watching a heavyweight champion such as Muhammad Ali being battered around by a younger, prettier and cleverer fighter. And, let's not doubt it, Mourinho certainly had the upper hand on Ferguson. By February 2005 he would have played against United five times and lost none. He was also very much the winner in the mind games and the charm war.

Of course, for all his looks, genius and money, José was only manager of Chelsea – not the biggest club in the world – but he had a massive cash war chest at Stamford Bridge, and he was a brilliant coach and motivator. He was also just 42 years old compared with Ferguson's 63. Both men had won the European Cup once, but Mourinho had the strength in depth of talent in his squad that was so obviously lacking in United's. OK, he did not have Rooney, van Nistelrooy or Ronaldo. Yet his second string would have rolled over Exeter in the first tie: that United struggled was the factor that set the alarm bells ringing in the first place.

Sure, it was a terrible day for a cup tie. Driving rain and hail, gale force winds and a biting cold enveloped Old Trafford at the start of January, but it was the same conditions for both teams. Exeter wanted a result more: they rolled up their sleeves and battled. I remembered sitting on the steps of Wembley in 1976, a mere boy devastated after United had surrendered to Southampton in the FA Cup final. Devastated but hopeful: a young United side had simply been overawed against Southampton's old men of war, including Mick Channon and Peter Osgood. They would come good again. This United team, including Miller, Djemba-Djemba and Bellion at its spine was, well, spineless. If this was a glimpse of the future, it was a nightmare.

Afterwards, captain for the day Phil Neville admitted, 'It would have been a travesty if we had won. We let the fans down, and we let ourselves down.'

Ferguson said sorry to the fans, after his team was booed off. He said, 'I apologise to the fans. They did not deserve that. In my 18 years at this club that was the worst performance we have ever produced in the FA Cup. It is hard to get your head around it. We are all very disappointed. If someone had told me before the game it would be 0–0 I would probably have hit them. I know we played some young players, but that is not an excuse: we expect more of them than that. This is Exeter's day, but I will play a much stronger team in the replay, and we will not make this mistake again.'

Rooney, wearing a pair of black gloves, returned for the trip to Devon. Again, conditions were pretty wild: a biting gale blew the ball all over the show. United redeemed themselves with a 2–0 win, Ronaldo grabbing the first and Rooney finishing the tie off with a couple of minutes to go. He coolly rounded the keeper and rammed the ball home. On a less welcome note, he was guilty of continually arguing and grappling with the Exeter midfielders. Surely a player of Rooney's stature and calibre did not need to let himself down like that? Especially with Conference-level lads. Come on Wayne, cut it out. Those sort of players would want your autograph more than to knee you in the balls. Couldn't you see you were a hero to them?

Afterwards, a relieved Ferguson said, 'There is no point saying we were brilliant or anything like that. We missed too many chances. We could have won by more, and at 1–0 they always felt they had a chance. At least we have a home tie now against Middlesbrough.'

United also had two Carling Cup ties in January: the home and away encounters with Chelsea. Four days after the depressing draw with Exeter, they travelled to Stamford Bridge and ground out an excellent 0–0 draw. Rooney almost netted on 40 minutes when he met a header from Darren Fletcher, but Carlo Cudicini pushed the ball to safety behind his goal. Ferguson brought on Scholes for the out-of-touch Djemba-Djemba, but the ginger head could not change the outcome. Eric 2DJ had earned the new moniker the 'Djemba twins' from the excellent fanzine *United We Stand* in the hope it would make him twice the player he was. That would prove to be wishful thinking.

The spicy highlight of the match came after the final whistle when Mourinho claimed Ferguson had influenced referee Neale Barry as they walked off together at half time. The Chelsea boss said, 'I see one referee in the first half and another in the second. If the FA ask me what happened, I will tell them. What I saw and felt made it easier to understand a few things. Maybe when I turn 60 and have been managing in the same league for 20 years and have the respect of everybody I will have the power to speak to people and make them tremble a little bit.

'The referee controlled the game in one way during the first half but in the second they had dozens of free-kicks. It was fault after fault, dive after dive. But I know the referee did not walk to the dressing-rooms alone at half time. He should only have had his two assistants and the fourth official with him, but there was also someone else.' The comments would earn Mourinho an FA charge for improper conduct and a £5,000 fine.

Unusually, Ferguson did not lash back at the Chelsea boss. He would only complain of a poor bottle of Portuguese wine Mourinho offered him after the match and promised to have a better quality vintage awaiting his opposite number after the return leg at Old Trafford. Ferguson appeared to have met his match in the world of mind games as well as football – although he did pour scorn on Mourinho's hopes of winning four trophies in the current season, saying, 'There's no chance of a club doing a Quadruple. A Treble is more feasible. But it is still very difficult to think that will be done again.'

In the return leg, there was little to choose between the teams. Yet in his programme notes, Ferguson sounded surprisingly downbeat and pessimistic – the first time I have ever heard him that way. His words would surely have struck fear into his own men:

> Our defensive record is good, but Chelsea's is better . . . as I said at the weekend it is Chelsea's title unless they throw it away . . . at times they look invincible. We are up against a well organised, disciplined and determined side. I must stop praising them before I frighten myself, never mind the players . . .

Astonishing stuff: have you ever heard Ferguson talk like that before?

The old man had also clearly been taken in by Mourinho's charm offensive. He added:

> I like José Mourinho. There is a devilish wit about him. We get on well – though it doesn't stop us standing up for our respective teams. I think he sees himself as the young gunslinger who has come into town to challenge the sheriff who has been around for a while. He was certainly full of it, calling me 'Boss' and 'Big Man' when we had our post-match drink.

Ferguson was more or less waving the white flag to the all-conquering newcomer and his undoubtedly fine team. Even when United lost 2–1 it was not the aggressive Fergie of old; he merely accepted defeat and enjoyed a drink with Mourinho. The defeat could have been avoided if Ferguson had maybe entertained less sweet talking with his opposite number and concentrated on the game. He dropped Rooney, for the second time that season, instead employing the eager but hardly as naturally gifted Quinton Fortune. United had lots of pretty play but no end result as they kept running into the brick wall of John Terry, and his hardline defence. Then the Reds fell for a sucker punch as Frank Lampard nipped in to put the visitors ahead on the half-hour mark.

Rooney replaced Fortune on the hour, and suddenly United looked a different side. The composed Terry and William Gallas found the teenager hard to deal with. Just eight minutes after coming on, Wayne had helped draw United level, Ryan Giggs chipping the equaliser over Petr Cech after Rooney had caused problems down the left wing. Chelsea stole the game five minutes from time when Damien Duff's inswinging free-kick beat the United defence and keeper Tim Howard to end up in the back of the net. Howard was the scapegoat for not stopping the 25-yard curler, but his defence was just as culpable. My feeling remained that Howard was the more naturally gifted of United's two senior keepers and that, given a boost to his confidence, he could still make it in the top grade as a reliable back-up to a real top-quality number 1.

A valid point here: United had the third best keeper in the world of the last 40 years when Peter Schmeichel kept goal. Could it not be arranged that he return to Old Trafford to coach the likes of Howard? Tony Coton had had his chance – now why not bring back the master? And if you're wondering who were the top two keepers: in my humble opinion, Gordon Banks and Peter Shilton.

Ferguson's only consolation after the loss – his first ever in a domestic semi-final with United – was the bottle of plonk Mourinho brought with him to celebrate his 42nd birthday. A true connoisseur of fine wines, Fergie admitted the taste of the 1964 vintage Barca Velha helped slightly to take away the bitter taste of defeat.

The questions would not go away. Why had Fergie dropped his best player again? Why was he running from another manager for the first time in his career? Ferguson later admitted, 'I thought we looked a lot sharper in the second half, particularly when Wayne Rooney came on.' Again, there was no one else on the United bench who could have made a creative difference in the absence of the injured Ruud van Nistelrooy and Alan Smith.

Even the Chelsea fans won the war of words against United. The refrain they started off in the old Scoreboard Paddock showed they possessed a rare wit: 'Stand up if you've won the league, stand up if you've won the league!' Well, I suppose to all intents and purposes they had. United fans joined in the chorus, unaware that it had been started by the mob from the Bridge.

Later, a United insider put an interesting set of thoughts to me. It was, he said, not so much that Fergie was running from Mourinho but that he accepted he deserved respect. Also, and here's the big one, he claimed Ferguson's dropping of Rooney and cosying up to Mourinho was yet another snipe, albeit indirectly, at Arsène Wenger. The insider argued that Rooney was dropped to ensure he would be available for the crunch Premiership match on 1 February at Arsenal, and that the compliments to Mourinho were part of a subtle campaign by

Ferguson to say: he is everything that other foreigner Wenger is not.

I am not so sure. Maybe there was a bit of mind games in it, but my gut reaction was that Ferguson had indeed met his match in José. The crunch match was the one United had just lost. Ferguson also desperately wanted to beat Chelsea to inflict some psychological scars that would hopefully affect their Premiership campaign. Yet even an almost full-strength side, in what Ferguson had traditionally dismissed as a 'nothing competition', was not good enough to see off Mourinho. No, the old firestarter was mellowing a little at last. He had finally found an adversary who was his equal and who could conceivably go on to surpass his own remarkable achievements.

Mourinho continued his own mind games to keep Ferguson buttered up after Chelsea's win, tipping his hat to the United manager for being a good loser. It was classic stuff and must have left Ferguson both puzzled and off-balance: 'I am learning a lot with him to the point where I need to improve myself. He is helping me to improve because I am a bad loser. When I lose I am not very keen to be with other people. He showed me a lot of respect and quality in that sense. He was in his office waiting for me and my staff with a bottle of wine I gave him before the game.

'He lost a semi-final and that feeling is not good but he was there completely open and respectful. When I have this kind of teacher, then, one day when I lose, I must open my doors for the winner. He is a football man and he likes to share opinions. There was Spanish football on his television after the game so we spoke about it and the Champions League. It was very nice for me to start learning that you must be the same when you win or lose. Maybe one day he will beat me, and I have to behave the same way. In our culture, when you lose a game, you don't want to share the next half-an-hour with the manager who beats you. I think it is great when you can have that kind of relationship before and after the game, respect and communication. I started in England because of your culture. Sir Alex's way is a fantastic way to be. He knows everything about football.'

So to recap: Sir Alex knows how to lose well, he is a good teacher and a man in control of his emotions. Really, José? Try putting that to Wenger and the players who have come under the dreaded hairdryer these last 18 years. The Portuguese was proving himself to be both a brilliant manipulator and a brilliant coach. The first manager to take on Fergie at United in 18 years and win, hands down.

The Red Devils were still chipping away in the Premiership, hoping Chelsea would have that blip. Two matches loomed for United that would normally have decided who would end up first or second, but suddenly they looked mere sideshows in the light of Chelsea's massive ten-point lead at the top. The first was at Liverpool in mid-January, the second at Arsenal at the start of February. The Kop showdown was, of course, Rooney's first return to Merseyside in a United shirt since his controversial move from Everton the previous August. Security was tight: Wayne was escorted by his own bodyguard and arrived under the watchful eye of the local constabulary.

He had been back and forth from Liverpool to Manchester over the previous four to five months to see his and Coleen's family and mates, but the trips were becoming less frequent. That was down to an edict from manager Ferguson, who was determined Rooney would settle in Manchester. He did not want him back in a place where he could be prone to doing silly things like visiting massage parlours, or where he might be led astray by some of his old mates. The boy was safe in Manchester: in Liverpool there were no guarantees, especially as some Everton supporters remained disgruntled about his 'sell-out'.

On a scale of one to ten, Rooney's day out at the Kop turned out to be a nine in terms of security fears and crowd anger. In the light of the hassle he received, you couldn't have written the script any better. He returned triumphant, scoring the only goal in a tight contest. Naturally enough, that did not go down too well with his fellow Scousers on the Kop. They had goaded him throughout – about his weight, his girlfriend and for being a 'Judas' – and it was probably divine justice that he would have his revenge in the best possible way. Sure, his celebration of the goal was foolish: right in front of the Kop, hands raised behind his ears, a defiant face taunting the home fans. The reaction from some of those in the old Spion was equally as foolish, as a mobile phone was thrown at Rooney. It would not take the police too much difficulty to find the culprit now, would it?

Rooney's winner came after 20 minutes: a thunderbolt from 30 yards that caught out the error-prone Jerzy Dudek. The shot skidded through the Pole's fingers into the back of the net. Again, Rooney's strength of mind deserves praise. He ignored the continued jibes of the Kop to help United hold on to their lead. His chasing back and harassing the likes of newly-purchased Fernando Morientes and his old pal Stevie Gerrard was a credit to him – although he did pick up a silly booking for taking a kick at Luis Garcia.

Even his now regular habit of mouthing off to the referee was kept under lock and key for most of the match – essential after United were reduced to ten men when Wes Brown was sent off for a second bookable offence. It was left to United's 2,000-plus faithful in the Anfield Road end to have the final words, mocking their counterparts on the Kop with the chant, 'City of culture, you're having a laugh'.

The win had been essential as United battled with Arsenal for that second place spot and an automatic berth in the following season's Champions League. They did not want to have to qualify again. Former Old Trafford hero Frank Stapleton had voiced the now common belief that United's title quest was all but over. He said, 'If United had lost or drawn, then you're looking for Chelsea to really mess up. It would have made it really difficult for the league – it would have been almost impossible. United players still talk about overhauling Newcastle a few years back, but there's a bit more resilience about this Chelsea side. It's a long haul against a team of that calibre.'

Stapleton's views on Rooney were not quite as well thought out. He was averaging a goal every two games and had become an essential cog in Ferguson's new tactical set-up: one that, funnily enough, owed its copyright to Mourinho at Chelsea. Just as Chelsea played 4-3-3, for the moment so did Ferguson, generally employing Rooney, Giggs and Ronaldo up-front in a flexible formation that allowed them to swap, from the centre to the left to the right, at will. In much the same way as Duff, Robben or Cole and either Drogba or Gudjohnsen did at Chelsea. The only difference was that Ferguson also liked to tinker with the more cautious 4-5-1.

Stapleton had claimed, 'We are still waiting for Wayne Rooney to fully emerge. Generally his performances haven't been up to scratch: perhaps we still expect too much from him. That's the thing with big-game players.'

The win at Anfield meant the United class of 2005 would not go into the record books for one particularly unwanted statistic. They had been on the verge of notching up a record number of consecutive 0–0 draws after the three goalless encounters with Spurs, Exeter and Chelsea. Only once before in their history, back in 1921, had United drawn three games on the trot without a goal being scored.

Rooney's goal secured United's second double over Liverpool in three seasons. It was also their third victory in succession at Anfield – a new record – and their seventh successive clean sheet, which equalled another club record.

Ferguson later admitted he would love to have Kop skipper Steven Gerrard on board to fill that troubling central midfield area when Keane finally hung up his boots. Ferguson said, 'We would show interest if we thought there was any chance of getting him. But there is no chance because he is captain of Liverpool and the two clubs simply do not sell to each other.'

One player who, surprisingly, admitted he would like to play again for United was David Beckham. The former United idol had lost a lot of credibility and affection since his move to Madrid. He was no longer a hero of the Stretford End, but he did himself a power of good in building bridges by declaring that he would want to return to United if he ever left Real. He admitted, 'I would go back to United and work with Sir Alex, definitely. Manchester United were the club I grew up with and felt that I would always be there my whole career.' They were sound words: well done, David, old son.

Rooney had other things on his mind before United concluded their January programme with the Premiership match against Aston Villa and the FA Cup fourth rounder with Middlesbrough. He was as 'sick as a parrot' when the boy band Busted split up. He had asked them to play at his 19th birthday party and at first did not see the funny side of it when his United teammates plastered his locker at Carrington with articles about the bust-up. He ripped them down and only just managed a smile when he was then jumped on by a bunch of taunting United players.

Also, both he and Coleen are animal lovers, and she was almost in tears when a paper accused her of having a wardrobe that would have led to the death of 70 animals including pythons, rabbits, chinchilla and mink. The obsession with football's new number one celebrity couple showed no sign of abating. In reality, they were simply two council-estate kids who were enjoying the money and the lifestyle that came with Rooney being the major British footballing talent of recent times. They did not court publicity like the Beckhams, but publicists continued to court them. The public could not get enough of Wayne and Coleen: they sold newspapers.

Even the greatest-ever football maverick wanted his say on the boy wonder. Just before the Villa match, the great Diego Maradona admitted that Rooney was his favourite player of the current generation but warned him of the pitfalls of success. Maradona said, 'Wayne Rooney is a phenomenal talent and has already achieved a lot. He could go on to be as great as Bobby Charlton and help England win the World Cup. To do that he needs to concentrate totally on his football – if he does this he has almost unlimited possibilities. That can be hard, as there is even more pressure on players today than when I was playing.' Maradona certainly knows about the pitfalls – he battled against drug addiction throughout his playing career, and since retiring from the game has struggled with his health and weight.

Sir Alex also weighed in for good measure, saluting his boy's ability to turn it on when it really mattered. Ferguson said, 'Wayne is a big-game player. He is going to relish the challenges ahead over the next few months. We saw how much he liked the big games in Euro 2004.'

In the home Premiership match against Villa, Rooney was overshadowed by Ronaldo, but he would certainly make up for it in the final match of January, against Middlesbrough. Villa arrived at Old Trafford looking for a point and nearly pulled it off. David O'Leary had put together a reasonable team, and they attacked well. Unfortunately for them, Ronaldo attacked even better, grabbing a well-deserved opener in a 3–1 triumph that enabled United to leapfrog over Arsenal into second place, their highest position of the season, but still 11 points behind Chelsea. Louis Saha, with his first league goal of the campaign, and Paul Scholes tied up the points after Gareth Barry nipped in for Villa's consolation. It was United's ninth win in their last 11 Premiership outings.

Rooney wrapped up the month with a miraculous second half brace against Boro in the fourth round of the FA Cup. The striker left Boro keeper Mark Schwarzer bemused with the first one: a clinical chip from 40 yards out that would have left Beckham, in his prime, purring. The second was just as magical as he connected with a Louis Saha knock-on to volley the ball home from the edge of the penalty area. It was reminiscent of the goal scored by Marco van Basten in the 1988 European Championships: the one that won the tournament for Holland as they overwhelmed the USSR 2–0 in Munich.

The performance had been coming for a good while: it was Rooney's most deadly since he personally demolished Fenerbahçe on his debut. The boy had done as Ferguson had asked him, playing right, left, central-attacker, without a murmur of complaint. His attitude contrasted sharply with that of the whingeing Welshman Craig Bellamy, who had been booted out of Newcastle after refusing to play on the wing. His ability was but a speck in comparison to Rooney's, yet he had mistakenly believed that he had a God-given talent. Again, it went to show that Rooney's approach and attitude were not as bad as some of the cosseted egos in Fleet Street's ivory towers would have you believe.

Afterwards Rooney was bubbling about his mighty double.

He said, 'The first was a good ball from Gary Neville. I managed to stay onside and when I looked up and saw the keeper was off his line I chipped him. The second was a long ball that Louis Saha did well to head my way. It could have gone anywhere, but I had a bit of luck.'

Boss Ferguson was also elated, 'Wayne is a big-game player. It just seems to come naturally to him. Some youngsters wilt when they go out at Old Trafford in front of 67,000 people and I understand that because it is not easy. Thankfully every now and again you get players for whom facing such an intense atmosphere is the most natural thing in the world. Wayne is one of those players, and, as he scored with a superb chip and a stunning volley, he took us right back to his debut hat-trick against Fenerbahçe.'

United were drawn out of the hat for a fifth round tie at Everton: as the excellent columnist Richard Littlejohn might say, you couldn't make it up. Yes, another trip to Merseyside but no pussyfooting about this time, just straight into the lion's den for Rooney with a first return to Goodison. Yet that was neither United nor Rooney's immediate worry. First up, would be a rematch with the bruisers of Arsenal at Highbury and a journey to Manchester City's new home.

Still, there was good news to end January 2005. Ferguson finally admitted the error of his ways by selling Eric Djemba-Djemba to Aston Villa for a fee of £1.35 million. Sure, it was a loss of over £2 million on his original fee, but it showed Sir Alex had returned to the real world. Which was more than could be said of the Djemba twins, who, astonishingly, claimed to be as good a player as Roy Keane. Straight-faced, he said, 'A lot of young players are scared because Sir Alex is a big, big manager. I told him I needed to play. The problem is that I don't know when Roy Keane will move on. No one knows if he will be playing this season and next, and I can't wait that long.' A little word to the wise here, Eric, old son. Your problem was never Roy Keane standing in your way. It was about getting the nod over half a dozen others blessed with talents mightily similar to your own for a regular spot in United's reserves.

12

MEET THE FOCKERS

FOR THE FIRST DAY OF FEBRUARY 2005 EVERYTHING WAS beautiful in the world of Wayne Rooney and Manchester United – as long as you did not mention Chelsea or Malcolm Glazer. It was time for the return grudge match against Arsenal at Highbury and a highly welcome double over Uncle Fester and his men. It was also the beginning of a busy two-week period that would see the City derby match relegated to the role of relative second-rater (such was the ferocity and fallout of the battle of Highbury), the refusal of Chelsea to suffer the 'blip' Ferguson was praying for and, of course, the damned stubbornness and continued advances of the American predator who refused to go away.

Sir Alex had started the mind games with Arsène Wenger almost a fortnight before the Arsenal encounter. Like a mischievous stirrer, he stoked the fires of anger in the Frenchman's belly in an interview with *The Independent* newspaper, claiming once again that the Gunners had got away with murder in October's Battle of the Buffet. The canny Ferguson said:

> Wenger is always complaining the match was not played
> in the right spirit. They are the worst losers of all time;

they don't know how to lose. Maybe it is just Manchester United . . . [Arsenal] don't lose many games to other teams. We tend to forget the worst disciplinary record of all time was Arsenal's up until last season. In fairness, it has improved, and now they are seen as paragons of virtue. But to Wenger it never happens: it is all some dream or nightmare.

Ferguson then went for Wenger's jugular, adding:

In the tunnel Wenger was criticising my players, calling them cheats, so I told him to leave them alone and behave himself. He ran at me with hands raised saying, 'What do you want to do about it?' To not apologise for the behaviour of the players to another manager is unthinkable. It's a disgrace, but I don't expect Wenger to ever apologise, he's that type of person.

The press helped the already simmering brew along by confronting Wenger with Ferguson's words just after his side had lost 1–0 at Bolton's Reebok Stadium. They pushed the button on cue, and Wenger simply exploded. He said, 'I've always been consistent with that story and told you nothing happened. If he has to talk, he talks. If he wants to make a newspaper article, he makes a newspaper article. He doesn't interest me and doesn't matter to me at all. I will never answer to any provocation from him any more. He does what he likes in England anyway. He can go abroad one day and see how it is.'

The last line struck a chord of sympathy if you looked at it this way: here was a man in an alien country being bullied and provoked by a local bruiser whose only aim was to destroy him. Yet, on the other hand, Wenger was no hopeless, helpless immigrant, was he? Educated, knowing and a self-confessed man of the world, he himself had not been adverse to dishing out the same treatment to Ferguson on many occasions. No, in the final analysis he had simply been 'Keeganed' by Ferguson, a phrase and verb now widely accepted in the language of football battles.

Just as Kevin Keegan had once waved the white flag at Newcastle with his, 'I'd just love it if they lose' rant against Ferguson, so Wenger had lost it now.

A couple of hours after promising he would never again speak about Ferguson, Wenger was doing just that, a sure sign that his head had gone. Here was a delirious boxer, battered and bloody, stumbling senselessly around the ring. Wenger told a small group of journalists, 'I have no diplomatic relations with him. What I don't understand is that he does what he wants and you [the press] are all at his feet. The situation [about the food battle in the Old Trafford tunnel] has been judged, and there is a game going on soon.

'The managers have a responsibility to protect the game before the game. But in England you are only punished for what you say after the game. Now the whole story starts again. I don't go into that game. We play football. I am a football manager, and I love football above all . . . no matter what people say. I don't respond to anything. In England, you have a good phrase. It is "bringing the game into disrepute". But that is not only after a game, it is as well before a game.'

Ferguson must have struggled not to have spilt his bedtime cocoa as the news of Wenger's reaction reached him. No doubt he was giggling, waking his wife Cathy with the news that he had reeled in another major catch.

The row provoked moralistic headlines in the next week's newspapers. Rather than seeing it all as a fun sideshow to the main event, Ferguson and Wenger were lambasted as yobs who were wrecking the game with their vile behaviour. It was more than a touch over the top. OK, if it were to lead to violence on the terraces then let that be the end of it, but most fans I spoke with were not foolish enough to act on the sayings of two grumpy old men. No, it was more pantomime than warfare – a continuation of the entertaining banter provided by the likes of Muhammad Ali and other heavyweights to talk up their mammoth battles.

To his credit, Sports Minister Richard Caborn accepted it had simply become a regular part of the build-up to games between the clubs. He said, 'We have had the pantomime. Let's now have the serious stuff. They are two of the best managers in the world, and they are a credit to English football.' But the policeman in charge of match-day security at Highbury had his doubts and sounded a note of caution. Commander Barry Norman told the *London Evening Standard*:

> If there is intense rivalry between the two sets of fans, which there is, then anything which increases that is unhelpful. The difference with the United game is simply that the intense playing rivalry can permeate into the crowd. People can easily become more agitated and aggressive towards supporters of the other team.

Come the night of 1 February, there were 180 police officers on duty at Highbury: twice the usual number. The match was one of three Arsenal home Premiership fixtures designated as high risk, along with the visits of Tottenham and Chelsea. By now, Ferguson and Wenger had agreed to halt their war of words – at least until the match was over – but you could still have cut the Highbury tension with a knife. Not so much on the terraces, where the fans were commendably well behaved, but certainly in the general anticipation of the outcome, and in the dressing-rooms. Especially in the dressing-rooms. Sol Campbell had set the tone with this pre-match statement in *The Guardian*, 'Oh man, I'm looking forward to it. Everyone at Arsenal has been waiting for this game. We're up for this one.' Wenger tried to explain Campbell's seemingly out-of-character words, 'Sol feels he was done by Rooney. If that had not happened, we would not have lost.' The managers were at least agreed on one thing: if there were a loser, they would be out of the title race.

Rooney certainly looked up for it as the players entered the tunnel from the dressing-rooms. He had been going through a sticky patch temperamentally, with many commentators claiming he was a red card waiting to happen. Would he blow against the Gunners? After the game, he would be lambasted for using the f-word more than 20 times in a minute after referee Graham Poll booked him. The film *Meet the Fockers*, starring Robert de Niro, had just hit the cinemas, and it was later suggested that Mr Poll, who had an excellent night in tremendously difficult circumstances, had no need to travel to his local Odeon for the meeting. There were many of them on the pitch, as curses aplenty abounded in a passionate, glorious match. Forget your Italian games of cat-and-mouse: this was football at its best, and, best of all, it was English football.

No quarter was given or expected. Even in the tunnel beforehand, tempers smouldered and grudges exploded. Big Pat Vieira was the man in the hot seat: he had decided to have a verbal pop at Gary Neville, asking him if he planned to kick Arsenal off the park again. Unfortunately for Big Pat, smaller but tougher Roy Keane got wind of what was happening and shouted at Vieira, 'Don't shoot yer fucking gob off.' Keane went straight towards the Frenchman and added, 'Pick on someone yer own size. Are you gonna have a go at me then?' Vieira panicked and headed towards the front of the tunnel, as far away from Keane as he could get. Keane then shouted, 'I'll see you out there,' but referee Poll quickly intervened, begging the pair of them to cool down and to 'keep it in here; don't take it out there.' The incident was beamed live to millions watching on television around the world and made dramatic viewing. It was just a mere aperitif to a mouth-watering main course.

Cristiano Ronaldo struck a fabulous double to spearhead United to a 4–2 glory win. The Portuguese winger grabbed his brace in four second-half minutes to end Arsenal's hopes of revenge for their Old Trafford mauling. The win also effectively ended the Gunners' hopes of retaining their Premiership title, and, as any football commentator worth his salt will tell you, a team that has never retained the title can never be called legends, unbeaten for a season or not.

Arsenal twice led through goals from Vieira and Dennis Bergkamp before Ryan Giggs and Ronaldo struck. Big, lovable John O'Shea nipped in for the fourth with a last-minute chip, and Mikael Silvestre got his marching orders for a foolish head-butt on Freddie Ljungberg, right in front of the referee.

It had all started at the speed of a runaway train, with two fouls in twenty seconds and a shameful attempt by Ashley Cole to win a penalty after three minutes. The England full-back pretended Keane had tripped him in the box and dived to the ground. Thankfully, Graham Poll was not conned. The passion was running sky-high, which leads us fairly naturally enough to Rooney and his aggression. OK, he was out of order, foul-mouthing the ref for almost the whole 93 minutes. That aspect of the boy definitely needs a thorough clean-up. The late, great Brian Clough never allowed his team to have a go at the ref, and it would enhance Alex Ferguson's reputation, and save him from unnecessary suspensions, if he would drill his own men in that way.

Yet Rooney's natural game and outlook needs only fine-tuning, not a massive overhaul. It is the fire in his belly that, allied with his unique skill and talent, makes him the physically exceptional player he is. Tell him to stay away from the ref and keep his hands off opponents; tell him just to concentrate on damaging any opposition – rather than his own team with enforced suspensions. Even his developing habit of taunting the opposition was nothing to worry unduly about: it merely showed them he was not scared of them or their reputations. Against Arsenal, Robert Pires was the stunned victim as Rooney goaded him over the bit of bum fluff he was growing on his face.

The spotlight will always be on Rooney, and it was sometimes easy to forget he was just 19. He was continually taunted by the Arsenal fans about his private life. In particular, they cruelly chanted, 'Where's yer grandma gone?' – a not too subtle reference to his massage-parlour visit – but he refused to let it get to him. His genius shone through when, after 18 minutes, he set up Giggs for the first equaliser. Rooney had shimmered through the Arsenal defence, and their stone-faced back four fully expected him to pull the trigger. Instead, he coolly passed the ball to Giggs, who duly blasted it home.

Playing as an out-and-out centre-forward, Rooney revelled in his role and the electric atmosphere. And, yes, when needed he slipped back into midfield – and even to left-back – constantly covering and closing down. This was no idle, slothful boy. However, the loose cannon in him meant he was booked two minutes before the interval for persistent fouling, and, on another night, without the generosity of referee Poll, he could have been heading for an early bath because of his dissent. On the 77-minute mark, Ferguson took off Giggs and brought on Saha. It may have been more provident to have substituted Rooney, who was still fired up, despite a half-time talking to from Ferguson and Roy Keane.

Vieira and Bergkamp netted for the Gunners, but it was a pale, haunted-looking Wenger who ran up the tunnel at full time, keen to escape the jubilant red face of Ferguson. The defeat left Arsenal ten points behind Chelsea, who also had a game in hand. Wenger said, 'We will not give up, but now we are too far behind. It is Chelsea's title now. United still have a slight chance, but there is too much for us to do. But we still have our pride and will keep trying to do as well as we can. We were poor overall defensively. The first, second and third goals were bad ones to give away and not the kind of thing we did last season. Mentally, we never recovered from the third one. You could see the confidence of the players start to fade, and in the end Manchester United got themselves quite a comfortable victory.'

Ferguson just about managed not to gloat over his arch rival's downfall but still could not resist an initial jibe: 'Both managers said before that whoever lost was out of the title race. Having gone behind twice, it shows the measure of our character. We had the mental strength, and on the night we were fantastic in terms of character and will to win, and we played some fantastic football.' As for the pre-match Vieira incident in the tunnel, Ferguson said, 'Vieira was well wound up for it. I've heard different stories. Patrick Vieira has apparently threatened some of our players and things like that.'

Some of the key protagonists on the pitch also wanted to have their say. Vieira said, 'I didn't threaten anybody. They are big enough players to handle themselves. I had a talk with Roy Keane and that's it. Gary Neville is a big lad, he can handle himself. They just played better than us and deserved to win.'

Keane, inevitably, saw it all rather differently. He said, 'Patrick Vieira is 6 ft 4 in. tall and having a go at Gary Neville. So I said, "Have a go at me". If he wants to intimidate our players and thinks that Gary Neville is an easy target, I'm not having it.'

Neville admitted he had not enjoyed the game: he had found it all too tense, too edgy and too unpleasant. He said, 'There were a couple of things that did happen before the game which disappoint you. Especially from players of that calibre, but it's a tough game, and we've been around a long time. I thought it was a horrible game in the first half, and it was not much better in the second. There is no way that should have happened in a football match.' The FA later confirmed it would be taking no action over the tunnel incident after referee Poll had told them he was satisfied he had dealt with the problem at the time.

A piece by United legend Peter Schmeichel, writing in the *Sunday Times*, also confirmed something: that the ex-goalkeeper was a man who could read a person's character as well as he once read a forward's instincts in the penalty box. For most of this book, I have been arguing that Rooney is much stronger mentally and emotionally than the majority of critics would have you believe – and that he and fiancée Coleen deserve a break from the barrage of envy about his talent, their lifestyle and his money. Schmeichel had himself been belittled by some elements of the press for, apparently, not being as slick and insightful as Gary Lineker and Alan Hansen on *Match of the Day*. Yet here he was in print telling it straight about Rooney and McLoughlin in a way that was much more insightful, understanding and incisive than his critics had ever managed. He wrote:

> Rooney has shown his class, not just as a player but as a person, at United. Before he arrived we knew he was a great individual talent but now we know he's also a great team player. To go to Old Trafford and crack it straight away at his age is some achievement. He deserves more credit for what he's done.
>
> He was, by a million miles, England's best player in Euro 2004 and yet he gets so much criticism from his

country's media it's unbelievable. If he has a bad game, his £30m transfer fee and the size of his weekly wage are thrown in his face, and there are comments about how much he paid for the car he's driving.

Reporters think they can follow his fiancée Coleen around shopping in Manchester, and slag off the type of boots she's wearing. I feel sorry for them. They're a young couple who've come into a bit of money and are trying to enjoy their life together – there's no crime in that, is there?

Yet whatever criticism Rooney faces, you never see it affecting his performances. Mentally, he's got to be the strongest player in the league. The pressure he's under would break a 30-year-old player but Rooney, at 19, just deals with it. I meet him from time to time and my impression is that if Wayne had to choose his perfect day, it would involve training, going home and playing a game of football in his back garden. That's all he wants to do: play. He's a genuine person. The money, the nice car and fame – I don't think they mean anything to him.

It was a brilliant assessment. As far as I can remember, it was the first time any critic – apart from myself, of course – had come out on Rooney's side since I had started shadowing him for this book. Schmeichel had no axe to grind, no resentment, envy or jealousy about Rooney to elucidate.

As if to highlight what I am talking about, the day after the Arsenal match, the *Daily Mirror* gave us two 'Arse reports'. One on the back page, spotlighting how Rooney and Co. had destroyed the Gunners; the other with a massive picture of Coleen's behind on Page 3 accompanied by the words, 'Wayne Rooney's girlfriend certainly looked big into pink as she went sales shopping.' The obvious comment being that she had got a fat arse: ha, bloody ha. It was a terribly cruel, cheap jibe and so unfair on a pretty young girl. Unfortunately, it was also typical of the envy-based negative publicity Rooney and his girl constantly received and were continually forced to endure during his dynamic first year at Manchester United.

Three days after the Arsenal match, the barbs continued to head the way of Rooney, with the press claiming he spent £18,000 on clothes in a few hours. The truth is it was more like £5,000, and it was not, as was also claimed, a sign of his so-called obsessive personality disorder that needed a fix to counter his aggression. No, it was just a young lad out spending some of the readies he had earned. OK, it wasn't 50 quid, but then he doesn't earn a £1,000 a month, does he? It's all so relative, isn't it?

The focus turned away from Rooney to Ronaldo by the time of United's next match, a routine-looking Premiership fixture against Brum at Old Trafford. Ronaldo was 20 on the eve of the game, and it focused my mind on the impact he and Rooney as a duo had had on United. During the season before, his first at Old Trafford, Ronaldo had flitted between genius and inconsistency. However, this term he had shone brightly, helped, no doubt, by the capture of Rooney, whose presence took away the pressure of the press spotlight from him. The two of them were a nightmare for opposing defences. They swapped wings and attacking territory at random and were virtually impossible to keep on a rein. They also had an indirect benefit to the team: their speed and skill ignited the early season spark that had been missing from Ryan Giggs and Roy Keane's game. Both golden oldies found more space and zest as the two new speed kings created space and took worried opposition players with them.

Keane, in particular, enjoyed the freedom of Old Trafford against Brum, driving his men on and grabbing his 50th goal for the club just before the hour. Rooney scored the second, yet again demonstrating his instinctive ability as he chipped keeper Maik Taylor after a shot by Ronaldo had been charged down.

Rooney's busy week continued with his involvement in England's friendly against Holland at Villa Park. Another routine match, another routine result – 0–0 – as both sides struggled to work up steam. Rooney played left-wing and had a fairly quiet match. There again, so did everyone else. It was another of Sven-

Göran Eriksson's inept performances in friendlies, riddled with incomprehensible tactics and decisions. Eriksson commented on Rooney's display, 'I was saying to myself on the bench that Wayne was coming too deep, that he was working too hard, that I don't want to see him at left-back.' Try telling the boy next time, Sven. England's best hope of glory next summer at the World Cup in Germany would still appear to be with Rooney playing down the centre with Owen or Defoe, flanked by Shaun Wright-Phillips on one of the wings to supply the ammunition.

More praise came Rooney's way after the game from the legendary Dutch hitman, and now Holland's national team coach, Marco van Basten, who said the Croxteth kid was better than he was as a teenager. Van Basten said, 'Wayne Rooney is a great forward. A great player. He is a better player than I was at the same age. His all-round game is strong. He's quick, he's clever and he's got a good technique. What more do you want in a footballer? People will ask if he can be a world-class player in the future. Well, as far as I am concerned, he's world-class already.'

Another Dutch master, Johan Cruyff, could also not hide his admiration. He said, 'Has someone made a mistake with this guy's birth certificate? As he is only 19 you might be fooled into thinking he's a kid, but he is one of the men already. When I saw him make his Champions League debut at Old Trafford, it was like a dream. A right-foot goal, a left-foot goal and a fine free-kick. What I loved was that he pushed his way to the front of the queue to take the free-kick and demanded the ball. The United players stood aside out of sheer respect. Any other player who tried that at a new club would have been sent to the back of the queue.'

The small matter of a derby match at Manchester City loomed after the England fiasco. Rooney had sat out the start of the game at Old Trafford earlier in the season, but it was clear Ferguson would not make the same mistake again. Apart from the still injured van Nistelrooy, the irreplaceable Rio Ferdinand and the creaking genius of Roy Keane, Rooney was now the first name on the United team sheet.

City were aiming to make a bit of history in the 132nd League derby between the clubs. A win would mean they had recorded three successive home victories over United for the first time in half a century. But there was to be no early birthday present for City boss Kevin Keegan on the eve of his 54th birthday. Instead, United, aided by a fine performance from Rooney, set about chalking up another vital Premiership win with the sharp efficiency that had been a key component of their excellent league campaign over the previous three months. There was a wee bit of trickery from Rooney and Ronaldo, but the general feeling was that here were another three points needed to stay on Chelsea's tails, so forget the wizardry, even forget the fact it was a derby, it was just another match and another away win.

As I have mentioned earlier, the derby games no longer felt as important as, say, encounters against Liverpool, Arsenal or Leeds. It had a lot to do with City's decline over the last decade and the lack of derby matches during their struggles. The heart seemed to grow fonder as the absences became more frequent. When City finally returned to the big-time, I felt there had been an essential climatic switch from a United perspective. It seemed wrong to treat the City match as a meeting of equals any more. It was almost like welcoming back an old foe who had cheated death at the eleventh hour. You wouldn't bully or taunt a man who had done that, would you? You almost felt compassionate.

Needless to say, City fans did not see it that way. They had a fiery welcome for United and their supporters at the City of Manchester Stadium. Rooney, in particular, suffered with chants about his private life and the inevitable, 'You fat bastard'. He laughed it off, even bowing to his tormentors after helping United to a 2–0 win with his sixth goal in eight games. He was also booked for a tackle from behind on Richard Dunne, which earned him his fourth yellow card of the season, but there was little of the temper tantrums that some critics argued were harming his game. It had even been claimed a few days earlier that he was seeing an anger counsellor, but that, like many of the barbs aimed at him, was mere conjecture. His counsellor was someone both you and I know, a man not given to soppy sentiments or excuses: no, Sir Alex was hardly a gentle therapist, in the mould of a Beechy Colclough. It was more a case of 'Do as I say – or you're dropped' – and that was probably the best therapy for a lad such as Rooney who lived for his football.

Having said it was no derby match of old, there were a few appetite-whetting sideshows. The continual grudge match between Gary Neville and Robbie Fowler was one. A true case of Manc and Scouse not existing contentedly side by side, with a history going back to the days when Fowler had almost as exciting a future as Rooney in front of him at Liverpool. The two were at each others' throats for much of the match, and I tried to feel compassion for Fowler. Here he was, bloated and dispirited, playing his final days at Keegan's retirement home for knackered old nags, but it was hard to feel for the boy. Like his old sidekick Steve McManaman (another put out to grass with Keegan), he was drawing over £2 million a year for services he often was not rendering, and he had a highly profitable portfolio of terraced properties to bring in the cash when he retired. He was an example to Rooney, if one was needed, of how not to grow old gracefully.

Then there was Ryan Giggs – coming on in a pair of bloody tights. Apparently, he wore them to ensure his hamstrings did not suffer in the cold. Imagine telling that to the likes of Big Jim Holton back in the '70s, or the great Duncan Edwards in the '60s.

Rooney shoved the taunts of the City fans back down their throats on 68 minutes. They had been chanting non-stop, 'Once a Blue, always a Blue' at him, just before he latched on to a pass from Gary Neville at the near post and lashed it home off the boot of Richard Dunne. The second, seven minutes later, saw Rooney as the master again. He hit a cross over from the right that Dunne could only deflect into his own goal. Later, Rooney cheekily tried to claim it as his goal.

United had now notched up 13 wins in an unbeaten 16-game run in the league – 42 points from their last 48. It was championship form; unfortunately, Chelsea had been matching them over the same period and still had a nine-point lead at the top.

It was a sickener: a real soul and morale destroyer for Ferguson's troops, but they vowed to continue the chase. Afterwards Rooney claimed the man-of-the-match bubbly but bristled when it was suggested he had done well to keep his temper in check. He said, 'There's nothing wrong with my discipline. I've had four yellows this season and I had eleven last season. It was a good result – with Chelsea winning we knew we had to win to keep in the title race. We have got to keep winning.'

Ferguson also backed Rooney's disciplinary record, laughing off claims it had become his Achilles' heel. He said, 'Wayne has been fantastic all season, and he's getting better all the time. What great players can do is raise their game when it really matters. He rises to the challenge, and his temperament is fantastic – you've seen it today.'

One interesting issue emerged from Chelsea's win – a 1–0 triumph at Everton. James Beattie was sent off for head-butting William Gallas and Everton boss David Moyes shamed himself by defending Beattie and claiming Gallas had play-acted. He said, 'I used to be a centre-half myself, and I'd have been ashamed to have gone down as easily as Gallas.' To his credit, a day later he admitted he had called it wrong and that Beattie was guilty: Gallas an innocent victim. That contrasts with Sir Alex's continued defence of Rooney for pushing Bolton's Haim in the face, even after he had seen the video replay. Maybe the United boss can even learn something from a young pretender like Moyes – although he would go purple if you suggested it – and rethink his attitude to so-called injustices that aren't really unjust at all. It would make him a more admired, respected and fair-handed individual if he added a little more grace and humility to his repertoire as he approached the end of a glittering, if controversial, career. Just a thought.

13

SOD'S LAW

WHY IS IT THAT WHEN YOU ARE IN THE MIDDLE OF A LONG supermarket queue they always open up a new aisle that benefits the punters at the back but never you? Or why, when you get on a train or a bus and you just want a kip, is it you alone that gets the life story of some off-the-wall nutter, when all you want is to be left alone? And why was it that Malcolm Glazer just could not get the message that he was not wanted at Old Trafford? By the management, the players or the fans. Why was the American so thick-skinned, stubborn and contrary that he would not just walk away from Old Trafford and leave the club in peace?

Simple: money, and lots of it. Plus maybe an unwillingness to be beaten in a very public transatlantic battle of wits. He was like the wasp that would not leave you alone, however many times you shooed it off. He had to have the final say: the final sting. Heading towards March 2005, Glazer re-emerged, having shrugged off his defeats in two earlier battles, and made it clear he wanted to win the war. He had a fresh plan – or so he claimed – that would involve more investment from himself and less debt for Manchester United. Yet, looking at the plans in finer detail, it quickly became clear that Glazer had merely camouflaged the debt with another of his schemes: in reality, the debt, like the song he was singing, remained the same.

The truth of it all was this: Glazer was planning to buy Manchester United Football Club with a large chunk of the cash coming from Manchester United Football Club. The club had already rebuffed him twice, yet here he was again, this time offering a price of 300 pence per share, a figure that was 10 per cent above the then closing price of 270 pence. He also argued that the amount of debt in the £800 million proposal had dropped from £550 million to £300 million. That had been achieved by the use of preference shares, which would raise at least £250 million. To everyone connected with the welfare of United, it appeared the debt had simply been repackaged.

Glazer was jubilant as he surveyed the scene from Florida. Having been written off just months earlier, after his bankers had pulled the plug, here he stood on the brink of buying the biggest football club in the world. He had defied the critics and had persuaded his bankers, JP Morgan, to bankroll the entire £300 million debt, even though they had previously walked away from him. He claimed he would not sell Old Trafford and lease it back, nor would he get rid of Sir Alex Ferguson. Hey, he was a good guy!

Shucks, he would even provide cash for Sir Alex to buy new players, thus ending the spending freeze imposed after the signing of Wayne Rooney. One little question: if he had the readies to spend on players, how come he couldn't invest them in buying the club to lower his debt?

The American wasn't home yet though. Not by a long way. This one would drag on and on. The very day of his new bid, United chief executive David Gill bravely stood up to him, issuing a statement in which he made it clear the board could not back the bid.

In an extraordinary statement to the Stock Exchange, made without Glazer's approval, Gill granted the Tampa Bay Buccaneers owner 'limited' access to official club accounts but lashed out at his plans for United:

> The board believes that the nature and return requirements of the capital structure [of the bid] will put pressure on the business of Manchester United, particularly if Glazer's business plan was not met. The board continues to believe that Glazer's business plan assumptions are aggressive and that the direct and indirect financial strain on the business could be damaging. If the current proposal were to develop into an offer – and there can be no certainty this will occur – the board considers that it is unlikely to be in the best interests of Manchester United.

It was a sensational riposte and an apparently endearing professional suicide letter from the United boss should Glazer take command. For all his faults, Gill had shown he had the club's interests at heart – even if it meant he would surely be the first out the door if Glazer grabbed control. It was hard to imagine Peter Kenyon, now at Chelsea, issuing such an immediate statement of intent if he had still been in charge at United.

A further blow for Glazer came the same evening with a brief, abrupt statement from Ireland and major shareholders John Magnier and J.P. McManus, who owned 28.9 per cent of the club, through their Cubic Expression Ltd investment vehicle. A Cubic spokesman said, 'Today's announcement changes nothing in relation to Cubic's position as long-term investors in Manchester United.'

Despite the American's refusal to back down after successive bloody noses, it still seemed likely that his campaign would end in ultimate defeat, and he would not get his hands on Rooney and Ronaldo. Glazer had perhaps been salivating at the prospect of how the youngsters could be used to make more money for him – from increased personal appearances and more extensive use of their images for marketing purposes. Then, his heart would have jumped an extra beat when, shortly after his new bid, it was revealed that United were still officially the world's richest club, with revenue of £171.5 million for the 2003–04 season.

Now United players, from the past and present, were coming forward to add their names to the anti-Glazer camp. Ole Gunnar Solskjær became the first member of the current Old Trafford playing staff to voice publicly his opposition to Glazer. The Norwegian striker, a hero to United fans, became the patron of Shareholders United. He said, 'I am honoured. I think it is important that the club remains in the right hands. I am absolutely on the supporters' side and think the club is in very good hands as it is today. I am a United fan myself and only want what is best for the future.'

Then Ryan Giggs and Rio Ferdinand joined the ever-growing bandwagon. Giggs said, 'The general feeling is that the club is in good hands. This club cannot get any better than it is at the moment. We sympathise with the fans, of course we do. Nothing needs to change; we hope that continues.' Ferdinand echoed those sentiments while admitting, 'It's unsettling for the players. No one knows what this guy will be bringing to the table. A lot of people want the club to be with the people who have grown up with the club and have its interests at heart. We'd like to see the situation resolved.' Even King Eric chipped in to the debate. Monsieur Cantona said, 'If Glazer were to come here, we would lose everything.'

A couple of things started to worry me as his bankers began their period of 'due diligence' – their two-week opportunity to go through the books. The campaign against Glazer had, for the most part, been well thought out and executed by Shareholders United and the United board, albeit in their own limited way. Yet as emotions started to run higher, as the American refused to go away, some rather dubious underhand tactics appeared to be emerging.

In the first instance, it was claimed Glazer released information about his new bid plans on 6 February, the 47th anniversary of the Munich air crash in which eight of the 'Busby Babes' lost their lives. A club insider revealed to me that it was actually the United board who had released the information on that date. After all, why would Glazer's publicity men be working on a Sunday? The implication was that the United board wanted to dump on the American. If that was the case, it certainly worked. The outrage was universal and heavy. Glazer was accused of being insensitive and out of touch with the feelings of the club he hoped to buy.

As Sean Bones of Shareholders United said, 'I think it is totally disrespectful for this bid to come out on the Munich anniversary weekend. It is disgusting and it goes to show that Glazer knows nothing about this club, what it means to the fans, and it confirms our belief that we don't want him to have anything to do with United.'

The second worry concerned the so-called Manchester Education Committee (MEC), another organisation determined to thwart Glazer, but with rather more sinister methods of going about it. After his latest bid, the MEC warned him, 'It's clear the consequences of any bid need spelling out. No matter how large the phalanx of bodyguards, we'll always outnumber you.' Their statement added:

> Malcolm Glazer's continued pursuit of MUFC indicates he has paid no attention to the wishes of the overwhelming majority of ordinary supporters of the club.
>
> We remind the directors of the duty of care they are expected to show towards the traditions and history of MUFC, and of the promises they have made in the past.
>
> Any failure to maintain a rejectionist position in the face of Glazer's overtures will be regarded as an act of treachery that will place board members in an extremely vulnerable position for years to come.

It was the language of terror and threats, and it prompted Greater Manchester Police to say that 'appropriate measures' would be taken to deal with any incidents. It was a worrying development. History frequently shows that public sympathy can turn to disgust when protesters resort to violence. United's campaign against Glazer was going just fine without the need for a militant breakaway group to throw a spanner in the works, or without the alleged involvement of the board to smear Glazer. The American didn't need anyone else to alienate him in the eyes of the general public: he could be relied upon to do that himself.

It was also worrying to hear the normally measured and intelligent Oliver Houston, vice-chairman of Shareholders United, discussing the dispute in terms of a military battle. He said, 'We promised at the start that a civil war would be unleashed if Malcolm Glazer were allowed to proceed. Emotions are running extremely high. People will go to extraordinary lengths to defend their club.'

Glazer did not go away as February turned into March, but at least he remained out of sight. It was rumoured that he would eventually approach Cubic for talks, but that would have to remain on the back burner until at least the end of the month, as the last thing the Irish duo of Magnier and McManus wanted was the MEC disrupting their beloved Cheltenham horse-racing festival.

On a lighter note, Rooney and Coleen were increasingly enjoying themselves in Manchester. Sir Alex had taken a shine to Coleen; he thought she was a sweet, down-to-earth lass, so unlike Victoria 'Posh' Beckham with whom he had suffered countless fallings-out. He told her to ignore the press reports about her shopping trips and fashion sense and to enjoy the fruits of Wayne's labours. Ahh, it was almost like a protective, lovable old granddad throwing an arm around his beloved granddaughter. And, to give the knight his due, it was remarkably civil and charming of him to keep an eye out for her. She particularly appreciated his support after one tabloid claimed she was the 12th most hated 'celebrity' in Britain, backed up with this reasoning from the website that had compiled the distasteful list: 'Jumped up Chav who has nothing better to do than spend her future husband's money. I hope one day he sees the light (doubt it though, he's thick, too!)' Coleen certainly needed the support from the likes of Ferguson and her beloved Nan as the media refused to leave her alone.

By now, Wayne was almost like a long-lost son to Ferguson. Forget any alleged early-season disagreements, the two were now extremely respectful of each other. Ferguson loved him for his outrageous talent and his Keane-like short fuse while Rooney loved the way Ferguson stood up for him – whatever the problem. A source close to Rooney told me, 'Wayne would run through walls for Fergie. He is the dominant footballing figure he always needed to keep him on the right track. He would be devastated if Fergie quit the club.' That reminded me of Georgie boy and Sir Matt – how, despite their occasional fallings-out, Best always delivered while Busby was there for him.

It was suggested that Wayne and Coleen could be the first couple to marry at the new Wembley, when it opened in 2006. That made the youngsters giggle – as did the suggestion that Coleen had asked number one boy band Westlife to play at their wedding. Err? Sure, they were favourites of Coleen, but the only problem was that there was no wedding to speak of.

While that was amusing tittle-tattle, the constant claims of the London media that he was overweight began to niggle at the boy wonder. It would lead to him regularly removing his shirt at the end of matches for the next month: to prove that he did not own an ounce of fat. In fact, Rooney was one of the fittest players at United. His boxer's frame just made him look big.

The barbs against Rooney continued, this time from a more surprising source. A head teacher in Wales claimed Wayne was setting a bad example for schoolchildren and claimed that Rooney was to blame for their indiscipline. Dr Chris Howard, head teacher at Lewis Boys School, Pengam, near Caerphilly, said, 'Young people behaving like Wayne Rooney does on the football pitch are increasingly finding themselves in front of an exclusions panel. In a recent Manchester United v. Arsenal game, seen on TV by more than ten million people, the referee told Wayne Rooney to stop swearing at him or he would be sent off. But Rooney used a tirade of four-letter words and kept doing what the ref had told him not to do and yet he stayed on the pitch. He's an 18-year-old role model for millions of youngsters.'

Dr Howard also claimed that children saw Rooney getting away with bad behaviour and that consequently, they also believed they could. He added, 'Teachers face it in the classroom and police face it on the streets. It's gnawing away at us.'

Rooney was soon to face another test – the biggest so far – of his temperament as United prepared for their FA Cup fifth round clash at Everton. Staying with the language so despised by headteacher Dr Howard . . . if Glazer had refused to sod off, Rooney's return to Goodison was witnessed by a bunch of mostly miserable local sods, and his natural talents were severely tested by a sod-awful pitch.

The boy wonder made all the right sounds as the tension built up towards the big day. He admitted Everton were still close to his heart: 'I keep in touch with a few of the Everton boys – people like Stubbsy [Alan Stubbs, the skipper] and Tony Hibbert. I always phone them up and see how they got on and how they are doing. My whole family are Everton fans and it was a tough decision to leave. But it was one I had to make. And I made the right decision for myself and my career.' That was clearly correct: he had scored only 17 goals for Everton in 77 matches but had already notched 13 for United in 26 games.

The noises emanating from across Stanley Park were not nearly as conciliatory in their tone as Rooney's. Everton fans, on local radio dial-in programmes and websites, promised their former idol a rough old reception. It prompted the Goodison hierarchy to warn their fans of the consequences if they stepped over the line with Rooney. Spokesman Ian Ross admitted they were already being monitored after two pitch invasions during the current season. He said, 'We appeal for common sense.' Ross added that police and stewarding would be stepped up: 'The last thing we want is anyone coming over the barriers on to the pitch. We've made a succession of appeals, through the manager David Moyes, chief executive Keith Wyness and our safety officer. We have done all we can to tell the fans they must not do this.' But would their efforts be enough?

There was another worrying aspect: the 5.30 p.m. kick-off. Chief Superintendent Mike Langdon of Merseyside Police feared the prospect of fans arriving early and getting boozed up. He said, 'There are numerous requests to change kick-off times, and each kick-off time has its own potential and dynamic. The fact that millions will be able to see the game live is a consideration when planning the timing. There will be a strong Operational order in place to deal with every eventuality on the day.' In fact, he admitted, the police presence was likely to be the largest ever witnessed at the stadium. And all for one young lad's homecoming.

This particular young lad tried to laugh off his nerves as the United team coach ploughed its way past Stanley Park through the growing mass of fans at 4 p.m. Sensibly, he was sitting in an aisle seat, his image shielded by the protective black-tinted windows. Rooney would never in his wildest dreams have guessed that one day he would be turning up at Goodison for a cup tie in the colours of the Red Devils. Nor would he have anticipated the never-ending chants of 'Judas' and 'You fat bastard' as he stepped off the coach at the players' entrance. A sea of faces crumpled with hatred and anguish pushed against fences that separated them from the kid they detested with a bloody vengeance.

No, he would never have expected that kind of reception – nor the ten-strong mounted police guard, nor the police helicopter shimmering purposely overhead. Is this what it had come to? Really? Do these people not have children of their own or any moral code? Well, yes, they do have kids: inside the ground every other forty-odd-year-old bloke seemed to be with a son or daughter of between six and fifteen. And here's the saddest aspect of the lot from this disgraceful day: the kids' faces were also contorted with hatred, mouthing obscenities like their misguided, shamed parents. Some wearing blue Everton shirts emblazoned with the word 'Traitor' and Rooney's old number, 18. Others held blow-up pigs, much to the delight of their gloating dads. Is this the legacy these blokes wanted to leave Everton or, indeed, their children? Fans who would grow up believing that hate, envy and burning anger were the name of the game.

At the warm-up the booing and profanities continued, only occasionally blocked out by the amusing ditty the United fans would chant all through the match: 'Once a blue, always a red, once a blue, always a red'. One thing Rooney has in abundance is guts: the reception knocked him slightly off balance and unnerved him, but he did not hide from his tormentors. Then came another shocker. As he walked off from the warm-up, a woman dressed to the nines and a bloke in a suit – part of the Everton match ball sponsors' party on the pitch – moved towards the boy and unleashed a mouthful of abuse. The bloke seemed to say, 'You fucking traitor', but it was hard to decipher the woman's bile. Rooney stopped, turned, looked at them and, clearly angry, shouted, 'What?' Then, thankfully, as the couple prepared to unleash more venom, he walked off down the tunnel to the sanctuary of Ferguson, the United lads and his personal former SAS bodyguard Ginger.

Ferguson gave Rooney a warm hug before he trotted out for kick-off, telling him just to go and play his normal game and to ignore the catcalls. Beforehand, the United manager had made it clear he expected the return to go off without major crowd problems. He had said, 'When Eric Cantona went back to Leeds, it was volatile, but nothing spilt on to the pitch from the terraces. I just hope the game passes off the right way without anything stupid happening.'

Well, it didn't. Paul Ince admits he still gets upset when he thinks about his return to West Ham in February 1994, but Rooney had it worse. Having been pictured holding aloft a Manchester United shirt before he had even signed for the Reds, Ince was tormented on his first match back at the Boleyn. Rooney received at least the same in terms of derogatory chants and vitriolic atmosphere, but the Everton crowd also felt the need to throw coins, mobile phones and anything else they could lay their hands on when the youngster approached. It was a 19-year-old boy you were abusing, for Christ's sake!

From one hail of missiles, keeper Roy Carroll was momentarily felled by a coin that hit him in the head. And what is this thing with the Scouse fans and mobiles? Just a month earlier, a nutter in the Kop also threw one at Rooney after he scored the winner at Anfield.

Today, there would be no winner from Rooney: those came from the magic feet of Ronaldo and the impressive Quinton Fortune, their goals separating the sides and sending United into a quarter-final tie at Southampton. Rooney, who had arrived at Goodison with four goals in his last five matches, was fairly subdued. Inevitably perhaps, but at least he kept his head while all those around him in the home supporters' stands were losing theirs.

United had done well to maintain their passing game on the terrible, mudbound pitch, with Roy Keane and Paul Scholes dictating in midfield. They went ahead on twenty-four minutes when Ronaldo's cross from the right was met by Fortune, six yards out, and he headed firmly past Nigel Martyn in the Everton goal. Rooney should have scored ten minutes after the break when Fortune's chip put him clear in the box, but Martyn was out quickly to block the shot. Ronaldo sealed the win on the hour when he lashed in the loose ball after a free-kick by Paul Scholes had rebounded off Martyn's body.

Wayne left the pitch applauding the fans in the Gwladys Street End who had tormented him for 90-odd minutes, then he walked over to the United fans, finally applauding the Everton fans in the main stand as he went up the tunnel.

One bit of light in an otherwise dark day: some of those Blues supporters in the main stand had the strength of mind to give him a round of applause back. Sort of restores your faith in humankind, doesn't it?

Amazingly, Sir Alex did not appear to think Wayne had had too bad a deal from his former fans and that the atmosphere of hate was also not that bad. He said, 'Having experienced players helps you in that respect. Players like Paul Scholes and Roy Keane in the centre of midfield: they've been through that; that doesn't matter to them at all. I think we played professionally, we had good discipline, good concentration, because on that pitch you need good concentration, and our possession of the ball was very good.' And no, he had never considered leaving Rooney out: 'I think there was talk of leaving him out; that was just ridiculous, he's got to return to Everton at some point whether that's today, the next game or next season. I think the supporters were pretty fair actually. Of course they are going to boo him because that is the nature of the game.' That's another thing we must agree to differ on then, Alex.

The hate mob waited around until the United coach finally left Goodison: as one they bellowed 'Fuck off Rooney' as the Reds made their way home to Manchester. The boy had helped save their club from financial ruin, thanks to his £27 million transfer fee, and this was their welcome for a hero. Later, some of those Everton fans would be involved in running battles with United diehards and police as the huge snake of supporters from Manchester wound its way towards Lime Street Station. It was a violent way of getting that intense anger and hatred towards Rooney out of their systems. Thirty-three fans were arrested and five policemen were injured as they tried to break up groups of fighting supporters. The United fans eventually boarded their trains at Lime Street shortly after 9 p.m. Rooney, meanwhile, had simply breathed a sigh of relief and played with his Gameboy as the coach swept out of Merseyside and back on to the East Lancs Road. His ordeal was over – at least until the next time United played at Goodison.

Next up was more European adventure, with the first leg of the knockout clash against AC Milan at Old Trafford and the return leg a fortnight later at the San Siro. But more of that in the next chapter. For the moment we will concentrate on the two league fixtures sandwiched in between those two exotic encounters. Portsmouth were due at Old Trafford, and United were keen to avenge the 1–0 defeat at Fratton Park from October. Since that setback United had embarked upon a run of fourteen wins and three draws in the league and this was another must-win game. Chelsea were otherwise engaged in the League Cup final the same weekend, and Ferguson knew only victory would keep the Blues on their toes in the Premiership. Typically, he applied mind-game pressure on José Mourinho and his men, claiming that Chelsea were struggling for form and that Liverpool could well beat them in the Cardiff final. Indeed, in the previous week, they had gone out of the FA Cup in a 1–0 loss at Newcastle and had lost 2–1 at Barcelona in the first leg of their Champions League knockout match.

Ferguson believed – nay, make that prayed – that this was the blip he had predicted all along. Trying to hold back a gloating giggle, he said, 'Anything I say nowadays is treated as psychological warfare or mind games, but if you look at the facts, and even Chelsea might have to agree with this, well, they might do, they are not playing as well as they were four or five weeks ago. Plus they've started to lose important players through injury. They have three London derbies, including Arsenal to play, as well as Newcastle, Bolton and ourselves away and right now they are grasping for form.'

United were still nine points behind Chelsea, with an inferior goal difference making it a virtual ten, but if they were to beat Portsmouth and Crystal Palace, a week later, it would close the gap to three points before Chelsea played at Norwich later the same day. As Ferguson summed it up, 'We cannot allow this opportunity to go. Our form is good. If Chelsea lose a couple of games, then the cat's out in the open and you know what cats are like . . . sometimes they don't come home. Chelsea have resilience about them, and you know they will defend for their lives if they have to. But that's not necessarily going to win them the league. It might save them the odd draw, but winning games is important now. Drawing is not much better than losing.' The last line of the big man's quote about drawing is the key here. OK, United had just about enough in their tank to grasp three points against Pompey, but they could not break down the Palace defence, a failing that really ended their Premiership challenge.

Rooney was the hero against Pompey. He scored twice: two fabulous goals in a man-of-the-match performance – the first on seven minutes as he swept home a cross from Gary Neville, the second a more individual effort nine minutes from time that saw him speed through the beleaguered Pompey defence and coolly slot the ball into the net. Gary O'Neil replied for the visitors, but it was Rooney's all-action show that earned him the accolades.

Rooney said, 'We possibly should have killed them off before they equalised. It was a tough game, as we knew it would be. They beat us down there, and we knew it would be the same sort of match. When they scored, they put men behind the ball to make it difficult for us. We knew we had to win today to give ourselves a chance of being only three points behind by the time Chelsea play again. All we can do is keep winning games and hope they will slip up. When they do, we will be there to pounce on them.'

Even Ferguson, who normally avoids singling out individuals for praise, purred when he made a special mention of Rooney. The United boss said, 'Rooney picked up the baton and dragged us over the line.' Just as he had done in previous games against Birmingham and Manchester City. His performances had also earned him the Premiership Player of the Month award for February 2005 and Ferguson the Manager of the Month award.

So, can anyone explain to me why Ferguson dropped the boy for the vital match at Palace? It was a game that United needed to win, a game that could shape their season and indeed Chelsea's if that gap had been narrowed to three points. Don't give me that crap about resting Rooney for the return Champions League tie in Milan. Surely, Alex Ferguson, who had made a series of baffling tactical decisions over the season, could understand that you play your best men when you need a win? Especially, the boy who, Ferguson himself had admitted, was carrying United at that stage of the season. No, Sir Alex did not see it that way. He had taken to wearing a black tracksuit top underneath his black coat during games: it made him look more like an Irish priest than a Scottish bruiser as he prowled the touch-line. This was to be the day that Ferguson would read the last rites for United's Premiership title hopes in the 2004–05 season.

He left out Rooney, Ronaldo and Paul Scholes and threw in the unfit Ruud van Nistelrooy and Alan Smith, both returning from injury. United laid siege to the Palace goal but did not have the craft or guile to break them down. Ferguson brought on Rooney with 17 minutes to go but it was too little, too late. He instantly transformed the visitors and almost scored himself against Palace's ten men, a consequence of Vassilis Lakis being sent off for two bookable offences. Rooney was United's best player in the short time he had to prove himself – surely he would have lifted the Red Devils to a win if he had started? It was the third time since his move to Old Trafford that Rooney had started on the bench, the third time he had come on as a late substitute, and guess what? It was also the third time United had drawn 0–0 in those circumstances – the other blanks being against Brum and Manchester City.

By the end of his 17 minutes, both Rooney and United fans realised the game was finally up for the title challenge. It led to him momentarily losing it, foolishly charging up to the referee and arguing at the final whistle when he had already been cautioned. United were now five points behind Chelsea, but two hours later that had increased to eight as the Blues romped to an easy 3–1 win at Norwich. Of course, Mourinho had sent out his best side at Carrow Road. Silly old Alex; clever young José.

14

HERNAN MONSTERED

ONE SPECIAL MAY NIGHT IN 1989, THREE-YEAR-OLD WAYNE Rooney was busy crawling around his mum and dad's council house in Croxteth, Liverpool. His dad, also called Wayne, was slumped in his usual favourite spot on the couch in the living room, slowly working his way through a six-pack of lager and a big bag of peanuts, keeping one eye on his tot, the other on the box. The final whistle blew, and the triumphant AC Milan players punched the warm Barcelona night air with joy, their job done with an emphatic 4–0 win, the club's third European Cup crown now in the bag.

The disillusioned Steaua Bucharest players stepped up first for their losers' medals. Wayne snr cracked open another lager to celebrate with the winners as they then proudly mounted the podium. There they were, in all their glory: the goalscoring Dutchmen Ruud Gullit and Marco van Basten, each having netted a brace, followed by fellow countryman Frank Rijkaard. Last up, of course, was their heroic skipper: the hard-tackling Italian hero Franco Baresi. However, before lifting the cup, the tough guy embraced the young defender who had walked up before him, affectionately tousling his mop of jet-black hair, telling him he had done well. It was a handsome gesture: the 20-

year-old full-back was new to this level of football, but he had let no one down, playing a rugged, technical game to earn his first European Cup medal.

Fast forward 16 years and the young hero of yesteryear would come face to face with our very own boy wonder. Paolo Maldini, now 36 and captain of the *Rossoneri*, had heard much about Rooney and liked what he had seen of him in Euro 2004 and United's current European campaign. Now the holder of four European Cup-winning medals, seven Serie A-winning medals and one *World Soccer* Player of the Year award, Maldini was a living example to Rooney of what could be achieved in the game. Achieved, that is, if he lived up to the very top of his potential; if he could channel that fearsome temper into the good of his game rather than in the face of referees and opponents; and if he lived and trained well. The alternative was to end up like a Paul Gascoigne: so much promise, the player of his generation, but rewards few and far between. Ultimately, a criminal neglect and waste of a divine gift.

Maldini admitted he was relishing his first competitive game against United and said he felt certain Rooney would not end up the way of Gazza: 'Rooney is still very young but already he has done great things in this competition. He scores beautiful goals. We will have to wait and see just how good he can be. But, at 19, you can already tell there will be great things ahead. It will be a wonderful experience to go up against him and to play United at Old Trafford. It is something I am really looking forward to.'

This was undoubtedly a key stage of the campaign for Rooney, United and boss Ferguson. The two games against the Italian champions would shape their season. The league was already lost, barring a miracle. Defeat against Milan would mean that only the retention of the FA Cup would be left as a viable proposition, and that would not be at all satisfactory after the massive outlay on Rooney, Heinze and Smith. Ferguson's very ability to coach, coax and cope tactically in Europe would again be called into question.

Of course, no one is doubting the great man's overall influence or impact upon the club, or the domestic domination he had brought to Old Trafford after all those relatively barren seasons. Yet, a bit like Cantona, he had still not convinced us that he could consistently hack it in foreign fields. If 1999 was his undoubted peak – when he won the Treble – the following six years would provide ample evidence of doubt for the prosecution. Some would even argue that the 1999 European Cup triumph was as much down to brute passion and an unwillingness to lay down than Ferguson's tactical acumen. For the two seasons after the win in Barcelona, United had gone out in the last eight to Bayern Munich and Real Madrid. Their best chance to win back the trophy came in 2002, when they blew it on away goals against an inferior Bayer Leverkusen in the semi-finals. As Ferguson said, 'We have been very unlucky at times, and the Bayer Leverkusen semi-final was one of those times, but generally I can look back and be proud of the achievements of the team in terms of performance. Yes, sometimes we have been disappointed with the outcome of matches in the latter stages, but, at the end of the day, our performance level over the past decade has been one of the highest level in Europe.'

Highest level for a decade? Was the big man kidding himself again? The defeat by José Mourinho's Porto in the last 16 of the Champions League in 2004 still left a bitter taste for many at Old Trafford. It was apparent that this two-legger against Milan was as vital for Ferguson's own self-esteem as his team's chances of glory. It was an opportunity to prove he could live with the best coaches Europe had to offer: indeed that he could outwit them at the highest level.

It was at least some consolation to Ferguson that he had already done just that with his opposite number at Milan. Six years previously, Carlo Ancelotti had been coach of the Juventus side that earned a 1–1 draw at Old Trafford only to lose the second leg of their Champions League semi-final 3–2 at the Delle Alpi stadium. That was the wondrous dawn for what would become United's greatest triumph since the 1968 European Cup final win over Benfica.

When Rooney walked out on to the Old Trafford pitch against Milan, Maldini shook his hand warmly, encouraging him much like Baresi had done with him back in 1989. But that was the last of the pleasantries. The big question now was: could Maldini and Milan's ancient back four keep Rooney and Ronaldo at bay? And would those two – without the still recovering Ruud van Nistelrooy – be able to breach the Italians and their famed *catenaccio* system of defence? The history between the clubs suggested United's chances were not good. Milan were the first club United met in Europe after the 1958 Munich air crash and their European Cup quarter-final victory over Red Star Belgrade. In the semis, an inexperienced United team beat Milan 2–1 in the first leg at home but lost the return 4–0. Milan also ended United's reign as European champions when they defeated them 2–1 on aggregate in the 1969 semi-finals, the last time the clubs had met competitively. The Rossoneri had no fear of the Theatre of Dreams – after all, they had captured the Champions League trophy there two seasons earlier by beating Juventus.

Ferguson had predicted before the draw that fate would throw the two clubs together. They were the only major European side United had not met during his 18-year reign at Old Trafford. He had also predicted that Milan would surprise people: that they would come out and attack. In that respect, he was spot on although, unfortunately, the Italian league leaders also managed to shut up shop at the back in a mightily effective fashion. Rooney himself had something to prove against Milan. After his hat-trick against Fenerbahçe in October, he had not scored in his three other Champions League matches. United desperately needed him to deliver, and he had sounded confident enough before kick-off, even managing to take a pot shot at his old pals at Goodison: 'You won't take part in these games at Everton. That's why you move to a big club like United.' Rooney did not doubt he would face a tough struggle against Maldini. He said, 'Paolo is a great player. He's been around for years, and playing against someone of his experience will be a difficult task. He reads the game so well. But I'll concentrate on my own game and hope things fit into place.'

The boy wonder also conceded that playing in the Champions League had so far been a magical experience, in itself worth decamping to United. He said, 'My first game for United – in the Champions League – was a big moment for me. I knew I had to do my best to try and help us win. Then I got the hat-trick. I was pretty pleased with my performance, but it was a bit weird at first. It was different, standing there listening to the Champions League music.

'It took me five or ten minutes to settle into the game, but once that happened I was comfortable. I knew I'd get a chance, so I was just waiting to take it. Luckily I did. The match ball is in the house. I got all the players to sign it after the game, and I'm just waiting to get it mounted. My ripped shirt is in the United museum.'

There was to be no repeat of that Rooney goal bonanza against Milan. The visitors were far too canny for that. No, as Ferguson had predicted, they took the game to United, playing a series of short, smart passes that ensured they kept possession and had their hosts on the back foot for long periods. There had been some speculation that Jaap Stam would come back to haunt Ferguson, but the big Dutch defender – who was kicked out of Old Trafford after a row over his autobiography – hurt himself in the warm-up. His time to prove a point would come in the second leg at the San Siro.

Two other men had points to prove in the first leg, and the differing outcome of their efforts decided the contest. Hernan Crespo – or Herman Munster as some comics among the United fans referred to him – had been farmed out on loan to Milan from Chelsea. Unwanted by José Mourinho, he was playing for his future. In the absence of the injured Andriy Shevchenko, it was to the Argentinian that the Rossoneri were looking for goals. He did not let them down: yet, at the same time, he probably ended the United career of another man desperate to impress. Roy Carroll was still locked in negotiations over a new deal at Old Trafford – his latest blunder could not have come at a worse time.

With the clock pushing towards 80 minutes, Clarence Seedorf decided to have a punt on goal. It was a speculative effort with the match coming to an end. Both sides seemed to have accepted the inevitability of a draw and were going through the motions, but the hapless Carroll had been reading from a different script. He allowed the weak shot to bounce out of his hands on to his chest and into the path of the disbelieving Crespo, who belted the ball home. It was an elementary, schoolboy error, and it provided Milan with a 1–0 lead to take back to Italy.

To the United faithful, it was a body blow, bringing back painful memories of Tim Howard's blunder the previous season – the one against Porto that had put them out of the Champions League at the same stage. Once again, it highlighted Ferguson's folly in not investing in a top-class goalkeeper in the January transfer window. Say an outlay on the likes of Shay Given or Anti Niemmi would have set United back £5 million: well OK, that was money the board did not want to part with, but how much would be lost if United were knocked out of the Champions League early again? Certainly a lot more than that £5 million. It was poor vision on the part of the board and Ferguson.

To be fair, it would be too simplistic to lay the total blame for the 1–0 loss at Carroll's door. He was just the latest in a long line of keepers – believe it or not *ten* since Peter Schmeichel departed – to flop at Old Trafford, with only Fabien Barthez showing any sign of consistent quality and that just for his first season.

United also failed in front of goal with Paul Scholes and Quinton Fortune the main culprits, both knocking clear-cut chances wide. Rooney, the lone striker for an hour, was bereft of decent scoring opportunities as Milan took control of central midfield. Scholes, Fortune and Keane struggled against the powerful trio of Clarence Seedorf, Andrea Pirlo and Gennaro Gattuso. With Gary Neville and Gabriel Heinze tucked up with defensive duties, as the brilliant Brazilian kid Kaka wove his spell, it was not easy to get the ball up to Rooney. Then, on the hour, Ferguson made one of those decisions that leaves you scratching your head. OK, it was a fair enough gamble to send on van Nistelrooy to get among the Milan back-line, but why take off your most productive attacker on the night? The old heart sighed at the sight of Ronaldo leaving the field of play so prematurely.

Milan jetted off from Manchester content with a job done, having inflicted United's first home defeat in Europe since a 3–2 victory for Deportivo La Coruña in October 2001. The stats showed how the visitors had dominated. United had two corners to Milan's eight, one effort on target to Milan's four and nine goal attempts to Milan's twelve. The only blemish for the visitors came off the field when one of their backroom staff – a 44-year-old doctor – was arrested for alleged indecent exposure to a woman worker at the Lowry Hotel, near to Old Trafford, where they had been staying.

Ferguson had much more to ponder and worry about. Admirably, he did not publicly blame Carroll for the defeat. The United boss said of the goal, 'Seedorf should have been closed down. We directed him into the middle of the park and should have closed that area down and forced him out to the side. After that no one closed him down, and he has got a free shot. That's all I'm going to say on the matter. I've said what the mistake happened from, and that's it.' As per normal with this remarkably contrary man, it would not be as straightforward as that. From defending Carroll one minute, he then inexplicably dropped him the next, saying, 'Roy made a bad mistake and at the moment is better off out of it.' The Northern Irish international's season – and his career at United – appeared over.

Ferguson seemed to have been watching a different game to the one in which his team had just been comfortably put in their place by Milan. He said, 'We had some good chances, but we lacked that composure needed to finish it off. The match was [of] a marvellous quality; every player had to produce a performance of a very high standard. In the second half, I thought we got hemmed in around their box; Milan started making some mistakes and giving the ball away for the first time in the game. At that point, we were ready to make a substitution – bringing Louis Saha and Mikael Silvestre on – then they scored. We have got to make sure we don't make mistakes over there, and if we score the game changes.'

The impressive Maldini offered a more measured view, saying, 'I believe we deserved to win. We had many, many chances and had the wish to score. We made a great game, Manchester United too, it was very balanced. We have many, many great players but Manchester too has a great team, and I do not believe we have qualified already.'

United's loyal fans refused to believe their European dream was over for another season. More than 9,000 of them travelled to Milan for the return leg, and that was just the official figures. The red army took over the city centre before the match: the bars and cafés were crowded with red and white. Milan learned just how big a pull their visitors were as the turnstiles clicked on the night; they had sold all of the available 79,103 tickets, pulling in £1,687,498 in receipts, and almost beating their record attendance in the Champions League of 79,855, set in the semi-final second leg against Paris St Germain in 1995.

Ferguson knew he was up against it – Milan had never lost at home to an English team – and he tried to find a balance in his Press conferences between gung-ho verbosity and a more measured realism as the match loomed. He even admitted it would take a bigger performance than the win in Juventus six years earlier if United were to progress. The United boss said, 'It was a great performance in Turin: the best of all time, easy. But this is above that game; they have such experience at the back in Maldini, Cafu, Nesta. If we can score then that can change the game, and that is obviously going to be our intention. I'm aware of the difficulty because I am trying to think of the last time they lost two goals at home. They don't lose many on their own ground. The issue will be: can we score? I just wish we hadn't let that goal in.'

But Fergie had words of encouragement for Tim Howard. He said, 'We hope he can get his form back. He started the season as our goalkeeper and did very well [but] then started making one or two mistakes. The boy is ambitious enough and hungry enough. It is just like everything else: there is a lot of pressure and a lot of spotlight on the goalkeepers here simply because of us having [had] a keeper like Schmeichel, and there are always comparisons for everyone who comes here.'

The United boss then set the final scene for what should have been a classic with the words, 'I think that this is the final. I think that the team that wins this could win the Cup, I really do.' While Mourinho and Rijkaard may have argued that the game between Chelsea and Barcelona was the real final, Fergie had a point. But would his men be the ones to go on to win the Cup? Or would they be heading once again for that lonely exit marked 'also-rans'? It was announced that man-mountain Jaap Stam would be back for the Rossoneri in a defence that read like an international dream team picker's choice: Brazil keeper Nelson Dida in goal, centre-backs Stam and Italy international Alesandro Nesta, flanked by full-backs Cafu, the former captain of Brazil, and Maldini, skipper of Italy. Not bad, hey? And this was the fortress Rooney and van Nistelrooy had to breach twice for outright victory.

Easier said than done, especially as, after 20 minutes, it was apparent that Ruud was simply not fit enough for this level of play. It was like watching a vintage car being shunted out for action from the garage after a long lay-off. The classic motor went chug-chug rather than va-va-voom *à la* Thierry Henry. Ferguson's gamble on the big Dutchman had backfired, but it had been one worth taking given van Nistelrooy's awesome scoring record in the Champions League. Again, there is an argument that Ferguson could have switched it around more quickly when everyone could see how 'Rusty Ruud' was suffering, maybe employing Rooney as a lone striker and throwing on Smith to get among them in the hole behind. As it was, Ferguson's first substitution – apart from the enforced one of Quinton Fortune for the injured Giggs – came just nine minutes from the end, with Smith's appearance. It was too little, too late, or maybe a reflection of the genuine lack of class Ferguson had at his disposal on the bench.

Scholes and Keane were again suffering in midfield as Seedorf, Pirlo and Gattuso worked not only tirelessly but so successfully in blunting the cutting edge of the two United legends. Keane had done well in the middle part of the season but now it was plain to see that his legs had gone. He simply could not compete with Milan's battlers and was lucky not to give away a penalty towards the end when his creaking body fell on to the ball in the box. Similarly, Scholes was having one of those matches when you wondered if all was well physically with him.

What United needed were goals and a clean sheet: in the event, they managed neither objective. Ryan Giggs came closest to scoring, but his shot from the left zipped agonisingly on to the post. Apart from the winner, there were only three shots on target in the whole match: the Giggs effort against the post; a stinging volley from Kaka that skimmed the crossbar; and a shot from Crespo that Howard saved.

The winner again came from Crespo: this time a superb swirling header that fizzled into the back of the net. At first glance, Howard seemed to be at fault positionally, but later it was clear even Schmeichel would not have saved it. It was a beauty.

United's Champions League campaign was over for another season and the inevitable inquests began. Over two legs against the Italian champions they had failed to score while, at the same time, they had conceded twice. That convinced Ferguson that the gap between the teams was only slight. He claimed, 'If you look at the two games we had six good chances, and we didn't take any of them. The margins at this level are very fine, and that is what has decided the tie overall. I'm disappointed to go out, but we've gone out to a very good team.'

He continued, 'We didn't get the break we needed when Ryan hit the post. We needed to score the first goal. That was the key to the whole contest; that was the chance, and unfortunately we didn't take it. If we had taken the first one, it would have been a different game. Our decision-making could have been better, but you only get that through playing, and my players will get better. We had a great spirit tonight, and it took a fantastic header from Crespo to decide it.'

I have read those two sets of quotes over and over, and I still cannot get rid of that feeling of sadness deep in my guts. If Ferguson truly believed that United were in the same league as Milan over those two ninety-minute periods of football, the end must be nigh. United were just not at the races: they were outclassed by a much better team, and, let's not forget, Milan were without European Footballer of the Year Shevchenko for both legs. If it puts it into some sort of perspective, think of Crespo in terms of Diego Forlan – referred to as Jordan by United fans due to his similarity in appearance to the famous Page 3 model – and Shevchenko as van Nistelrooy, only better. Also, don't forget United were the only team in the last 16, apart from Monaco, not to score.

I felt compassion for Ferguson as he clutched at straws but concern for United's foreseeable future in Europe. United had become Alex's personal fiefdom, but was he now the right man to take the legend further? Or would it all end in tears? Look at that second quote from him again: 'Our decision-making could have been better, but you only get that through playing, and my players will get better.' Be honest: isn't that nonsensical babble? How will the decision-making of Keane and Scholes get better? Haven't they played together enough: what, almost ten years?

Fair enough, Rooney and Ronaldo did not show on the night in Milan. The youngsters both froze, particularly Rooney. One of his most passionate moments in the San Siro came when he mouthed, 'Fuckin' hell' at Ronaldo late in the second half, as the Portuguese burned another opportunity over the bar when Rooney was clean through, awaiting the final pass. They will both get better together, that's for sure; they are the future and a magnificent one at that. But for Keane, Scholes, Howard, Giggs and even Silvestre? These were the men Ferguson had to think about replacing – or at least find quality stand-ins for them if they were injured, off-form or simply suffering from burn-out – if he were to complete his final great team: the team that could win the European Cup for him one more time. However, there was no transfer cash for the following season and not much in the way of star quality to generate cash from sales – unless he flogged van Nistelrooy, Smith or Saha. No, it was a sad, worrying night in Milan as the hordes of United fans – already disgruntled after an hour's lock-in by the police after the match – hopped on to the number 16 trams from the San Siro for the half-hour journey back to the city centre and a consoling glass (or two) of beer.

Some were now openly mouthing what would become a common grumble over the next fortnight: that Ferguson had also got it wrong in the group stages by fielding his second eleven for the final match at Fenerbahçe. That 3–0 defeat left United stranded behind Lyon in the final table but also provided the French with the rather more attractive prospect of a knockout clash with Werder Bremen. Lyon thrashed the Germans 10–2 on aggregate to set up a quarter-final date with, on paper at least, the weakest team still remaining: PSV Eindhoven. If United had won that earlier contest in Turkey, they would have topped Group D by a point and sent Lyon to play Milan while they, surely, would have also demolished Bremen and made the quarter-finals.

It was too late to worry about it now, although it was perhaps another indictment of Ferguson's tactics and thinking at a crucial part of the season. The main concern remained: how would United bridge the gap between themselves and the likes of Milan and, although it pains me to say it, Chelsea. Maybe United needed a benefactor after all, if the PLC refused to sanction cash for Ferguson to rebuild? Of course, not a businessman such as Glazer, but someone with the club's interests at heart, and someone who would put vast amounts of cash in, rather than take it out. Or maybe Ferguson should give the board an ultimatum: give me a fistful of readies or I walk. It could prove to be the best option for him personally: simply because it was impossible to see how he could prosper with the players at his current disposal. His transfer turkeys – Bellion, Miller and Kleberson – were not up to it, and, with a new goalkeeper, central midfielder and left-winger on the agenda, major surgery was required. A plaster across the festering sore would not be enough.

If this was Ferguson's roll of the dice now, how would the same roll of the dice bring a different outcome in a year's time? The big man was in big trouble, and surely only a massive transfer pot in the summer could save the back end of his wonderful career at United descending into acrimony and an earlier-than-expected departure. These were the random thoughts spinning through the old head, trying to make sense of it all, as the misery of another night of European collapse by United sunk in.

Milan coach Ancelotti did not put the boot in but told it straight, 'The first half was balanced, but after the break they started to push forward a lot more, and that gave us space to exploit. But I thought we controlled the game.'

Phil Neville went and spoilt it all, by backing Ferguson's blinkered view that all was well and that just a bit of tinkering was needed to get United back to the very top. The younger Neville told MUTV, 'There's nothing wrong with this team or squad. In the past, people have said we need certain players, but I can't see a player at the moment that would come into the squad and improve it. We have to accept we were beaten in Europe and get on with it. It's probably true: we've probably underachieved in terms of the knockout stages [in the Champions League]. In terms of getting to the knockout stages, we're one of the most consistent sides in Europe, but when it comes to the crunch we've consistently over the years slipped up. Not through being beaten by a better team: it's probably through naivety, lack of experience or, sometimes, not learning from our mistakes. Eventually that will have to change.' Neville was wasted in football: surely, with such a talent to spin, there was a place for him in the Government's dark publicity machine.

There were some bright spots amid the self-deluding darkness. It had emerged that Milan's midfield general Gennaro Gattuso would fancy a move to United, if the board got their fingers out and came up with, say, £10 million in cash. Now we're talking hope: in both matches against United, the Italian battler shone like a beacon. He was Keane in his prime: aggressive, determined and a fantastic leader. Remember how he urged the Milan *Ultras* to get behind their team in the San Siro when it was still 0–0: raising his arms aloft to them; passionately drumming up their support.

This man was no Djemba-Djemba or Kleberson. Here was the real thing: he was just what United – and Ferguson – needed if they were to return big-time to European competition. Gattuso, who used to play for Glasgow Rangers and is married to his Scottish sweetheart Monica, told the *Mail on Sunday*:

> My dream is to play for Manchester United in England. I have always been fascinated by them. I would love to have a new experience, even in the next year or two. I would choose Manchester United ahead of Chelsea because the stadium has a very special atmosphere and the club is world famous, like Milan.
>
> When a club has been good to you, as Milan have been to me, and they say you are not for sale, it is difficult to know what you can do. I have always been happy at Milan and I still am. But I think you need a new stimulus in your career. It is a question of the circumstances being right. I am sure Sir Alex knows all about me, because last year his assistant was Walter Smith, who had faith in me when I was young at Rangers.

Those words were a massive boost, especially after Keane had changed his mind, confirming that he planned to hang up his boots when his current contract expired at the end of the 2006 season. The United skipper had said, 'I feel good. My hip feels good; my left knee had been a bit sore, but overall I am not too bad. Mentally I am enjoying my football. But when I signed my current contract I believed it would be [my] last playing contract and I still believe that to be the case.'

The campaign against Glazer was also progressing well: a groundswell of support was helping to attract new converts against the American. Before the home match against Portsmouth, supporters took their battle to the skies above Old Trafford. A light aeroplane trailing the banner 'Stop Glazer – Join Shareholders United' circled the ground. Shareholders United now had 25,000 members and was aiming to push that figure towards 100,000 as they continued their publicity campaign. Another boost to the cause came with the backing of arguably the most influential football figure the group could have hoped for: Sepp Blatter. The FIFA president had his critics, but here he could only be applauded for sticking his neck out. Blatter said, 'I have sent a letter to the fans' organisation of Manchester United supporting them in their fight against this takeover by Mr Glazer.

'This is only our philosophy because we cannot intervene in the market: here we are powerless in the commercial forces of the market; we can do nothing. But the fans' organisation have received a letter because the basis of a club is its supporters. Football started in England in 1863, and a club was attached to, and part of, a city. Now because of the universality of football the club is an industry. But we have to make sure that it is not only an industry; we have to protect the club ethic because football is a game for everybody.' Great stuff, Sepp.

It had been a good few days in the fight against the predator but a very bad few days on the playing front. From 5 March to 8 March, United had crashed out of the European Champions Cup and out of contention for the Premiership title with that disappointing draw at Crystal Palace. All that was left, after the excitement of Rooney's signing and wonderful Champions League debut the previous August, was the FA Cup and a fight for second spot in the league. Again.

God, surely United were not becoming the new Liverpool and Ferguson the new Gérard Houllier? Scuttling about for an automatic Champions League place and dreaming of domestic Cup glory had been the hallmark of the Frenchman's reign at Anfield – until he was finally rumbled and sacked.

15

SAINTS AND SINNERS

OFF THE PITCH, UNITED WERE SPEEDING PRECARIOUSLY towards Easter like a rally car bumping along on particularly rough terrain. The ride would get worse for Ferguson as he continued to try to defend his tactics and decision-making, and Rooney would also suffer a rocky time, both in his relationship with Coleen and over an alleged punch-up in a nightclub. The upside, of course, was on the field as Rooney dragged United into the semi-finals of the FA Cup and inspired England to thumping wins over Northern Ireland and Azerbaijan. He was rapidly becoming, and becoming widely acclaimed as, the key man for club and country. Remarkable, when he was still just 19 years of age.

The FA Cup quarter-final at Southampton could not have arrived at a better time for the Red Devils. After the morale-sapping loss against Milan, United had a swift chance four days later to get the defeat out of their system at the St Mary's Stadium. They certainly did that, dumping Saints out of the competition with a 4–0 triumph and setting up a mouth-watering semi-final against Newcastle. It was Southampton's biggest home defeat since they moved into their new home in August 2001.

FA Cup holders United kicked off without Ryan Giggs, who was still out with a facial injury from the Milan second-leg, as they set about moving one step closer to retaining the trophy for the first time in their history. The adaptable Quinton Fortune was chosen to replace Giggs and boss Ferguson made sure his team was not complacent: reminding them that his Saints counterpart, Harry Redknapp, was something of a bogeyman as far as Old Trafford was concerned. In 1984, Redknapp had engineered a massive giant-killing act as his Bournemouth team, then in the Third Division, knocked United out of the FA Cup with a 2–0 third-round win. Afterwards, 'Arry was asked if he had any sympathy for then United manager Ron Atkinson. His reply? 'No, none at all. He has all the highs in the First Division. This one's for us.' That served as a warning to Ferguson: he could not afford to lose the match. Defeat would end United's season well before Easter, and Easter had come early that year. Ferguson himself had also suffered at the hands of Redknapp – back in 2001 when a single Paolo Di Canio goal earned victory at Old Trafford for West Ham. That was the famous moment when United keeper Fabien Barthez attempted to out-psyche the Italian by holding up his hand as if to signal the forward was offside. It was to no avail: Di Canio ignored Barthez, coolly slammed the ball into the goal and only then checked for any offside flag.

Yet overall, United had the edge on Saints in the FA Cup. Fair enough, Tommy Docherty's young team had frozen in the 1976 final to go down 1–0, and Saints had also beaten United on penalties in a subsequent fourth-round tie, but the Red Devils had knocked them out on six of the eight occasions they had been drawn together since the Docherty final loss. United had also won the Cup a record eleven times and were unbeaten in their last ten ties. So, there was only the expectation of victory as they settled quickly into their stride at St Mary's. Admittedly, Saints were dire on the day – it was a walkover for United – but maybe Ferguson and United deserved fate to deal them a kind hand after drawing Milan in the Champions League.

United were ahead after two minutes. Beanpole Saints striker

Peter Crouch had scored in every round, and he continued that run against the Reds. The only problem for him was that it was in his own net, as he haplessly helped in a volley from the aggressive Roy Keane. Three minutes later, the impressive Rooney almost helped to make it 2–0, sweeping past 18-year-old Martin Cranie – the skipper of Saints' youth team and a mighty fine prospect for England – and crossing a lovely ball in for Fortune, who failed to convert the chance. Paul Scholes was also in fine form, making up for his tired display in Milan and proving his decision to quit the England camp the previous summer had been the correct one. United were benefiting from the little man's less-stressful lifestyle. OK, he might have one poor showing in, say, four or five, but generally he had more energy, and his first-time touches and passes were a delight. After the game, it was revealed that Sven-Göran Eriksson was desperate for him to return to the England fold: if that were to happen it would be very bad news for United, who could ill afford for him to suffer again, particularly given their poverty of resources in central midfield.

Scholes and Keane were both playing much further forward than in Milan, prompting questions on the terraces as to why United had not set out their stall this aggressively in Italy. Simple, really: they were not allowed to; there was a world of difference between this Saints 11 and the magicians Milan paraded. Southampton made clear their limited game plan early in the first half, continually punting balls up to Crouch, all the time ignoring the ability of the twinkle-toed Camara.

United were two up just seconds before the interval: a goal conjured up by Rooney and converted by Ronaldo. Rooney had made a run into the box: his determination took him past two defenders, and Ronaldo fired home his pass into the left-hand corner. It made me think how far the two of them had come: Rooney, the street footballer from Croxteth, and Ronaldo, the yokel wizard from Madeira. Amazing to think that this superb speed king had learned his trade on that Portuguese holiday island for geriatrics. Again, all credit where it is due to old man Fergie for spotting the boy's potential.

Scholes made it 3–0 just after half time: the goal again set up by Rooney who lobbed a perfect pass into the six-yard area to van Nistelrooy. The Dutchman's shot was deflected into the path of the ginger man, and he gratefully hammered the ball into the net. For some reason, a nutter in the United end then threw a flare on to the pitch, delaying the re-start. What purpose did that serve? It nearly hit young Saints keeper Paul Smith and could have brought United serious punishment. United would later pledge that the imbecile would be banned for life when caught. Quite right, too.

The fourth and final United goal was one of the goals of the season, and again Rooney was at the very heart of it. Lobbing the ball delicately with the outside of his right foot, he found van Nistelrooy, who crossed to Scholes on the far post. The chip beat the defence, and Scholes gently headed home on the line. An absolute cracker. United were home and dry and had also maintained their run of not conceding a single goal in that season's FA Cup. The United fans now turned their humour on to their Saints rivals, who had persevered with one particular chant throughout the match: 'We support our local team'. To the same tune of 'You're not singing any more', the United hordes now warned, 'We'll be back to send you down', a reference to the last league match of the season for both clubs, again at St Mary's.

Rooney had just about secured the man-of-the-match award from Saints keeper Smith, who also had an outstanding game despite the scoreline. Old 'Arry Redknapp also deserved a bottle of champers for his classic touch five minutes from time. Rooney approached the United bench and Redknapp rushed over, pleading with Ferguson to take him off, a move which brought a smile to both Ferguson and Rooney's faces.

United were heading for their 24th FA Cup semi-final, and a relieved Ferguson admitted, 'It was unthinkable that we didn't get a win tonight. We had a setback on Tuesday in Milan, but we have recovered from that and got ourselves into another semi-final. It would be very easy to look upon Tuesday as a disappointment that takes us no further. You could look at it as putting us up against a brick wall, but I believe it will only lead to better things. I think what happened in Milan will prove to be the start of a long road to future success in Europe. We are not far away now, and I firmly believe this team will get that success in the future.

'We are just one win away from another FA Cup final, and I find that quite exciting. I actually love the FA Cup, and you could see from the support we received tonight how much it means to the fans.'

Ferguson's comments on the Cup were fair enough, if you conveniently forget he had treated it as a distinctly second-rate competition when United had given it a miss for a year in 2000. But give him his due: United fans still had something to look forward to, albeit only a consolation prize. It was just the words about the club's and his future that jarred. Was he really sincere in his belief that United were almost the finished product? Did he not consider his own future could be at risk if United continued to be also-rans in the Premiership and the European Champions Cup?

Well, it certainly seemed that way, and some of his comments in the week after the FA Cup win over Saints reinforced the view that Ferguson was living in his own world: that he and he alone would decide when he would leave United. He said, 'I have no idea when I would want to quit. When you are my age, your health controls you. But at the moment I am fit and healthy, so there is no reason why I should be thinking about retiring just yet. We have some of the best talent in the world and some youngsters who will be sure bets in this game and also this business. Why would I retire?

'Sometimes I ask: "Do I still have energy?" But then I look to my side, and I see businessmen in their '80s, full of energy, clarity and strength, who continue to work and I think: "If they, at 82, can, then why can't I at 63?"'

It was all getting a bit out of hand. Of course, United had a duty to give a more than fair chance to the man who had led them to 16 major trophies since his arrival in 1986. But did he have the right to imagine that he, and only he, would decide when was the best time for him to depart or move upstairs into an ambassadorial role? Surely, if only out of respect for the club, he could understand that talk like that was slightly arrogant? That the board of directors at Manchester United should also probably have a say, however minor they might seem?

Well, his words did not bring the expected backing of the board. In fact, if anything, they seemed more than slightly irked by the great man's pomposity. Chief executive David Gill temporarily put him in his place by telling the BBC, 'He is sackable. We live in a very pressurised sport. The pressure will be on next season, and we wouldn't want that pressure not to be there.' The stunning words were delivered as it was confirmed in the City that United's pre-tax profits for the six months to 31 January were down from £26.8 million to £12.4 million. Falling media revenues and the cost of buying Rooney, Smith and Heinze were blamed for the losses. How ironic that the magnificent purchase of Rooney would turn out to be one of the very reasons behind the pressure mounting on Ferguson's wondrous 19-year dynasty.

Gill added, 'But [removing the manager] is not something that has entered our discussions at boardroom level. It would be detrimental to the club to make a knee-jerk reaction for not winning the league for a second season in a row. The manager's record is second to none; we still have a chance of winning a major trophy this season in the FA Cup, and we are very positive about the future.'

A United insider told me that within 30 minutes of his quotes on Radio 5 Live, Gill encountered an unpleasant ear-bashing on his mobile phone from a very irritated Ferguson, who claimed such talk by Gill was unsettling for the team at a vital part of the season. Gill was quick to backtrack in public. He claimed, 'I was trying to state the obvious, but the comments have been portrayed in the wrong way. There is nothing in our plans about changing the manager. The issue has not even been discussed. Who is to say what will happen in three, five or ten years' time, but for now we have great plans to work together in the future to ensure the club remains strong as it goes forward.'

However, the damage had been done. For the first time since the late '80s, the word 'sackable' had been employed in relation to Ferguson. The United manager then did his cause no good by continuing his pleas for more time, in the *United Review* match programme for the home game against Fulham. This was how obsessed he had become about his own position and survival: for the first time under his management, he neither welcomed nor mentioned the opposition of the day in his programme notes. No, Fulham and their bright young boss Chris Coleman may as well have not existed as Ferguson talked haughtily about how he was moving on from the Milan defeat, how he was building a new empire and how wrong the critics were to have a go at him. He said, 'It's very easy to be overcritical in face of the disappointment and when expectations are so high, but I think our supporters understand and appreciate that we're working hard to become a power in Europe.' Maybe he would get around to mentioning the Cottagers next time they came to Old Trafford and apologise for the self-absorption and defensiveness that had caused the oversight in the first place. Then again, he probably wouldn't give a damn.

Ferguson completed his 'I am the king of all I survey' speech by again anointing Carlos Queiroz as his ideal successor. He said, 'Can he be the next manager? Why not? He knows how to be one, has experience, he is very bright. There are many Portuguese people in football but I have the best one here in Carlos Queiroz.' No doubt a clever dig at José Mourinho, the *real* top man in football from Portugal. But a few days later, Fergie once again highlighted his own unpredictability by changing his mind and nominating Roy Keane as the next boss. He told *Management Today* magazine, 'I can see him as manager here. He's intelligent and decisive. What's the most important thing you need as a manager? To be willing to make a decision. That's his nature.' All this talk of being decisive and then immediately spouting contrary words was making my head spin.

A bit of decisive action on the pitch was what was needed, and Ronaldo was the very man to provide it in the Fulham clash. Domestically at least, only Chelsea had the upper hand on United at this stage. Ferguson's men entered the fixture still in second place and on an unbeaten Premiership run of 18 matches. Victory over the Cottagers would also be their fourth consecutive win at Old Trafford. It went without saying that a win was now also vital to United and Ferguson's future: that runners-up spot in the league guaranteed riches that were essential to the club's progress, balance sheet and stability. Fulham had held United to a 1–1 draw at Craven Cottage earlier in the season, much to the chagrin of Ferguson who had seen chance after chance go begging. It was a similar story in the Old Trafford return, although at least Ronaldo's winner this time secured all three points.

The Portuguese winger's eighth goal of the season, midway through the first half, ended the contest, but it was very much a worthy winner. Keane found Ronaldo with a clever pass and the Portuguese cut dynamically inside Liam Rosenior and hammered home a glorious pile-driver into the top corner from 20 yards. United then fluffed numerous other opportunities and were hanging on as a late Lee Clark shot hit the post. It left Ferguson fuming. Already feeling the heat in one of the most pressured weeks of his United management career, he uncharacteristically let rip at his players. He raged, 'It was farcical at times: laughable. We totally lacked a killer instinct. We have an FA Cup semi-final coming up and if our form doesn't match up to our expectations, I will make changes. If it doesn't get any better than that level of performance, it is something I will have to think about. We have fresh players like Alan Smith, John O'Shea and Phil Neville ready to come into the team, so we will see what happens.'

The victory would go down in the stats as United's 19th league game without defeat, but here was the rub, the aspect of it all that made a growing number of fans and directors fearful for the future: not only were United out of the Champions League before the quarter-finals for the second successive year, they also still trailed Chelsea by eleven points, with only eight matches of the campaign remaining. Sobering stats indeed. By now, Kevin Keegan had quit as boss of Manchester City, and the bookies were quick to speculate on the future of Sir Alex. William Hill were offering odds of 100–30 that he could walk out on United before the start of the 2005–06 season, and Martin O'Neill was the 5–2 favourite to take over at Old Trafford, with the dark horse David Moyes shortening to 16–1.

It was a good time for a two-week break for Manchester United Football Club. A chance for Ferguson to regroup and for the club as a whole to catch breath after the dramas over the manager's future, Glazer's serial bids and Rooney's powerful impact. Talking of Rooney, there would be no respite from the front or the back pages for the boy wonder. No, for him it was time for England's spring internationals, two World Cup qualifiers against Northern Ireland and Azerbaijan, the first at Old Trafford, the second at St James' Park.

Rooney had established himself on a steadier footing after the run-ins with referees and the bust-ups with other players. He was making a big effort to keep his temper under control, and his sponsors had told him they would not drop him from their advertising campaigns but warned him that he now had to keep his nose clean. So what happens next in the Rooney saga? Rather than keeping it clean, he nearly gets his nose put out of joint in a nightclub 'incident'. Or did he?

The day before joining up with England at the Lowry Hotel on Salford Quays, he had 'gone out to play' with Rio Ferdinand, Wes Brown and Roy Carroll. To be fair, the lads were on their own time and only shared half a dozen glasses of Budweiser apiece when all hell broke loose early on the Tuesday morning. But this was no Sven-Göran Eriksson approved bonding session, and, legally, Rooney should not even have been there: the club operated a strict over-21s only licence.

Here's what happened: Rooney and the three United players went for a relaxing drink at Tiger Tiger, one of Manchester's most trendy nightclubs. They kept to themselves, and, according to Wayne, a bloke came up to him and started being abusive, taunting him about his move to United from Everton, with the words, 'Once a blue, always a blue, eh, Wayne?' Wayne says he walked away, but the bloke – a 22-year-old student at Manchester University – continued hassling him. The student then approached the tabloids with his side of the story, claiming

Rooney had thumped him. He only later reported the incident to the police. When quizzed by the police, he retracted his statement. The episode had all the ingredients of a sting. A close friend of Rooney told me, 'No way did he hit that bugger – although I wouldn't have blamed him if he had done.'

Sir Alex Ferguson entered the debate like a Rottweiler who had been let off the leash. He praised Wayne for his mental strength in not reacting to the bloke and said it was an example of how Rooney would avoid the pitfalls that had derailed George Best and Gazza. The United boss, who was picking up a lifetime achievement award at the HMV Football Extravaganza held in support of charity, said, 'None of what happened surprised me. Human beings today are not stupid. They go into a nightclub, spot a footballer and see a pot of gold. They see a nice earner. That's the sad part. When this guy went to the police station to complain, there was a newspaper guy with him. That's when you ask yourself just what's going on. Wayne, as usual, has been different class. He has been terrific. It used to be Paul Gascoigne, George Best and David Beckham. They're gone now, so people are looking for someone else.

'Wayne knows how to behave. If you're drinking with a couple of friends in a bar and somebody comes over and bawls at you but you ignore them, then I don't really know what else you can do. He's 19, what do you expect him to do? Stay in his house all day and night? I think they should charge the other guy. The whole thing has been a waste of everybody's time. There were CCTV cameras in there and nothing happened.'

Ferguson had proven once again that when it came to standing by his players he was without peer.

The Guardian did make light of Rooney's nightclub moment. For most of the season, they had been running a weekly cartoon on Mondays called, 'On The Wayne (with football's teenage ace Wayne Rooney)'. It was clever enough, if predictable, typecasting Rooney as a dimwit, but it hardly had me falling off my seat in stitches. Wayne had proved he could have a laugh at his own expense, always smiling when he had chance to cast an eye over it. This particular week the cartoon had Ferguson asking him the truth about what had happened in Tiger Tiger. Wayne recounted the story: it emerged he had got involved in a stand-up row with a tough-looking cookie in the gents and had cut his hand lashing out at the tough guy. The punch-line? The tough guy was actually his own reflection in the mirror. Hilarious, hey?

However, it was no laughing matter when Rooney finally joined up with England for the match against the Northern Irish in Manchester. Eriksson quickly advised him to keep a low profile. He did not ban him from leaving his room, as was claimed in some newspapers, but, when training at United's Carrington complex was over, Rooney himself decided it was a good idea to spend most of his time there, playing with his PlayStation and watching TV. He also spent a good amount of time on the phone to fiancée Coleen, who had nipped away for a week in Tenerife with two girlfriends.

Her absence did affect him, leaving him down and lonely. After the nightclub incident, he had phoned her to explain what had happened and to keep her sweet, but, by the weekend, it was she who was having to keep him sweet. Rooney was none too pleased by her antics on the sunshine island, and a source told me he let her know it in a series of phone calls. She had been plastered over the tabloids having a riot of a time, but that in itself, apparently, did not provoke the boy wonder. It was when he saw pictures of her in the *News of the World*, holding hands and dancing with a barman in Lineker's Bar in Playa de las Americas, that he, supposedly, hit the roof.

A source close to Rooney said, 'Wayne was fuming. He did not take kindly to seeing his fiancée having fun with other blokes, however innocent it might be. To him, it just made him look a fool. He loved her, treated her like a princess, was giving her everything, and here she was making him a laughing stock in front of everybody back home.'

Coleen was no fool. Within 24 hours she had cut short her holiday and was back home in Manchester with Rooney. It was their first falling-out since the massage parlour revelations. The source added, 'Coleen is a lovely girl and she knows which side her bread is buttered.' Maybe, but she was also becoming a celebrity name in her own right. Many commentators continued to dismiss her as talentless and a professional layabout, but they were in for a shock. It was becoming clear that Coleen would soon be able to make a career for herself as a model or a television presenter, maybe on children's TV. Some envious women writers might still be knocking her, but large chunks of the public were growing fond of her.

She had been voted one of the world's top 25 sexiest women by the readers of men's magazine, *FHM*, and was even being mooted to appear on the cover of *Vogue* magazine. *Vogue* editor Alexandra Shulman was put in the unusual position of almost having to beg someone to star in the magazine when Coleen initially turned down a plea from one of her lackeys. Shulman said, 'A fashion-struck teenager who didn't want to appear in Vogue didn't really ring true. So I got on the phone to say . . . where would she ever have better pictures taken? We went backwards and forwards over a few days and eventually a deal was struck.' The pictures were taken by the man responsible for the Prada campaign, Robert Wyatt. Coleen did not make the cover, but Shulman no doubt appreciated the sales boost her mag received from Coleen's appearance.

The little Scouse girl we had seen wearing an anorak when she was still at school was now turning into an in-demand young woman. Even her fashion sense was changing – her holiday in Tenerife confirmed that. Coleen had secretly employed a personal dresser, and the results were clear to see. Her clothes had changed dramatically: the pink tracksuit and the Uggies were gone, replaced by the 'boho chic' femininity favoured by actress Sienna Miller. Pretty skirts, blouses and the like.

Coleen was still in Tenerife as Rooney earned man-of-the-match plaudits for his superb showing against the Northern Irish on Easter Saturday, but she was back for the following Wednesday and the Azerbaijan game. England – and United – needed a settled, contented Rooney. His family, Coleen and her family provided the stability. Whereas Gazza had Jimmy 'Five Bellies', and other drinking cronies, Rooney had a sound base from which to launch his God-given talent.

213

As expected, he proved to have far too much in his tank for Northern Ireland. The two nations were meeting for the first time since 1987, with England clear favourites to maintain their position at the top of the qualifying group. Northern Ireland had chalked up just six wins in ninety-six attempts, and, with an inspired Rooney, Eriksson's England were about to make it six in ninety-seven.

After a goalless first half, Wayne took England by the scruff of the neck and set about destroying Lawrie Sanchez's scrappers. He set up all three goals after Joe Cole's opener, the Chelsea man having curled a shot past Maik Taylor into the bottom right of the Northern Ireland goal two minutes after the interval. The first Rooney-led strike came five minutes later: he exchanged passes with Frank Lampard and Michael Owen powered the ball in. Just four minutes later, Rooney refused to be kicked off the ball at the corner flag. Determinedly, he swept past two defenders, and his cross was deflected in for an own goal off poor Chris Baird. The final flourish from the boy wonder arrived just after the hour mark: his crafted pass setting up Lampard, who belted the ball home from 25 yards.

Mission accomplished. For some inexplicable reason, Eriksson then took off Rooney ten minutes from time, sending on Jermaine Defoe. It did not make much sense to take off your best player. It also meant Rooney had yet to finish a match for England and that, despite his match-winning efforts, he had still to find the net for the national team again after Euro 2004. However, his name was up in lights again with Gary Neville claiming that if Rooney remained fit, England could win the World Cup in Germany in 2006.

Rooney admitted that he believed in himself and his ability as a match-winner as much as teammates like Red Nev did. It wasn't arrogance, just acceptance. Rooney said, 'It's nice when your teammates are saying things about you and what you can achieve in the future. I just try to learn from the senior players around me in the England squad. Obviously I think everybody feels pressure, but as soon as you go out on to the pitch you've got to do the best you can.

'I love playing, so from the first whistle I'm 100 per cent focused on the game. I've never doubted myself. I'm a footballer who is confident in myself and my ability. From the first time the manager picked me for England I've thought I'm worthy of playing on this stage.' He admitted that he had the jitters during the Euro 2004 quarter-final against Portugal. Rooney said, 'That was probably the most nervous I've ever been. I don't really go back and analyse what might have happened if I hadn't got injured. Obviously I'm just disappointed I couldn't stay on the pitch and help us win the game. I look back at the tournament as a whole and think about what it has given me: a lot of experience, which helps when I play big games now.'

Rooney admitted that his England strike partner Michael Owen was one of his early heroes. He said, 'For the 1998 World Cup, I used to watch all the games on TV at my Nan's house and then go outside afterwards and play football in the street. I used to pretend I was one of the England players. Now, obviously, it's amazing to be playing with some of those same players. Michael's goal against Argentina was brilliant. The way he took the ball was amazing, and he was so composed in front of goal. I probably pretended to be Michael Owen that night.

'Obviously, I've done things in some big games so people tend to label you in that way. But I prepare for every game in exactly the same way. Beforehand, I try to have a picture in my head of what I'm going to do. I'm always picturing myself scoring a goal. I start preparing mentally two days before a game, so I know exactly what I want to do come kick-off.'

Wayne also admitted his physical strength is a vital aspect of his game. He said, 'It probably comes from the fact that I went to boxing for four or five years. Strength is important because I like to hold defenders off and run with the ball. But I don't do weights now because I don't want to get too big, as it's important to be able to move around the pitch.'

Rooney partnered Owen for the second match of England's spring assault – at Newcastle against Carlos Alberto and his Azerbaijan boys. The visitors had been swamped 8–0 in Poland five days earlier, and England fans were licking their lips in anticipation of a potential 10–0 hammering. Inevitably, it was not to be. Azerbaijan defended much more steadily, and Michael Owen wasted at least five goal-scoring opportunities. The little man was rusty from sitting on the bench at Real Madrid, and clearly, from England's point of view, he would need to find regular first-team football there, or elsewhere, in the season leading up to the World Cup finals in Germany. Newcastle had been suggested as a possible destination, but he would surely prosper more at Arsenal, or even Manchester United?

Even with Owen off target, England managed a 2–0 win with goals from Steven Gerrard and David Beckham. Rooney set up Gerrard for the first with a far post cross, and Beckham sped clear to score a fine solo goal. Rooney and Lampard also hit the woodwork as England coasted home. Afterwards, Eriksson heaped more praise on Rooney, saying he could be the one player to make the difference for England's World Cup hopes. Eriksson said, 'All the teams who win a big trophy have one star who can do something extra. I think we have more than one star, but Wayne Rooney is something extra and in one and a half years, when the World Cup finals come around, hopefully he will be even better. I feel privileged to work with him. As a striker, Wayne is something very special, and he will be better and better.'

Special praise indeed, but there was no time for the golden boy to rest on his laurels. Two key Premiership matches – which could go a long way to deciding if United or Arsenal would finish runners-up – loomed, along with that FA Cup semi against the Toon army. Plaudits from his national coach and Ferguson were all very nice, but Rooney wanted medals and plenty of them. No way did he want to end up as a Gazza or Shearer: the greatest players of their generation but with little to show for it on the mantelpiece.

16

ROONEY TOONS

THE GEORDIE HORDES WERE TOO BUSY DROWNING THEIR sorrows in Cardiff's city-centre pubs to worry about yet another crushing defeat. All they wanted was the temporary oblivion from grim reality that pint after pint brought to their nerve-shredded systems. Yes, it was a potent mix of gallows humour and ingrained cynicism that reigned among them in those packed bars the night *before* their team's semi-final against Manchester United. It had got that bad on the Gallowgate: the loyal supporters of the Toon were rapidly becoming fixed with the same brand of resigned acceptance that had come to typify the equally suffering fans of Manchester City over the past decade.

No, of course, they did not realistically expect their patched-up team to beat Manchester United the following afternoon. Yes, they would never stop following their boys, and, yes, they would do their best to drink the city dry before heading back 'oop' north. The FA Cup had now become the last-chance saloon that season for both teams and their fans. For Newcastle, it represented a last shot at getting into Europe without having to enter the embarrassing InterToto Cup; for Manchester and Rooney, it was the sole avenue of winning a trophy in a season that had promised so much yet, ultimately, looked like leaving an unpleasantly bitter taste.

Sir Alex was by now becoming more and more like that Iraqi bloke from the Gulf War, Comical Ali. Remember him? Saddam Hussein's spin doctor, otherwise known as Information Minister Mohammed Saeed al-Sahaf. His brief was actually disinformation: daily, he would tell the world's media that Iraq was winning the war and the infidels of America and Britain would soon surrender. He was the last member of Saddam's Ba'ath party to abandon his post, giving his final briefing on the morning the tyrant's statue was toppled in Baghdad.

That day he claimed, 'There is no presence of American infidels in Baghdad. They are going to surrender or be burned in their tanks.' As he was speaking, US tanks and troops were steadily appearing into view behind him. Similarly, in the build-up to the FA Cup semi-final, Sir Alex was now taking a note out of his 'We are winning' book. In the two Premiership games before the Cardiff encounter, he may have inhabited a magical world of his own, where all was not only well at Old Trafford but wonderful. In reality, the two results – a 0–0 at home against Blackburn and a 2–0 loss at bottom club Norwich – were yet another disaster in a torturous season for the boss.

United huffed and puffed against Blackburn after Ryan Giggs pulled a hamstring when making a routine pass to van Nistelrooy just four minutes into the match. It was the latest in a series of blows – especially as the Welshman would now likely miss starting in the semi. Without him, United simply messed up against a physically strong Rovers, managed by that former United bull in a china shop, Mark Hughes. Fluffing chance after chance, Rooney came closest to breaking the deadlock with a scorcher from 30 yards in the first half, but, generally, United seemed as if they were playing out a meaningless end-of-season get-together. It was hardly that: the 0–0 draw and Arsenal's 4–1 win over Norwich the same day sent the Gunners above United in the battle for second place in the Premiership and that automatic Champions League spot.

Yet Ferguson had surely sown the seeds of that complacency

by writing in his programme notes, 'To win a trophy a season adds up in my book to a satisfactory season.' This is the man who had in previous seasons fielded weakened sides in the FA Cup and whose tunnel-vision obsession remained one more triumph in the Champions League. Later, he would even go on to say that winning the FA Cup was more of a tribute to his skills than automatically getting into the Champions League: 'We have no chance in the league because Chelsea are out of sight, and, while we want to finish second, winning the FA Cup is far more important.' Really? Who are you trying to kid, sire? I doubt if David Gill would agree.

Even the fans had a go at Ferguson. His decision to leave terrace-hero Alan Smith on the bench for an hour was bemoaned by chants of, 'All we are saying – is give Smith a chance'. They had a point: Ruud was still suffering from a lack of match fitness, and the abrasive Smith would be more of a pest to the Rovers back-line. Ferguson eventually acquiesced and swapped the two.

That selection choice would be the least of his problems in the actual week leading up to the Newcastle clash. The 2–0 setback at Carrow Road was again of his own making. He dropped another of his now customary selection clangers by leaving out Rooney, van Nistelrooy and Ronaldo. Second-half goals from Dean Ashton and Leon McKenzie destroyed United. Ferguson's response was typical: he refused to speak to anyone, including, for the first time in seven years, United's own TV station, MUTV. The defeat left Arsenal – who won 1–0 at Middlesbrough – in the driving seat for that Premiership runners-up spot. Finishing third would cost United £2 million in domestic prize money, plus the problem of having to qualify for the Champions League.

Norwich's delirious fans chanted, 'Can we play you every week' and, 'Come on, let's be having you' – a reference to co-owner and celebrity TV chef Delia Smith's half-time appeal to the Canaries fans to cheer on their team during the recent game against Manchester City.

By sending out a scratch outfit – with a midfield of Phil Neville, Kleberson and Quinton Fortune – Ferguson had taunted Norwich and cranked up their motivation. Canaries boss Nigel Worthington said, 'United were a little bit blasé – thinking, "We are only going to Norwich, it will be three points."' Peter Schmeichel also felt Ferguson should have started with his strongest line-up: 'I don't know what Fergie was thinking about. I don't think some of the players he put in are good enough in terms of their mentality. The squad is not good enough. It was quite a bench at kick-off. The FA Cup semi is still a week away and their last game was last weekend – I just don't understand it.'

When the United boss finally recovered from his paddy, he only compounded his own shortcomings during the season by saying, 'When you look at the season as a whole, we have dropped points to Norwich [3], Portsmouth [3], Fulham [2], Crystal Palace [2] and Blackburn [4]: it is not something we are going to accept. We have done very well against the top teams, but we expect that, so we are left looking around for reasons why we have lost so many points to teams in the bottom half of the league.' The reasons, Alex? Simple again. You took the opposition too lightly. You did not play your best team. The players you threw in instead were often not up to the job. No need for an in-depth inquest when the answers are so obvious, is there?

It was not just the fans starting to put the boot in about Ferguson's puzzling decisions. Former United midfielder Lou Macari and striker Jimmy Greenhoff also waded in, questioning the boss's tactical acumen. Macari argued, 'This club is all about up-and-at-'em football played at 100 mph. This is a club based on attacking football and flair, balls into the box and goalmouth scrambles.' Greenhoff agreed, saying, 'We don't want to go the way of boring Italian football with five in midfield and one up front.'

They were unimpressed by Ferguson's decision to play 4-5-1 instead of 4-4-2. My belief was that United would be best served by a 4-4-1-1 system. This would include a midfield of Ronaldo, Keane, Scholes and Giggs, with Rooney playing as the link-man between attack and midfield, and Ruud up front. The problem was that Ferguson was obsessed with playing Keane and needed five in midfield if he were to continue to employ the rather restricted services of the Irishman. He needed an extra runner, like, say, Darren Fletcher, to hold Keane's hand. You could almost envisage a day when Ferguson would send Keane out in a wheelchair, with Fletcher pushing him around.

In an ideal world, the answer would have been to buy Gattuso from Milan – a man who could do his own running and covering, thank you very much – and use Keane as a back-up when needed. But these were far from ideal times at Old Trafford.

The Newcastle semi was just seven days away, and United's woes increased as the fans began the countdown to a weekend in Cardiff. The first blow came out of nowhere, but the sharp right jab left Ferguson reeling. The second was a hammer blow that would cause Rooney all sorts of problems.

Ferguson's season *horribilis* continued with the revelations that the man he had nominated as his successor had gone and put his foot in it. Yes, Carlos Queiroz, Ferguson's very own special one who could not succeed with Madrid's *galacticos*, was now getting far from rave reviews at Old Trafford. It emerged Queiroz had coached and picked the team for the Norwich debacle, and, in the light of the result, the news was hardly a powerful entry on his already questionable CV. United's senior players were unhappy with his slowly-does-it training methods, their dismay echoing that of Beckham when Queiroz was his boss at Real. Beckham had claimed the Portuguese's timid fitness sessions had left him out of condition for Euro 2004.

Several United players now approached reserve team boss Brian McClair to have a word with Ferguson, but McClair's efforts only earned him a bollocking from the boss and the clear message that Ferguson believed in Carlos. The central problems were the training and the tactics: like Macari and Jimmy Greenhoff, the players wanted to revert to a 4-4-2 formation rather than the Queiroz and Ferguson favoured 4-5-1. They believed it better served their attacking instincts and would open the floodgates goals-wise. They also wanted a more intense level of activity on the training pitch.

Sir Bobby Robson appeared to back the United stars in his weekly column in the *Mail on Sunday*. He said:

> There have been reports of some players being unhappy about Sir Alex Ferguson's assistant, Carlos Queiroz. He succeeded me at Sporting Lisbon, and I was told his coaching exercises were sometimes static and left some players feeling restless. They would remain still while he went through the correct positional play. Somebody remarked that it was suited to a good climate but might not work in England where players like to move about, if only to keep warm!

Ferguson had gone to ground in the week leading up to the semi-final, and an alleged incident involving Rooney on the Sunday kept the limelight firmly off him until United arrived in Cardiff. All hell had broken loose when a tabloid newspaper claimed Rooney had slapped fiancée Coleen McLoughlin in a nightclub – a claim they both denied. As this book headed for publication, Rooney had decided he would sue the newspaper for libel, so legal constraints limit what we can say here. However, the main plank of the story had been confirmed by both Coleen and Wayne. They had had an argument in Brasingamens nightclub in Alderley Edge the day before she was due to fly out to Cyprus for a modelling assignment, paid for by Wayne as a 19th birthday treat. The couple's spokesperson had denied that Wayne raised his hand to Coleen. 'They did have an argument in public at the nightclub and left together and spent the night together,' he said. 'Everything is fine between them.' For the next few days the tabloids were full of counsellors advising Coleen to leave Rooney, if the allegations were proved correct, and urging him to seek help.

A couple of days later, Coleen said, 'Of course he did not slap me. Wayne would never hurt me, and if he did I would not be with him. I'm so in love with him, I'm going to marry him. He is such a talented man.'

The modelling trip was Coleen's second luxury break away in a month and would cost Rooney, according to insiders, the best part of a week's wages: £40,000. The bill included £10,000 for suites and meals at the five-star Amatheus Beach Hotel in Limassol for Coleen and an entourage of ten – including the likes of photographers, a make-up artist, a hairdresser and a stylist. The end result was worth the readies: the pictures were sensational and, a fashion journalist friend told me, could earn Coleen up to £1 million for publication rights. The young Scouse girl was rapidly carving out a niche for herself, albeit on the back of the Rooney cash carousel. She was no fool, despite what some envious women writers would have you believe. In her own way, she was as determined and as feisty as Rooney. Coleen was rapidly gaining the celebrity status and financial means to make her own independent way in the world.

Her fame was astonishing when you think 99 per cent of the population had never even heard her speak. The week after the allegations emerged, Coleen was on the front cover of three major-circulation women's magazines – *Closer*, *Grazia* and *Now* – and the front pages of all the British tabloids.

She also hoped to have a more tangible birthday gift awaiting her on her return to Manchester: a £67,000 Porsche 911. Still talking of money, the nightclub allegations looked as if they could cost Rooney heavily in the pocket with his sponsors. Coca-Cola were 'horrified' by the alleged incident. They still had bad memories of his visits to hookers and told him to deny the allegations in public if he wanted to continue their £1 million-a-year deal. Nike – due to pay him £5 million over ten years – also wrote to him, asking for his explanation of the events, his subsequent denial and potential lawsuit, to satisfy themselves that there had been no physical assault.

It was no way to prepare for what was now United's most crucial game of the season. Arriving in Cardiff, Ferguson broke his self-imposed silence and dubbed his team 'pathetic' for their showing at Norwich. His mood had hardly been improved by the sight of Chelsea and Liverpool both marching into the semi-finals of the Champions League in midweek.

His only consolation was that – as per usual – Newcastle's preparations had been equally, if not more, stormy. The omens had suggested this would be the year that they would win the FA Cup and give skipper Shearer that long-awaited first honour with his boyhood club. It was 50 years ago since Newcastle had last taken the trophy home and the same length of time since Chelsea had won the league. The double golden jubilee was not to be. Chelsea would keep their part of the deal by lifting the title, but the Geordies were simply not at the races in the semi.

Just four days earlier they had been swamped 4–1 by Sporting Lisbon in a UEFA Cup quarter-final, and they arrived in Cardiff knackered and missing key players. Lee Bowyer and Kieron Dyer were still suspended for their pitch brawl a fortnight earlier during the Premiership clash with Aston Villa at St James' Park. Trouble was nothing new to Bowyer: it had followed him like rats followed the Pied Piper throughout his career. Dyer had been just as culpable, yet the club amazingly tried to pretend he had done nothing wrong, in a desperate attempt to save him from a ban. Thankfully, the FA saw straight through that one, but it made a mockery of 'hardman' boss Graeme Souness's claims that he would restore order to the revolting peasants.

Of course, there was a bigger problem than that: the club was rotten to the core, not just in the dressing-room and on the pitch. How could you expect a player to take a bollocking when the man who was handing it out was just as much a bad apple? Yes, we're back to our old pal Freddy Shepherd, the man who helped deliver Rooney to Old Trafford. Trying to act the iron-fisted chairman, he had told Lee Bowyer he should, 'go down on his hands and knees and thank us for keeping him here'. He continued, 'We certainly considered sacking Bowyer. We could have done: it was gross misconduct. But we thought a fine and a final warning was fitting.' And on Dyer: 'Dyer was attacked, and he certainly didn't provoke the incident. It was down to Bowyer. What would anybody do? In my opinion, Dyer's had the raw edge of this.' And on 'hardman' Souness?: 'That's why we brought Graeme Souness in – to tighten things up.' Really, Freddy? Well, why didn't he and you use these two miscreants as an example? Bowyer should have been kicked out of the club and Dyer banned for a month. With his pay docked. That might have knocked some sense into the boy who likes to call himself Sixty Clicks in reference to his £60,000-a-week wages.

The Toon certainly needed a revolution – starting at the very top with the resignation of Shepherd and his cohort, vice-chairman Douglas Hall – if they were to finally awaken from their sleeping-giant status. The duo had survived by the skin of their teeth in 1998 after the *News of the World* had captured them on video and audio tape in a bordello in Marbella, making derogatory remarks about Newcastle's players, fans and women. At the time, Kevin Miles of the Independent Supporters Association had said, 'It is a massive miscalculation if they think they can ride out this storm. Every hour that they stay is another expression of their contempt for the fans of Newcastle and the people of Tyneside. Over 97 per cent of people on Tyneside, in opinion polls, have said they must go. They obviously think they are above public opinion, but they have made a big mistake. They have brought shame on the club, on the city, and they will not be forgiven.'

Yet the brass-necked duo did ride out on the storm, and here was Shepherd, seven years later, trying to lay down the law to Bowyer. The horrible little weasel must have been secretly laughing his balls off as Shepherd had a go at him. In an ideal world, the Toon needed the likes of Martin O'Neill to come in and sort out the mess. He was the ideal man to dispose of the dead wood and disinfect a club that stank from the top downwards. Those long-suffering fans certainly deserved that. There they were at the Millennium Stadium, out in their thousands, giving United's red army brigades a run for their money in terms of vociferous chants and loyal support. And not many sets of supporters can do that.

Of course, the Toon's continued demise was good news for Ferguson. He urgently needed a win in Cardiff if he was to have a case for remaining as boss at United for at least another season. With no title or Champions League triumphs for three seasons, he would already have been shown the door in Madrid or Milan.

But United owed him, and that was fair enough. One more season; one more chance to get it right.

It was his luck that Newcastle did not turn up for battle. Missing Bowyer, Dyer and the talented Jermaine Jenas, they were reliant upon Laurent Robert and Nicky Butt to give them an edge. The Frenchman inevitably disappeared for large parts of the game, and poor old Butty looked as if he simply did not have the stomach to batter his old Man United teammates. Once a red, always a red, hey Nicky?

For once, I felt sorry for Shearer. Now 34, he had committed himself to another playing season at the Toon and after this shambles must have wondered whether he should just commit himself full stop for making such a rash decision. He was taunted unmercifully by the Manchester fans and was the butt of punishing chants including, 'You should have signed for a big club', 'You're gonna win fuck all' and 'Cheer up Alan Shearer'. The Stretford End have long memories and still could not forgive Shearer for turning down a move to Manchester three times. But he was mellowing and, dare I say it, becoming a much more likeable, approachable character. Often seen as a big dullard, he had made something of an image/personality breakthrough in his regular spots as a TV analyst. Similarly to snooker's 'boring' Steve Davis, Shearer had proved he possessed wit, intelligence and a willingness to have a laugh. Yes, we were warming to him, and it was sad that he was let down by such a poor bunch in the semi.

The Magpies were playing in their seventeenth semi-final and their first in five years. It was Manchester's twenty-fourth last-four appearance, and the bad news for the Toon was that they entered the match with a 100 per cent record against Newcastle in this competition. The most recent of their three victories had come in the 1999 final, which they won with goals from Teddy Sheringham and Paul Scholes, on their way to the Treble.

That final at Wembley was one-sided and uneven: so was this semi-final at Cardiff. As in 1999, Manchester had the better players and the better spirit. Ferguson's bollocking delivered in the dressing-room after the Norwich game – and another one from Keane accusing his teammates of slacking – had motivated Manchester, and they were flying from the first minute. Ferguson was giving his team and the supporters a fair deal by putting out his strongest possible eleven rather than dabbling with Kleberson, Bellion or Miller. OK, Fortune was in for Giggs, but the South African provided the sort of gutsy, skilled show he is capable of at times. He and Darren Fletcher were now undoubtedly the best of the second string, but both needed to aim for a greater consistency.

For the record books, Manchester booked a final showdown with bitter rivals Arsenal by finishing 4–1 winners, with a superb, powerful show from Rooney down the left and an impressive return to the scoring charts for van Nistelrooy. The Dutchman latched on to a cross from Ronaldo on 19 minutes to put United ahead, and a glorious Paul Scholes header – from another Ronaldo set-up – made it 2–0 just before the interval. Van Nistelrooy slotted home another thirteen minutes after the re-start, and Cristiano Ronaldo's shot from close range after 76 minutes ended the contest. Shola Ameobi had pounced for the Toon's consolation on the hour, sliding the ball under Tim Howard's legs for yet another goalkeeping blunder in a nightmare season of them for Ferguson's men.

Afterwards, Ferguson was full of praise for van Nistelrooy, who had not scored in the previous eight matches. He said, 'Hopefully, now Ruud will maintain his scoring form and start to notch on a regular basis. When he does do that, he is unstoppable. The first goal was typical of him because it came out of nothing. Everyone is delighted for him.

'It has been difficult for Ruud and maybe we made a mistake rushing him back so quickly, but it was a sensible mistake – if you can call it that. We knew ten days' training before the AC Milan game was not enough but what do you do? Keep him in the stand knowing he could score a hat-trick?'

A 'sensible mistake' . . . What a great line from Ferguson. When he speaks like that and puts out his best team, he is still one of the greatest. But he can be so infuriating: someone who drives you around the bend with half-baked team selections and tactics yet someone who can also have you on the edge of your seat when he goes back to basics and gets things right. He certainly got it right after the semi-final win – which had kept United's season alive – when faced with a contract problem with Rio Ferdinand. The big defender, called the 'best centre-half in the world' by the United manager, was unhappy with his financial lot at Old Trafford, and talks about a new deal stalled.

The same week, Ferdinand had been pictured meeting Chelsea chief executive Peter Kenyon in London. Kenyon claimed the meeting was a coincidence, and Chelsea said they had no interest in signing Ferdinand. It was suggested Ferdinand had used the meeting to crank up negotiations with United. He wanted £100,000 a week to stay at Old Trafford – an increase of £30,000. Ferguson sensed Rio was playing a game and urged him to sign the deal United had put on the table. He owed the club, so he should show some loyalty, just as United had done when they had paid him more than £2 million for his eight-month absence when he was banned for missing a drugs test. Ferguson said, 'The best thing Rio can do is sign his contract and put the matter to bed. He says he wants to sign for the club, and he has an opportunity to do just that. We have offered him a good deal, and hopefully something can be done in the next few days.'

It was a classic call your bluff by the United boss. Ferdinand now had nowhere to hide if he genuinely did want to sign a three-year extension to a contract that was due to expire in 2007, effectively tying him to Old Trafford until 2010. It was an excellent piece of work by Ferguson in attempting to tie up the talisman whom he had earmarked to succeed Roy Keane as captain. Ferguson's ploy contrasted sharply with how Arsène Wenger had dealt with Ashley Cole's tapping up by Chelsea. Wenger had refused to blame the player, even when it seemed to become clear that he had in fact instigated talks with the Blues. The Arsenal boss had made Cole look bigger than the club, while Ferguson had brought Ferdinand down to size.

Funny, ain't it, to think that in 2010 Rooney will only be 24. If he remained at United, he would also, surely, be skipper one day. In fact, he had already asked Ferguson to make him captain for his first match back at Everton, in the FA Cup in February. Rooney admitted, 'There was no way that I wanted to miss that cup game. To go back to Goodison was special for me. I went up to the manager and said, "You should make me captain." I wanted to be the captain, but I'm not sure Roy Keane would have been too happy. I had to go there sometime, but to go in the FA Cup, and with so many United fans there as well, it was great. The fans were brilliant, and it was nice to come away with a win.'

Some youngsters reckoned Rooney would go on to even greater things. A poll of children aged between nine and thirteen put the United striker before Harry Potter as top choice to be Prime Minister. The boy wonder won 15 per cent of the votes, 3 per cent ahead of the boy wizard, in a survey compiled for the Cartoon Network TV channel.

He would certainly make a generous, if flawed, PM: Rooney was extremely free with his time and money. Not only was he bankrolling Coleen as a real 'footballer's wife', he was also splashing the cash on her family. He had given her mum and dad, Colette and Tony, his £1 million mansion in Liverpool and was also extremely kind to Coleen's severely handicapped adopted six-year-old sister, Rosie. Rooney had spent hour after hour visiting her at a children's hospice in Cheshire.

Another survey was not as complimentary to him. It showed fans believed Wayne was the most disloyal player in the Premiership for leaving Everton for United. Roy Keane was voted the most loyal, after 14 years at United, in the Britannia Building Society survey of 2,000 fans. It was unlikely to make Wayne lose any sleep, but the Premiership run-in, and the battle for second spot, was hotting up. Maybe the thought of another hairy return to Everton in United's next match *would* leave him having to count sheep for a good night's kip.

17

THE WONDER OF ROO

THERE'S SOMETHING ABOUT THE START OF THE MONTH THAT does not sit easily in the life of Sir Alex Ferguson. Take March, April and May 2005 for example. On 5 March, he dropped Rooney and effectively gave up the chase for the Premiership title by settling for a miserable 0–0 draw at Crystal Palace. On 9 April, he again left Wayne out and paid the price with a 2–0 defeat at Norwich – a result that gave Arsenal the upper hand in the race for the Premiership runners-up spot. Then, to compound his earlier errors, Sir Alex once again demoted Rooney to the bench on 7 May as his journeymen 11 stumbled to a disgraceful 1–1 home draw with relegation strugglers West Brom.

That result formally handed Arsenal the runners-up spot and condemned United to an early season start in which, still groggy after their summer breaks, they would have to qualify for the Champions League. Was it just me? Was I being too hard on old man Fergie? Or was it a fact that his team selections were becoming ever more unfathomable? Every time he sent out a second 11, or components of it, and every time he dropped Wayne, the outcome appeared to be the same grim one. Surely he could see that it only motivated the opposition when he wound them up with his second-raters?

Well, after the West Brom debacle, Ferguson's comments summed up his selection failings during the season but also prompted more questions than they answered. This is what he said: 'If you look at our record, all season it's about giving points away to the bottom half of the league. That's an embarrassment to the players and everyone at the club. I think we're going to have to correct that next year, and I think we have to play the right teams in these games. The number of chances they've had today is embarrassing.' There, I have not been too hard on the United manager: he himself admitted he had got it wrong for a good part of the campaign. But can I ask him this: why, Sir, if you know you will have to play the 'right teams' next season, did you not do so this season? And why, Sir, if you accepted goals were a must, if Arsenal were to be caught, did you not start with the boy Rooney against Albion? It was an incredible admission of guilt and culpability for the bulk of United's disappointing results, but I do not feel it was one resulting from a bout of humility. No, I am sure when Ferguson reads this he will be stunned that he even uttered such self-condemnatory words.

The draw meant United had now shipped fourteen points to the Premiership's worst seven teams and it left them trailing champions Chelsea by a massive seventeen points. Of course, they were more likely to have won if Rooney had started. The Reds had a total of twenty-seven shots on target to West Brom's three, but a midfield of Phil Neville, Kleberson and Quinton Fortune gave the Premiership's bottom club just the lift they needed. The Brazilian World Cup winner in particular proved, once again, he was not up to it: fluffing a number of chances, including a one-on-one with the keeper that my seven-year-old boy would surely have converted but that Kleberson could only heave over the bar. It drew a shout in the press box from former United boss Wilf McGuinness that echoed the thoughts of many on the terraces: 'What part of Brazil is he from and which sport did he win the World Cup final in?' It was a fair put-down: did this fella really play in a World Cup final? He certainly did not play like any Brazilian I knew.

Ryan Giggs had put United ahead, but Robbie Earnshaw

earned Bryan Robson's team a point with a penalty just after the hour when John O'Shea conceded a debatable spot-kick for bringing down Geoff Horsfield. Even United's most loyal fans had found it hard to contain their disenchantment. They would back Ferguson – the man they had dubbed 'The Wizard' on the terraces – to the hilt, but today they could not help but boo as he withdrew Alan Smith for Kleberson.

The West Brom match was at the back end of four Premiership games that had very much shown the 'Jekyll and Hyde' outfit United had become. The first of the quartet saw Rooney return to the jungle of Goodison. Wayne was still unhappy at the hot treatment the Everton faithful had dished out on his first return in a United shirt in the FA Cup in February. He admitted as much in his pre-match comments when he attacked those who had given him such a rough ride as ignorant. He said, 'You've got to block the abuse out and focus on the game. It's mostly people who don't understand the game who give you stick. People who understand know players move on. I'm not bothered if they never forgive me.' That did not go down well in the Gwladys Street End, and they showed their feelings towards Wayne by abusing him as the players ran on to the pitch to the familiar tune of *Z-Cars*, the Everton anthem. If the very sight of him spurred them into action, the vision of Rooney kissing the United badge on his shirt in response to their heckles only served to whip up their catcalls and hatred to a new level.

Let's stress this again: here was a tough young cookie. He was no Gascoigne in terms of durability and mental strength. He was much stronger, much more determined, and he was genuinely scared of no one. He knew he had done his best for Everton and that they were out of order to continue their campaign of hatred, but no way was he going to let them live rent-free in his head for the rest of his career.

Indeed, Rooney almost opened the scoring on five minutes when he blasted a 20-yard drive towards goal, but keeper Nigel Martyn was equal to it. There were fireworks on the pitch as well as off. Rooney ended up with a bloody nose a minute before his shot on goal – a consequence of his bravery in throwing himself in the way of an Everton attack. United also had two players sent off: Paul Scholes for a second bookable offence and Gary Neville for foolishly hammering the ball at a spectator who had been continually jeering him. Also, big, bad Gabriel Heinze was doing his best impersonation of Jack Nicholson in *The Shining*: the Argentine was the master of the evil smile after something had gone against him. Then big, bad Duncan Ferguson won the points for the Toffees with a trademark header just before the hour that left Tim Howard for dead.

It was a painful result for Rooney, for United and for English football. Everton had bustled and battled, but they were there for the taking. It was their first victory over United in ten years, and it was a sad indictment of the overall quality of the Premiership that they had been able to consolidate their push for fourth position in the table, and the final Champions League qualification spot. This team of scrappers stood 33 points behind leaders Chelsea, yet only 29 points from the third bottom team in the table.

Four days later, United entertained Newcastle at Old Trafford. The match was set against unusual comments from Sir Bobby Charlton and Rooney. Sir Bobby was in Beijing and gave the dreaded vote of confidence to Ferguson. He said, 'The only way we would ever be separated from Sir Alex Ferguson is if he decides. We have no plans to do that. He is the best manager there has ever been and the most successful, certainly in England, and we have no reason to change.' The archetypal nice guy had done his best to back his friend, but, of course, it had the opposite effect of merely emphasising that Sir Alex was treading on dangerous ground. It was something he could have done without: he needed the spotlight off him, not on, if he were to survive another season.

Temporarily, he gained some breathing space as Rooney spoke of his dismay with his own form. I found this a surprising outburst, after all, he was United's top scorer and their creative genius; he had lifted them out of mediocrity on several occasions lately. Rooney said, 'I've had chances where I should have scored and didn't or where I've been a bit unlucky, like against

Blackburn when I hit the post. I cost a lot of money, and with any player brought in to a new club there are always expectations to do well. If you're not performing well, you will get told.

'It has been a disappointing season here at Manchester United. You can't perform one week and not the next. I came to this club to play in the Champions League and to win things. The last thing I won was with the Copplehouse Under-13s. It still has pride of place at home, but I want to win trophies here.' Well, Rooney *did* perform *and* won a trophy during the weekend of Newcastle's visit.

The Geordies arrived determined to avoid a mauling similar to the one they had experienced in the FA Cup semi. They were helped in no small part by an United midfield lacking edge: Roy Keane looked drained and Paul Scholes was absent due to his suspension for being sent off at Everton. Newcastle took the lead on the half-hour when Tim Howard gifted them a goal. The American kicked the ball out to the effervescent Darren Ambrose, who marched in on goal and shot past Howard from 12 yards out. The Toon stoked up the pressure with the rotund Patrick Kluivert – doing his best to impersonate the late, great Barry White – getting well stuck in.

But, once again, Rooney would drag Manchester back from the dead. His stunning goal – a marvellously executed 25-yard volley – helped extinguish the spirited Geordie challenge. It came out of the blue on the hour. A stray header from Peter Ramage dropped into Rooney's path, and he swerved it home with all the exquisite skill and power of the great Brazilian forward Rivelino.

It was Wayne's 16th goal of the season and had the effect of propelling United into a different gear. Wes Brown headed the winner on 75 minutes from a Ryan Giggs corner. The only setbacks were a booking for Rooney just after half time for going in studs first on James Milner and the agonising sight of Gabriel Heinze being taken off on a stretcher with an ankle injury that would cost him an FA Cup final spot.

Afterwards, Wayne – who had played a far more central attacking role than usual – was bubbling about his performance.

He claimed the goal was his best yet: 'I struck it sweetly, and it's gone in the top corner. If you can hit the ball as hard as you possibly can, you've always got a chance because the keeper might not be able to hold on to it. Then, even if he does save it, there's a chance of it rebounding for someone else to score. You concentrate 100 per cent on the ball rather than where the keeper is. Any forward will tell you, they always know where the goal and the keeper are so, as long as you concentrate on the ball and catch it nicely, you've got a chance of it going in. It's my best-ever goal.'

Ferguson was lavish in his praise of the boy. He said, 'We had the bit between our teeth more in the second half, but it took a fantastic goal from Wayne Rooney to change the pattern of the game. It was phenomenal – a fantastic strike.' Fergie then scored one of his, by now traditional, own goals by complaining about referee Neale Barry's display. He was annoyed that Barry had refused Alan Smith a penalty – and claimed it all dated back to United's 2–0 win over Arsenal in October when Mike Riley awarded his team that disputed spot-kick.

The United boss said, 'Since that penalty kick, it seems to me we are not going to get another one, no matter what the circumstances. It is getting ridiculous now. I am not sure if they are instructed, but it is looking sinister to me. One of our players will need to get shot for us to get one.' It led to the FA writing to Ferguson to ask him to explain his comments.

Rooney had no time for such distractive sideshows. While his boss was running into another row with authority, Wayne was picking up the Young Player of the Year award. OK, you might say it wasn't the Player of the Year award, but that will no doubt follow. Plus, don't forget, he had to beat off a rather impressive list of rivals to secure the honour, including men such as Jermaine Defoe, Arjen Robben, Cristiano Ronaldo, Stewart Downing and Shaun Wright-Phillips.

Wayne was grinning like the proverbial Cheshire cat at the awards ceremony in London. He said, 'Obviously for any footballer to receive any award is a great achievement and especially so when it is one voted for by all your fellow professionals. As a footballer, you are always looking to improve and learn from the people around you. If I keep learning, and keep my feet on the ground, then hopefully I can start winning more trophies.' He spoke with admirable humility: further proof that he was hardly the tearaway angry young man some would have you believe.

Rooney would also admit such splendid goals as the one against Newcastle were no flukes. In fact, they were not at all down to luck. No, it was a simple consequence of hard graft. He said, 'Me and Paul Scholes stay behind after training sessions and have someone cross the ball in for us to practise shooting and volleying. The first-team players stay to knock the ball in, so it's always high-quality delivery. Most of our shots go over or wide, but, luckily enough, the one against Newcastle flew in. Working with Sir Alex Ferguson and all the players at United can only benefit me. I'm a young lad.'

Although he had 'loved' his first season at Old Trafford, Wayne conceded United had not done well enough. He said, 'You have to look to win things at United. The fans and everyone has that expectation on Manchester United to win things. The season we have had in the league hasn't been what we wanted. If we can win the FA Cup – though we know it will be a tough game against Arsenal – that will be something.'

Rooney was of the opinion that England could also lift the World Cup in 2006. He said, 'Looking at the England squad now, we've got a lot of young and good players. We've definitely got the players to win it. It's going to be a tough tournament, but we feel we can go all the way.' From nowhere, he then said something which was almost worthy of Ali G, but maybe he was just being his usual mischievous self: 'Speaking to the masseurs, who have been around the England squad a long time, they tell me this is the best spirit they've seen with the England team.' Masseurs, indeed!

Away from the pitch, Wayne and Coleen still hogged the tabloid headlines. Rooney had apparently 'done a Beckham' by having the word 'Coleen' tattooed on his right arm, above an enormous Celtic cross. Some cynics suggested it was a peace offering after he and Coleen had argued a few weeks earlier. After more serious allegations that Beckham had cheated on his wife, the Real Madrid midfielder had had a four-by-six-inch winged 'redemption' cross penned across the back of his neck.

Coleen's *Vogue* pictures had also emerged. They were impressive: the magazine had transformed her into a fashion icon in a ten-hour shoot. The pictures appeared in the *Sunday Mirror* and they commented, 'With her slicked-back hair, Stella McCartney skirt, Yves Saint Laurent scarf and Gucci top and earrings, Coleen is transformed into an Ava-Gardner-style sex symbol.' Rooney was said to be 'blown away' by the pictures, allegedly telling her, 'They are phenomenal. You look amazing.' Away from the pitch, Wayne was, surprisingly, often shy and insecure. Indeed, a source close to him confided that Wayne was wary of Coleen's growing fame, fearing she might one day grow out of him.

An interview accompanying the pictures showed the admirably strong Miss McLoughlin to be a far from happy bunny at the treatment some members of the press had meted out to her. She complained:

> I haven't set out to be famous, but I'm beginning to feel like I can't win. Sometimes I wonder if I'm being punished for something that Wayne has done. In the end, what matters to Wayne is what appears on the back pages, the sports pages. He can go out and be a hero again on the football pitch. I can't.
>
> I'm not the person the newspapers think I am. And there's all this hype, but I didn't seek it. And I don't understand that chav label. I don't know what it's supposed to mean. When you see someone in the paper, it's so different to real life, isn't it? Yes, I go shopping, and I buy what I want. But sometimes I'm photographed and there's a story that says I've been on another spending spree, when all I was doing was popping round to my mum's or buying a friend a birthday card.

All right, it sounded like she was playing the victim, but, to an extent, she had a point: she had become the victim of hardened media operators. Take the *Vogue* shoot, for example. What struck me there was how the magazine's editor, Alexandra Shulman, had pulled off a classic sting and still emerged whiter than white. Shulman had basically used Coleen to boost her magazine's sales for one month. On the pretext of providing Coleen with the best modelling photos she could ever hope for, she had got the big one: the first media interview with Rooney's girl. Yet Shulman then washed her hands of her, putting in the boot in an interview in the *Daily Telegraph* with the words, 'An outrageous shopping habit . . . prefers her hair to be a bit too flash blonde . . . likes pink to an inadvisable degree . . . and enjoys dubious hair extensions and white-tipped manicure.'

Coleen found an unlikely ally as she complained about her lot. Feisty Welsh songstress Charlotte Church said she sympathised with her: that it could not have been easy being thrust into the public limelight so suddenly. But that dopey girl from *Big Brother*, Jade Goody, could only stick an envious boot in. The Miss Piggy double was annoyed she had not been chosen for the *Vogue* shoot. She said, 'To be honest, it has left me gobsmacked. If she weren't dating Wayne, she would never have got in the magazine. It's not as if I don't shift mags. I'm a big seller, so I'm told.'

The debate about Rooney's girl continued to rage in the newspapers, on websites and on phone-in talk shows. Even the blokes got in on the act. Unlike the women, they were generally appreciative of her looks, and one cracked an amusing gag about how Coleen's relationship with the world of football could pan out:

> Imagine if Wayne Rooney's beautiful girlfriend Coleen McLoughlin got friendly with legendary Italian referee Pierluigi Collina, married the bald-headed legend, before starting her own colonic irrigation practice in the beautiful ski-resort of Cortina. She would then be Coleen Collina the Cortina colon cleaner!

Enough frivolity. United headed for Charlton and another brush with mediocrity. Like Everton, they were an advert for how disappointing the quality of the Premiership had been that season. Take away the top three, Liverpool and maybe Spurs, and most of the other teams you would not rush out of bed to watch. Charlton duly collapsed, allowing United to romp to a 4–0 victory. History had suggested United would have an easy day at the races. The Londoners had lost their last five matches against them and had never beaten them in the Premiership, collecting just two points from a possible thirty-three. They had lost the last three at the Valley against the Reds, and their last home victory over the visitors was in 1989, when they won 2–0.

So, even without Ruud van Nistelrooy, who had injured an ankle in training, Ferguson knew this would be a day he could savour. The goals in the walkover came from Scholes, Fletcher, Smith and Rooney. Wayne's goal, the final of the four, came on 67 minutes. He exchanged sweet passes with Scholes and powered forward to lob the ball over stand-in keeper Stephan Andersen. Considering it was such an emphatic win, the main talking points, surprisingly, were not the goals but incidents involving Scholes and Rio Ferdinand.

Scholes had been very lucky to stay on the field five minutes after he scored. His crude tackle on Dennis Rommedahl merited a red card. Instead, a lenient Dermot Gallagher showed him yellow. Red would have meant the ginger man missing the FA Cup final. Rio also found himself in the wars – from the United fans. His continued delay in signing an extension to his contract was not going down well with the loyal Reds, and they frequently booed him and chanted, 'Rio, Rio, sign the deal', 'Chelsea rent boy' and 'Sign on or fuck off'.

Ferdinand was temporarily stripped of the vice-captaincy by Ferguson and warned by the United boss to knock the wild nights with Rooney on the head. Rio had been present at both of Rooney's nightclub 'incidents', and Ferguson wanted the 'playtime' couplings broken up. A United insider told me, 'Sir Alex has told them to cool it. He doesn't want them to end up on the front of the papers again because of their nights out. He's had enough.'

Ronaldo, meanwhile, was in the boss's good books. Ferguson had offered him a fresh deal that would more than triple his wages from £14,000 a week to £52,000 a week. The United boss had been spurred into action after reports that Real Madrid were greedily eyeing up the exciting winger. Ronaldo was having a good season, although he continued to infuriate Rooney by shooting over the bar when Wayne was in a better scoring position. The two were the future of United, but it did not stop them having a go at each other now and again. A source close to Rooney said, 'Wayne does get peeved with him. He thinks he can be too greedy and should pass more, but he also admires him for his skill and says he is on the way to being a great footballer.'

United struggled against West Brom and then, three days later, licked their lips at the prospect of making up for it by getting one over on newly crowned Chelsea and the cocky Mourinho. The Blues arrived at Old Trafford like proud peacocks: they walked in as though they owned the place. They had won the league with three games to spare, and victory over United tonight would see them setting a new Premiership record for points gained and total wins. Victory meant they would have 94 points, as compared to United's 91 in the 1999–2000 season, and 29 wins, compared with United's 28 at the start of the new millennium.

They achieved both against a United team that, save the injured Gabriel Heinze, was Ferguson's first 11. That selection meant no start for Ryan Giggs. You've no doubt heard of individual players being lauded as two-in-one stars: because they do the work of two men. Well, Giggs had been axed for United's very own one-in-two player: Darren Keane (or, if you prefer, Roy Fletcher). This unique innovation had been created by Sir Alex over the last month, since Fletcher's return from injury. Basically, it meant Keane could play on, even though his legs were almost gone. It was one of the boss's more unusual ideas of late: along with the 'guess-what tactics I'm going to use today' and the 'I'm having a laugh' selection of players not fit to pull on the coveted shirt of Manchester United Football Club.

That night Chelsea opted against the one-in-two man. Instead, they sent out their two-in-one battler, Claude Makele. He could tackle like Keane, run all day like Fletcher, pass like Keane and carry water like Fletcher. Old fashioned certainly, but maybe Sir Alex should think of getting his own model? Then he could drop one of Fletcher or Keane to the bench and bring in an extra creative player like, say, well, Ryan Giggs. The other problem for Ferguson was that by finally showing his best hand, he also emphasised the enormous distance that Chelsea had put between them. The Blues fielded a virtual reserve outfit – they were missing Cech, Paulo Ferreira, skipper Terry, Wayne Bridge, Duff, Drogba and Robben – yet still ran out comfortable winners.

Darren Keane worked hard in midfield but could not get the better of the inspiring Makele, and, after weathering an early spell of United domination, Chelsea's 3,000 fans were not far from the truth when they broke into chants of, 'Easy, easy'. It had started well for the hosts. They had formed a commendable guard of honour for the new champions and then set about them like a Rottweiler would a piece of meat. Twice in the opening minutes Rooney knocked Robert Huth to the ground with pile-driver shots.

Wayne was lucky his favourite referee Graham Poll was officiating. Poll had treated him in the way a lenient teacher might gently admonish an off-the-rails kid he has a soft spot for when they had met at Highbury in February. Rooney had sworn at him most of the night, but Poll had simply waved him away. Once again, Wayne owed a chunk of gratitude to the man who had been the best referee in town that particular season. He might even have sent our wonder boy off on 40 minutes for hitting out at Geremi and then swearing at him (again). Rooney and Geremi had shaped up to each other after scrapping for the ball and Wayne foolishly had a go. He was still wound up after chants from the Chelsea fans alleging he had mistreated Coleen and that he still had a liking for prostitutes.

Earlier Wayne had done what he does best: play magnificent football. He had sent in a steamer of a shot on seven minutes. It was heading wide, but van Nistelrooy backheeled it home. It was the perfect start, but it would not last.

Ferguson's folly in continuing to ignore his goalkeeping problem raised its ugly head again just ten minutes after Van's opener. Claude Makélélé laid the ball off to Tiago and, from 30 yards out, his swerving shot beat Roy Carroll. The United number 1 watched it go by as if under the influence of a magic wand: like he was observing a miracle happen before his very eyes. His prostrate body and open mouth only kicked into action when he realised he now had to get the damned thing out of the back netting.

Then, as Ronaldo jigged and lost the ball, you could not help but feel sympathy for Van the Man. How much he must still be grieving over the defection of Beckham, whose inch-perfect right-wing crosses had helped make him the marksman he was. United's shape was not right. Why wasn't Rooney playing in his best position – in the hole behind van Nistelrooy? Surely he had done his stretch – a large chunk of the season – out on the left? Ronaldo again lost the ball on the hour and was left sitting on his backside as Chelsea powered forward, with Eidur Gudjohnsen converting. Then Joe Cole nipped in for the third, after 82 minutes, when Wes Brown gifted the ball to the Blues with a dreadful kick from defence. Yes, Cole was offside, but by now the United faithful were on their way home, and those that had stayed behind didn't have the stomach for any more resistance.

It was United's first Premiership loss at home of the season, their third in all competitions: Chelsea again (in the Carling Cup) and Milan causing the extra damage. It also kept up José Mourinho's remarkable run against Sir Alex. The old master had now failed to get the better of him in six meetings.

The last home game of the season is traditionally party time at Old Trafford. The players and the fans applaud one another for a job well done over the previous nine months, but not tonight. Rooney and Co. appeared stunned as they walked around to a chorus of boos from a three-quarter empty stadium and the taunts of the Chelsea hordes. 'Boring, boring Chelsea', they gloated. Even hardcore United fans had booed Ferguson when he had brought on the struggling Saha for Fletcher, the chant in unison being, 'Alan Smith, Alan Smith, Alan Smith'.

Ferguson decided to keep his end-of-term speech for the fans in his pocket. There would be no need for it tonight: the cascading empty banks of seating around Old Trafford provided the United boss with a harsh, but honest, verdict on how the fans had viewed his season's work. Then, at the after-match press conference, he again claimed it wasn't really all that bad. He said, 'Tonight was about trying to keep our confidence up, and on the whole it was good. That is the one thing I can take out of the game. The tempo was fantastic, and anyone watching as a neutral would be thrilled by the football played. I thought we played some good football; the match was very competitive, and it was really a game for professionals.' His comments had brought a smile a month back, but now the spin was no longer amusing. In fact, it was all transparently painful.

Let's be honest, Alex. This was not the glowing Old Trafford Premiership sign-off you had envisaged. No marker had been laid down for Chelsea for the next season, only a disconsolate emptiness pervaded those rapidly emptying stands. A realisation was dawning that this and, hopefully, another FA Cup win might be as good as it now got in the latter days of your reign. Twenty points behind the new king and his glory boys, with little hope of catching them next term, given their resources and the brilliant tactics and man-management of the self-styled 'Special One'. Where did it all go wrong, Sir?

18

TWO BALD MEN AND A COMB

ARMAGEDDON. THAT'S THE WORD THE UNITED FANS' WEBSITES were running with on Friday, 13 May. Unlucky for some, particularly if you bled red, like many of the lads behind those sites. Glazer had made his move the day earlier, snapping up the shares of the so-called 'Coolmore Mafia', John Magnier and J.P. McManus. By close of business in the City on the Friday, he controlled 74.8 per cent of Manchester United. After the weekend, he had more than the all-important 75 per cent, the figure that would allow him to take the club back into private ownership for the first time since it floated in 1991.

It emerged the purchase would cost Glazer a total of £790 million. Red Football, the working title of his bid, would receive £275 million funding from preferred securities, which would not be secured against United's assets, but £265 million which would. Given the club's most recent half-year profits were just £12.4 million, the Tampa Bay Buccaneers owner would need to produce a massive increase in turnover simply to service the debt, with interest alone costing upwards of £20 million a year.

Those were the harsh facts of the situation: the central planks of an unpleasant saga that had dragged on all season. Glazer tried to sweeten it by promising the manager £20 million a year for signings. It showed just how out of touch with United he was if he thought it would have the fans exclaiming 'wow'. Twenty million a fortune? Not in today's game, Malcolm – merely a satisfactory tip at a restaurant for Mr Abramovich. I was initially puzzled why the Irish duo had taken their 30 pieces of silver and ran. Why did they do it? Simple, said my publisher: money and lots of it. Ninety-million notes split between two to be exact. But was it only down to that? Certain sources within Old Trafford alleged that this was their payback time after the dispute with Alex Ferguson over Rock Of Gibraltar. Well, if that was the case, they were wide of the mark.

If their aim was indeed to destabilise Ferguson's role at the club, it backfired spectacularly. The United boss, who had endured a nightmare season in which he had often lost the plot, was suddenly in a position of strength. Before Glazer's takeover he had been heading for the last chance saloon. One more season on his 12-month rolling contract, in which he had to win the Premiership or the Champions League, or he was out. Now, suddenly, he could almost dictate his terms to Glazer. The American believed the fans would riot if he sacked Fergie, plus he needed the volatile Scot's experience and hand on the tiller because he knew zilch about running a football club.

The Irish would now always be remembered as the men who had sold out Manchester United Football Club and the men who had plunged it into turmoil. Their seeming miscalculation in apparently seeking revenge on Ferguson could cost United dear if he did not manage to reproduce the magical management skills that had consistently deserted him that term. Unless he walked or clashed with Glazer, United could be stuck with a boss past his sell-by date tied into a longer-term deal, although Marcia Shapiro, Glazer's sister, warned Ferguson it would not be all cosy-cosy. She said, 'This Sir Ferguson will do Malcolm's bidding or he won't be managing the team.'

Another claim doing the rounds inside the club was that the Irish duo had been egged on to sell by Celtic supremo Dermot Desmond. It was alleged that Desmond persuaded McManus and Magnier to cash in because he was still angry at United for taking midfielder Liam Miller from Parkhead on a free transfer. Please tell us that is not true, Dermot. I am sure it can't be. United chief executive David Gill would gladly have driven the boy back to you, if that were the case. His impact at Old Trafford had been such that hardly anyone would have even noticed he had gone missing.

Beware a silent Glazer – or Glazier as Sir Alex continued to refer to him in private. He represents the modern-day Dracula of the beautiful game, intent on sucking as much of the lifeblood from it as he can. OK, Roman Abramovich was another of the silent breed, but at least he was bringing food to the table at Chelsea and plenty of it. Glazer was hosting his own version of the last supper at United with tables loaded with bread and wine he had secured on tick.

He now had control of Rooney and the rest of the gang. Wayne had even been caught up in some aggro on the Thursday night, hours after Glazer had made his move. He was heading into Old Trafford for a charity dinner but had to flee back to his car when an angry mob pelted VIP guests with missiles. Police warned him they were worried about his safety and that of other guests. Some protesters shouted, 'Don't go in there and put money into Glazer's hands by drinking the beer.' Police made five arrests as they tried to control the hotheads who had broken away from the 2,000 or so United supporters who had been protesting peacefully outside the ground.

Rooney was shaken up by the ill-conceived ploy. Just how did having a go at the club's only world-class player get at Glazer? How did disrupting a *charity* event get at Glazer, for Christ's sake? And what was the point of the mass sit-down by fans on a busy road into Manchester? Would that hurt Glazer in Florida? No, the United fans had fought an inspired campaign against the American, but now their frustration was beginning to show. Inevitably. They had seen their club plundered by the Yankee pirate, and you could only feel sympathy for them and for Manchester United. The dream scenario would be a situation whereby Glazer got sick of the hassle from the fans, walked away after a troubled year and the club supporters and members took control in a co-operative trust set-up similar, say, to the one in place at Real Madrid.

A couple of days later, when tempers had subsided a little, there was much more measured talk about organising a mass boycott of club merchandise and that of major club sponsors Vodafone and Nike, and attempting to line up a set of alternative commercial deals for fans. That was more like it: let Glazer destroy himself with the continual verbal garbage his family and PR people were putting out. Indeed, it only took 24 hours before Glazer's son, Joel, put his foot in it. He said, 'We are delighted to make this offer to acquire one of the pre-eminent football clubs in the world. We are long-term sports investors and avid Manchester United fans. Our intention is to work with the current management, players and fans to ensure Manchester United continue to develop and achieve even greater success.'

Avid United fans? Mark Longden, spokesman for the Independent Manchester United Supporters Association, had something to say about that on behalf of the real avid United fans. He said, 'That statement is an insult to human intelligence. Does this guy really think anyone will actually believe him? Maybe it should not be a surprise given what has gone before, but the ignorance of the Glazers about ordinary Manchester United fans is truly astonishing.' Indeed it was.

It then emerged that Joel would run the club and that he intended to be an 'active' owner in the style of Roman Abramovich. He promised he would sit in the directors' box for the first home game of the 2005–06 season: no doubt he would be amazed by the welcome he would get. I recommended he snapped up one of those hard hats builders wear on sites and some reinforced earplugs. Shareholders United's chairman Nick Towle also warned the Glazers they were in for a rough ride. He said, 'Life is not going to be at all easy for them. I don't think they realise the full scale of the reception that awaits them. We can't stop him gaining majority control, but the hardcore fans will not give in this battle.'

There were some voices arguing that Glazer – who had once been described by an American judge as a 'snake in sheep's clothing' – should be given a chance: that he would not sink £272 million of his own money into a club he would deliberately run down. Munich survivor Harry Gregg said, 'I can't believe the statements coming from some fans that the Glazer takeover marks the worst day in United's history. I think that is totally misplaced. Many fans are against him, but I won't prejudge anybody.'

Like Glazer, Rooney was also having a rough ride – literally – as the last Premiership match of the season at Southampton and the FA Cup final loomed. Not only had he been harassed by angry fans at the charity bash, but he was in trouble with the police after a crash in his BMW X5. He had been in a collision with a Nissan Primera driven by a 45-year-old woman, who suffered minor whiplash injuries. The United star, who had just splashed out £5,000 on a personalized number plate 'WAZ 8', escaped unhurt but faced a charge of driving without due care and attention. If found guilty, he could be banned and face a fine of up to £5,000.

Then, from nowhere, a voice emerged telling the world to leave little Wayne alone. It was from his beloved gran – a wonderful, spritely 74 year old called Pat Morrey – who had had a bellyful of the constant jibes directed in Wayne's direction. In a letter to the *Liverpool Echo*, she stormed:

> Wayne isn't as bad as people make out. There's a lot of goodness in my grandson. I don't know why the press keep picking on him. He just gets singled out for bad treatment all the time. OK, he gets angry on the football field, but he's a very shy person when you meet him and he never swears in front of his family.
>
> There are many football players that swear, but the cameras always zoom in on him. Why can't people see the good side of my grandson?

She ended the note, 'So please find the good in my grandson instead of pulling him down,' before signing off 'his loving Grandma'. She was spurred into action by reports earlier in the month that Rooney had been dropped from a schools Football Association match after officials ruled he was not a good role model for youngsters. It was touching and emphasised the bonds of loyalty that tied Wayne and Coleen closely with their respective families.

Forced to live in an almost *Truman Show*-style existence since the age of 17, the couple had coped remarkably well with fame and the ever-increasing demands placed upon them. Put it this way: by the age of 21, the much admired John Terry, the newly-crowned Player of the Year and future England captain, had done much more than swear and pull faces. He had disgraced himself by mocking US tourists during a booze bender with four other players at a Heathrow hotel the day after the September 11 terrorist outrages. And he had been arrested and charged – though eventually cleared – after a fracas with security staff at a London club. Now, in the same week as the Rooney grandma letter, he was pictured on the front page of the *Sunday People* urinating into a pint glass at a nightclub bar. The incident happened in 2002, when he was 21 – two years older than Rooney – so maybe it is time to get real with Rooney. As his old gran says, he is a good lad, not half as bad as some would paint him. And Coleen is a great girl, too. Give 'em a bit of credit.

Rumours from Old Trafford suggested the couple were thinking of getting hitched that year, maybe in a surprise ceremony in the summer. They would have to be quick. United's failure to finish as runners-up in the Premiership meant pre-season would start two weeks earlier on 27 June instead of 10 July.

On 15 May, Rooney and Co. headed for Southampton to bring down the curtain on a disappointing league campaign. It was an emotional day at St Mary's as United won 2–1, condemning Saints to life outside the top flight for the first time in 27 years. Rooney was again United's man of the match, continuing his excellent run of form in 2005. He didn't score, but he did pull the strings for those around him. A fine 19th-minute header from Darren Fletcher – prospering on a day he did not have to play nursemaid to the rested Keane – and a predatory goal on the hour from van Nistelrooy killed off Saints.

John O'Shea had put Saints ahead with an own goal on ten minutes. I was told that in Florida Joel had grumbled at Malcom for celebrating the goal. 'What you so happy for?' he said.

'Well, ain't that made it one to zero to our franchise?' Malcolm had apparently replied.

Funnily enough, United's other American, keeper Tim Howard, was also grinning. Despite an inconsistent season, and being left out for Roy Carroll against Saints, he was the first player to benefit from the Glazer takeover, winning a two-year extension to his deal. Ryan Giggs then signed a two-year deal that would most likely see him finish his career at Old Trafford.

Roy Keane was hardly in celebratory mood after the Saints match. He made a fool of himself while warming down. Keane, an unused substitute, had reacted to chants directed at him from the relegated club's disappointed fans by pointing down and waving goodbye. This was the man who would apparently be manager of Manchester United one day. In the event, he was escorted down the tunnel like a sulky kid.

Luckily, Cardiff and the FA Cup final was on the horizon. Memories flooded back of the 1979 final between United and Arsenal. Then, the Gunners led 2–0 with just five minutes left after first-half goals from Brian Talbot and Frank Stapleton. Gordon McQueen and Sammy McIlroy grabbed late goals to make it all square, but, with the final whistle imminent, Alan Sunderland sneaked in for the winner that broke Mancunian hearts. Could this year's showdown be as exciting? It certainly had all the ingredients with the bitter rivalry and the fact that one of the clubs would end trophy-less.

Here were two giants of the game desperately scrapping for the leftovers at King José's table, when they should have been loftily digesting the main course. It brought to mind one of the greatest ever put downs in football journalism from Euro 2000 when Germany and England met in a group match. Neil Rowlands, a colleague of mine on *The Sun*, working at the time for football365.com, made the brilliant observation that the match was akin to two bald men fighting over a comb. How the mighty had fallen. Similarly, Ferguson and Wenger had taken on the role of the baldies in combat for 2005's comb, both forced to eat humble pie after previously claiming the FA Cup was a tiresome irrelevance in their pursuit of world domination. No, now it was suddenly an important trophy, one that, if won, would prove their season had still been a success. Pull the other one, guys.

United, led by Keane, trooped on to the Millennium Stadium pitch with Ferguson's words of doom ringing in their ears. He told them they had to 'fucking win', it was as simple as that. Balls it up, and they would all be in the manure. It was claimed that they had already lost upwards of £25,000 apiece for their failure to finish as runners-up in the Premiership, and a defeat in Cardiff would cost them more hefty bonuses. The two truly world-class players on the pitch were Rooney and Arsenal's José Antonio Reyes. The Spaniard had criticised Wayne after United's October win over Arsenal, but by now he had realised the class of the English boy wonder. He went straight to Wayne to shake his hand before kick-off and had elaborated upon his growing respect before the match, saying, 'Rooney is an incredible player, especially when you think about his age. He is very strong and skilful, and I like the way he thinks on the pitch. He is the future of the game in England.' It was a commendable tip of the hat, and all eyes were on the two men as the match kicked off. If anybody could produce something out of the ordinary, it was surely one of these two.

In the event, they did. Rooney was the man of the match for a performance that was powered by tenacity, genius, vision, touch, skill and the force of a bull. If United had lifted the Cup, as they certainly deserved to do, it could even have ended up being known as the Rooney Final. Reyes, on the other hand, became the second man to be sent off in an FA Cup final for hacking down Ronaldo (again). Rooney, playing most of the match on the right wing, took Ashley Cole to the cleaners, and that is saying something, for the full-back is arguably the best at his job in the world. Cole was forced to resort to ugly tactics on 17 minutes. His horrible challenge on Wayne sent the teenager sprawling over on to his back and earned Cole a booking. Patrick Vieira had also attempted to psyche out Rooney as early as the second minute, his rough challenge bludgeoning him to the ground.

Wayne truly came into his own, for a five-minute period, twenty-seven minutes into the match. He had three tremendous efforts on goal that could all have easily penetrated the Gunners' defence. The first was the goal that never was. Rooney was set up by a fine lay off from the once again impressive Darren Fletcher, only for keeper Jens Lehmann to foil the Wazza and Dazza show with his outstretched foot. Rio Ferdinand slotted home the rebound, but Ruud van Nistelrooy was clearly offside. Two minutes later, Wayne was tormenting the Gunners again. This time Ruud set him, up but Lehmann was again the boy wonder's equal, clawing a thunderbolt over the bar.

Then, in the best move of the lot, on the half-hour, Paul Scholes brilliantly executed a training ground move, sending over a corner for Wayne to volley at goal. The thunderous effort was a re-run of Rooney's wonder goal against Newcastle – the one he dubbed 'his best ever' – only this time it soared over and wide.

Considering this was Wayne's first cup final, he was remarkably cool. He had been nervous before his United debut the previous October but admitted he felt no fear before this showdown. His other major contributions came just after the hour and three-quarters of the way through the game. In the first instance, he forced his way towards goal and beautifully camouflaged his movements, making out as if he were going to pass, and then rifling the ball against the right-hand post, much to the relief of the bemused Lehmann. In the second, he showed how respected he is in this team. Keane may have been the captain on paper, but Rooney was now its spiritual leader. Wayne and Roy both weighed up a free-kick on the edge of the Arsenal box and Wayne shooed his skipper away, as if he were the man. Well, he was really, wasn't he? Proof of it, if needed, was in Keane's reaction. The eternal tough guy simply walked away meekly.

It had been built up as the latest battle between Arsenal and United, but, for the most part, it never lived up to that billing.

Sure, it was a compelling fixture, but Arsenal's surprising lack of bottle and attacking motivation made it almost as one-sided a match as the one United had won 12 months earlier against Millwall. There had also been fears about pitch invasions to protest about the Glazer takeover. In the event, the United fans limited their protests to dressing in black and waving a few flags berating Glazer. As the team played in black, the shirts protest did not register with the Glazers, who had the match beamed live into their Florida home, at 10 a.m. their time. The only flag Glazer saw in the Millennium Stadium made him smile and assume all would be OK: it said, 'Manchester United Buccaneers'. Of course, he did not know it was a put down by the Arsenal fans, and son Joel would have been the last person to bring him in on the joke after persuading him to rack up £790 million to buy the club. Glazer also wore a wide smile at the end of it all. Sure, United had lost, but at least that saved him a tidy sum on win bonuses.

For me it was a personal hands-up time. I had knocked Ferguson over his persistent team tinkering and tactics, but in Cardiff, on 21 May 2005, he was spot on. Before kick-off, I had bemoaned the choice of Fletcher to nursemaid Keane, instead of Giggs, but the inclusion of the talented young Scot thwarted any ambitions of purposeful attacking play Arsenal may have entertained. I take my hat off to you, Sir Alex, it was an inspired move, although I still question your decision to often use Fletcher to do Roy Keane's leg work. Put him next to Michael Ballack or Gennaro Gattuso in the centre, play Rooney in the hole or as a striker and you could have one hell of a team.

Van Nistelrooy's poor vein of form had continued at Cardiff where he missed three sitters, including a howler in extra time. Would he ever be the player he once was? He deserved more time – another season – as did Ferguson: if only as a mark of respect for their extraordinary past endeavours for the club. It would be a tragedy for player and club if the plethora of injuries Ruud had picked up over the last five years were to curtail a remarkably gifted and brave career. One other point about the players: Rio Ferdinand had been so impressive, it looked as if he could easily have dealt with Dennis Bergkamp and Reyes in his favourite armchair and slippers (we'll forget the pipe). His tears at the climax touched me. Maybe this was a good time to move on for both the fans and the man some of them had caustically nicknamed the Peckham Penguin.

The stats pointed to the enormous attacking gulf between the sides on the day. Maybe inevitable, given the Gunners were without key man Thierry Henry. Arsenal had five shots (one on target), United had twenty (eight on target); the Gunners had just one corner, United had twelve. Yet Arsenal had won the 2005 FA Cup five–four on penalties after it had ended 0–0 after 120 minutes. It had been the first FA Cup final ever to be decided on penalties – with Paul Scholes missing for United – and the first to end goalless since 1912. One other rather surprising fact: the Gunners had also won the possession battle, with 55.5 per cent as opposed to United's 44.5 per cent.

Sure, United had been mugged, and Arsenal were hardly worthy winners, but, in terms of success, United had done worse this season than the one before. On both occasions, they had finished third in the Premiership, but in 2004 they at least had the FA Cup to parade around the city. Afterwards, Ferguson was bristling, promising his team would bounce back. He particularly praised Rooney, the team's top scorer that term with 17 goals and United's undoubted player of the season. Fergie said, 'We've always been the sort of team that is galvanised by defeat and adversity. We're that sort of team. We'll get ourselves off the ground; cup football can do that to you sometimes. We are a very good team, and in that form we can play against anybody. It was a really good performance, and we got our game together today. You could toss a coin for man of the match out of Wayne Rooney and Cristiano Ronaldo because they were great, the pair of them. There's a great future for those boys and Darren Fletcher as well. The season's over now, and we can reflect on what might have been as long as we like, but we have to look forward to next season now.'

United later drowned their sorrows at their hotel, the Vale of Glamorgan. Rooney knocked back a few beers and eventually managed a smile. Ronaldo was the star of the evening. He had persuaded two girls from the luxury hotel's leisure complex to join them during their 'celebration' meal. He couldn't stop chatting through 'a boring speech by the boss' and then asked the girls if they would like to carry on the night at a Cardiff club. They both smiled nervously at each other, and Ronaldo, picking up on their fears, pulled an older woman over to his side. 'It be OK', he pleaded, his face contorted like an innocent puppy. 'This is my mum, and she come everywhere with me.'

Sir Alex had much to think about as he headed for his summer holiday. Was this season merely a massive blip before the onslaught of further honours – as had been the case in 1998 when a blank season was followed by the Treble – or was this now going to be the norm for the world's biggest club? Football goes in cycles and United's uninterrupted monopoly at the top during the '90s was now under immense pressure. The genius of Mourinho, and the power of Chelsea's millions, were casting a huge shadow over Ferguson's dreams of a final winning flourish to a great career. My feeling was that, despite the potential highlighted in defeat in the FA Cup Final, Ferguson would never again win the Premiership or the Champions League: that Mourinho and the ever-impressive Rafa Benitez would call time on his reign. How ironic that Ferguson should be lauding a United display in defeat at Cardiff when supposed no-hopers Liverpool were preparing to lift the European Cup in Istanbul. Ironic and cruel. Ferguson had staked his reputation on winning the Champions League one more time, and it had impacted upon United's domestic campaign. Could he now be relied upon to resist the kind of domestic tinkering and tactical clangers that had cost United so dear this season? And, even then, could he outwit Mourinho? I doubt it.

A lack of future success, in turn, would eventually threaten Rooney's future at Old Trafford. As you've probably guessed, I love the boy. He has the talent to become United's – and England's – best player ever. As the season progressed, he reminded me more and more of Bobby Charlton: how the great bald one would break regally from midfield to attack and thunder home one of those mighty pile-drivers. Forget the red herring of Rooney's so-called suspect temperament, he has all it takes to line up alongside Maradona and Pelé as the greatest. We are all lucky to have him: to be witness to this remarkable man-boy's development.

But here comes the rub, and it makes worrying reading for United fans: this is a boy who was determined and *ruthless* enough to quit his hometown club – the club of his dreams – to join the hated red revolution up the East Lancashire Road. If he was ruthless enough to walk away from home comforts, he would also be ruthless enough to walk away from United to better himself. Even a middling talent like Steve McManaman has two European Cup medals on his mantelpiece after his stint at Madrid, while loyal old Alan Shearer's cupboard remains bare. Here was a boy with more talent than the two combined, who had left Everton for glory and ended up in his first season at Manchester United with his only 'glory' being that of finishing one Premiership place above the Goodison outfit. If it continued like that, you could hardly blame him for moving on again. Could you?

19

BROKEN DREAMS

'I'm not scared of anything. I just play my own game.'
— Wayne Rooney, February 2006

'When I saw the stretcher come on for Wayne, I thought,
"Oh shit."'   — Joe Cole, 29 April 2006

'It would be a disaster for England if we had to go to the
World Cup without Wayne. He is idolised around the
country and is our main man. I think it is impossible to have
a successful World Cup without Wayne.'
— Steven Gerrard, 30 April 2006

TWELVE MONTHS ON AND ROONEY PROVED HE HAD STAYING
power as far as Manchester United was concerned. He would not
be leaving Old Trafford – for the moment at least. But April 2006
was not a good time to be Wayne Rooney or, for that matter, even
a fan of England's best player. His domestic season would end
much as it had the previous year – in misery at the hands of Chelsea.
On Saturday, 29 April, Wayne and United's hopes went up in
smoke. They began the match against their now biggest rivals
believing they could win at Stamford Bridge and go on to snatch

the Premiership title in what would have been a footballing miracle. That proved to be simply a pipe dream – Chelsea thrashed them 3–0 – and Wayne Rooney's season ended in tears, his World Cup hopes hanging by the slenderest of threads.

A fairly innocuous challenge by Paulo Ferreira on Rooney, with 11 minutes left, signalled the nightmare United and England fans had dreaded. Wayne collapsed to the ground, his face anguished and tears welling in his eyes, his right arm clutching the same right foot he had broken in the game against Portugal in Euro 2004. He left the field strapped to a stretcher, and, as he was carried off, fans from both sides applauded him sympathetically, all hoping it would not be the worst-case scenario. It would: Wayne had broken the base of the fourth metatarsal on his right foot. He would be out for six weeks – which would take him to the day of England's opening World Cup match against Paraguay on 10 June. And that was just the diagnosis of how long it would take for the injury to heal – beyond that he would need time to get match fit and make sure there were no further problems with the foot. When he broke the fifth metatarsal of the same foot in Euro 2004, it had taken 13 weeks to play again, and this time the news kept getting worse. A second fracture of the fourth metatarsal was discovered a few days after the first.

Following the Chelsea match, his teammates would find him crying with rage in the dressing-room – hardly surprising when you consider his lifetime ambition was to play in football's greatest tournament. A United insider told me, 'He was angry as hell and was kicking out at bins and the lockers with his left foot. He knows his body well – he knew he would probably not be going to the World Cup. It took the boss [Sir Alex Ferguson] to calm him down, telling him he had lots of time on his side, that he could still play in three, maybe four, World Cups, even if he did not make this one. Eventually he calmed down, saying he would make the latter stages of the tournament, but it was clear to see that he was heartbroken.'

Not much of a way to end his second season at Old Trafford – a season in which, for many matches, he had once again carried a transitional United. A season in which his sparkling form and determination had seen a United side not in the same league as some of Ferguson's previous incarnations push Chelsea to the wire. They had become a one-man band – much like the English national team. That was why his domestic rivals – Joe Cole of Chelsea and Steven Gerrard of Liverpool among them – were so devastated by his injury. Domestic rivals maybe, but also England teammates who knew that their World Cup hopes would be threatened with no Rooney. Even Chelsea's celebrations at securing back-to-back Premiership titles were slightly muted after the United match: the injury had taken the edge off it, leaving players and fans gutted.

In many ways, the injury summed up what Rooney is all about, just why he had become arguably the third best player in the world after Ronaldinho and Thierry Henry. Chelsea had been coasting to the title, and some of Rooney's United teammates – Rio Ferdinand among them – had seemed to be treating the occasion as if it did not really matter. As if it were just another end-of-season encounter. It was clearly not that for Wayne Rooney – with United on the end of a hammering and just 15 minutes left, the wonder boy was still full of running, still full of that massive commitment and edge that marks him out as *the* English player of his generation. Would Ferdinand have made the run Rooney did? Or the increasingly languid Ruud van Nistelrooy?

Were his United teammates chasers of lost causes? Hardly. They were players with other matters on their minds: perhaps like steering clear of any injuries that could threaten their participation in Germany 2006. This is why Rooney is special – he never gave up, never lost that competitiveness. It brought back fond memories of that time he went for a kickabout in the street in Croxteth after Everton's match with Arsenal in 2002 – a match in which he had scored the winner, thus ending the Gunners' unbeaten record. The kid was now 20, but the boy within the man burned as brightly as ever: this was the flame at the heart of the wonder of Rooney.

The boy loved his football. Full stop. He once told me he had never worried about getting injured – that to do so would endanger his game. He said he was confident that other players could not hurt him easily: he had great balance and his muscular presence meant he could not be easily knocked off the ball. He admitted it would be a personal tragedy if he missed out on the World Cup – it had been everything he had been working towards since those days as a nine year old with Copplehouse Juniors.

Bookmakers Ladbrokes immediately lengthened the odds of England winning the tournament from 6–1 to 7–1 following the announcement of the severity of Rooney's injury. Sir Bobby Robson summed up the feeling of national gloom when he said: 'It's depressingly sad. Without him we would go from possible World Cup winners to outsiders. We can't replace him. I don't think there's another player like him in the country – or even in Europe.' England coach Sven-Göran Eriksson claimed he would take Rooney if there was a slight chance he would be fit, but Sir Alex Ferguson then stepped in to make it clear that it would be *he* who would make the final decision, saying, 'We will do our best to get the boy to Germany, but if he is not fit, he is not going to go. In six weeks' time, Rooney will have another two weeks to get fit to play in the quarter-final of a World Cup. That is a wild dream. Sven saying he'll take Wayne fit or not was something we didn't want.'

So much passion, so many opinions, so many words over one 20-year-old footballer. At such a tender age, Wayne Rooney had come to represent so much to so many people. A nation's very hopes lay with the chances of a miracle improvement in that injured right foot. And no wonder: his domestic season with Manchester United had proved once again that he was the man for the big occasion. While David Beckham may have been the England skipper and Gary Neville wore the armband at United, by the end of the 2005–06 season Rooney had become the real leader of club and country, the true talisman who could provide glory for both if fit.

Indeed, the 2005–06 season had been a very successful one for Rooney before he was carried off at Stamford Bridge with just two Premiership matches to go. He had played in a total of 48 games for United, scoring 19 goals. His form throughout the season had been consistently excellent, so much so that he had won the United Player of the Year award for the first time and the PFA Young Player of the Year award for the second year in a row. Indeed, some had argued that his season had been so sensational he should have actually won the PFA Player of the Year award instead of Liverpool's Stevie Gerrard, his best mate when players got together for England duty.

The Red Devils had, on paper at least, also enjoyed a better season than the previous one. They had finished a place higher in the Premiership (runners-up) and had won the League (Carling) Cup. The Premiership finish meant they would not have to begin the 2006–07 season early – they were parachuted straight into the group stage of the Champions League, so, mercifully, no qualifiers in early August would be required. On the debit side, in 2005–06 they had crashed out of the Champions League before Christmas – finishing bottom of their group – and there were, quite rightly, questions over Sir Alex Ferguson's claim that the team which lost 3–0 at Chelsea in April 2006 was essentially the third great side of his 20-year tenure at the Theatre of Dreams.

Many – including myself – feared they actually represented a false dawn rather than the ushering in of a new era of success. The team lacked invention and security in central midfield throughout the season, and some of Sir Alex's decisions and purchases were as puzzling as the previous season. Getting rid of skipper Roy Keane on 18 November was perhaps the most mystifying – along with the £5.5 million purchase of Patrice Evra in the New Year. Keane was clearly not the player he had been over the years, but the manner of his departure left a particularly bitter taste in the mouth of most fans. Here was a man who had served club and Ferguson for 12 and a half years – a man who had given his heart and soul to both.

Some believed Ferguson's once favoured one was jettisoned by the United boss so that his new blue-eyed boy, Carlos Queiroz – known as Qantas to Keane and the boys – could survive. Roy and the Portuguese had been falling out for a 12-month period before the ultimate rift. Keane told friends he did not appreciate the training methods of Queiroz – softly-softly rather than up and at 'em – and believed that his tactics were also faulty. In my book *Roy Keane: Red Man Walking*, Roy is on record as saying that he felt the team were going nowhere fast under Queiroz. The Portuguese was becoming increasingly influential – towards November 2005 he was actually picking the team and deciding the tactics as Sir Alex took a back-seat role.

Now, don't get me wrong. Queiroz is a charming man and delightful company, as Sir Alex will testify: the two liked nothing better in 2005 and 2006 than to enjoy a glass of red, a slab of stilton and a late-night natter. Arguably, though, in 2005 his influence had led United into a dead end that saw them exiting the Champions League before Christmas and trailing Chelsea by 18 points.

Queiroz had seen off Keane, but Roy would still haunt him. A month after the Irishman's departure, Ferguson would return to the fore and change United's fortunes. He dropped the safety-first tactics of Queiroz – the stifling 4–5–1 – and put United back into the role of entertaining cavaliers, the very attacking traditions the fans had been brought up with. Roy Keane's ultimate legacy would be to free United of their shackles and set up their season for an outstanding finish. His criticism of Queiroz's negativity would cost him his job at Old Trafford but save the season from being a total damp squib.

Rooney was shocked and upset by Keane's departure. He told a friend, 'Roy had become like an older brother to me. I loved him, he stood for everything I wanted to be – he was passionate and would have died for his football. He loved Man United. I will really miss not having him around the place. I will miss not having him there if I need a chat about things.'

Rooney missed Keane so much that he travelled up to Scotland for the Glasgow derby at Ibrox to see his old mentor in action on Sunday, 12 February 2006. Roy, perhaps inevitably, was booked as Celtic went on to win 1–0. Afterwards, Wayne confirmed, 'I had never been to a Celtic–Rangers match before but had always wanted to see one. With Roy moving to Celtic, it was the ideal chance to do so. I loved the atmosphere, and the fans were great. Also, it was really good to see and talk to Roy again.' The fans loved him, too – it was heartwarming to see the Celtic end applaud as he took his seat among them.

If letting Keane go was hardly a sensible move, not having a replacement lined up for the old master bordered on the criminal.

Ferguson not only had no replacement, he did not seem to have an idea of whom he could turn to. To give the United manager his due, he did manage to persuade the Glazers to change their cutbacks policy – during the season they had sacked blue-collar workers at Old Trafford and encouraged the policy of farming out players on loan – as the New Year of 2006 arrived. But then he blew the £12 million the Glazers – known as the Three Stooges to the Old Trafford faithful – had reluctantly parted with on *two defenders*!

Ferguson brought in Nemanja Vidić for £7 million and Patrice Evra for £5.5 million. I am sure Vidić will become a useful asset at the club: he is the sort of no-nonsense centre-back United have long needed. But Evra? How does he fit into the scheme of things? Is Gabriel Heinze not good enough? Ferguson mumbled on about maybe trying out Evra in left midfield or left-wing, but, and here's the rub, shouldn't the £12 million have been spent on a replacement for Keane? Or at least have been put by until the summer and then put towards trying to secure a top-notch new man?

Surely it was sheer folly to spend it on two defenders when the positions they both usually played in were well covered? The folly meant United had to progress from January 2006 until the end of the season with no recognised central midfielders. Alan Smith, himself not a natural holding midfielder but a natural forward, broke his left leg and dislocated his ankle after falling awkwardly in the 1–0 FA Cup loss at Liverpool in February, and by the end of the season they were having to rely upon a makeshift central midfield pairing of defender John O'Shea and left-winger Ryan Giggs: a journeyman and a man approaching the end of his best playing days. It was a pathetic situation for the self-styled biggest football club in the world to be in.

You might say, well, how could it have been that bad if United eventually finished runners-up? The answer is this: the level of quality in the Premiership was distinctly poor during the season overall (apart from Chelsea and Liverpool) and United were carried for long periods of the campaign by Rooney and, to some extent, the rampaging runs of Ronaldo. If Ferguson had buttressed that central midfield nightmare area, who knows what might have happened – but the results would surely have been even better. All we know for definite is that after Keane departed, Ferguson owed a huge debt to Rooney. The Liverpudlian revelled in his attacking role but was also good enough to help plug that central midfield area when he had the chance. He was everywhere – just as Keane had once been.

What was Rooney's highlight of the domestic season? Winning the League Cup, or the Carling Cup as it is now dubbed. Not surprisingly, Wayne was named man of the match after a superlative show. He led poor Wigan a merry dance – and his influence was behind that rather damning 4–0 scoreline. It was the second time in their history that United had lifted the League Cup – and Rooney set them on their way, scoring the first goal after 33 minutes and the fourth on the hour. Throughout, he drove the team forward like a man possessed.

Rooney, who also won the man of the match award in the FA Cup final defeat by Arsenal the previous year, was 'absolutely delighted' with his winner's medal. He said, 'To win any trophy gives you a big buzz, and this is the best feeling I have ever had. It is so long since I won anything, you can probably understand why I feel the way I do. Hopefully, it will be two medals this season, because we are going to the World Cup with England looking to win it.'

He had gone 12 games without a goal before the cup final brace but made no mistake with his first goal, firing the ball home after a mix-up between Arjan de Zeeuw and Pascal Chimbonda. He had already hit the bar and completed his personal super show by tapping home from close range on 61 minutes after latching on to a Rio Ferdinand header. Rooney added, 'I signed for Manchester United to win trophies. We were disappointed to lose the FA Cup final last year. We remember how that felt, and we didn't want the same thing to happen again. Everyone knew we were in a no-win situation, but we have put on a performance and got the victory. We want to win every trophy we go for, and hopefully we can do even better next year.'

But was winning the trophy such a big deal? Wasn't this the cup Ferguson had once described as 'the Worthless Cup'? All of a sudden, it was as if United had lifted the Champions League Cup itself – not just the ordinary old League Cup. Ferguson grasped at the straw like a dying man desperately gasping at oxygen. No, this was not an acceptance that United had fallen from the big league – they had still won a trophy, and in Ferguson talk that was a success – after all, hadn't one trophy a season always been his mantra? Well, yes, but that did not usually boil down to the l'il 'ol Carling Cup, did it?

To an extent, you could understand Ferguson hyping up the trophy – he clearly did not relish the unhappy prospect of successive seasons without silverware for the first time in 17 years – but surely he could have brought a little perspective to it all rather than trying to hype up success in a tournament he had previously referred to with disdain? The fans looked sheepish as they 'celebrated' the win, but Ferguson was full of himself, claiming that winning the trophy would be the start of a bright new era for the club.

He blustered, 'You have to take winning one trophy – no matter what it is – as a successful season, purely because of the competition we face nowadays. We had a phenomenal spell in the 1990s, but from the moment we won the European Cup, there was a catch-up by other clubs who realised what it was possible for a British team to do. Money is being thrown at the Premiership now, not just by Manchester United and Chelsea, but by a lot of clubs who are under pressure to deliver and win trophies themselves. We are facing far stiffer opposition now than we were before. We all only have four possibilities to win anything, and there will be some big, big clubs, with great histories, who will not win a trophy this season.'

Writing in the *Daily Mail* the day before the final in Cardiff, Ian Ladyman perhaps better than anyone got to the heart of the matter: 'Desperate men can convince themselves of anything and with the Glazer family in town . . . Ferguson is desperate to win at the Millennium Stadium.' In *The Guardian* on the same day, the excellent David Lacey's boot landed with an even harder thud. He proclaimed: 'It is safe to say that the last trophy Sir Alex Ferguson has ever wanted to win is the League Cup. Yet if Manchester United beat Wigan . . . the occasion may come to be remembered as the last trophy the club won under his management.'

By the end of the 2005–06 season, United had finished behind Chelsea (again), were knocked out of the Champions League before Christmas and out of the FA Cup by Liverpool. In the cases of Chelsea and Liverpool, they would both surely only get even better. Ferguson would certainly need to come up with a couple of world-class central midfield reinforcements in the summer of 2006 if United were not to lag even further behind. In Rooney, he had hit the jackpot – he had a gem, as long as the mercurial Scouser stayed at the club.

Winning the League Cup – in the absence of any other trophies – may indeed have been the highlight Rooney had claimed it to be, but, as we asked in the previous chapter, 12 months earlier, how long would he put up with chicken feed? How long would England's best player put up with being second best? Twelve months on and you could still hardly complain if he eventually said enough is enough and walked away. Well, could you?

In January 2006, Ferguson was at least honest enough to admit that normal rules did not apply when it came to Rooney – in effect, he was conceding that the boy was the greatest natural talent he had ever worked with. Ferguson has previously played an ultra-cautious game with youngsters like Ryan Giggs and even Ronaldo – resting them when he felt the need and keeping them out of the spotlight as much as possible. He admitted that would not be the case with the unique talent known as Wayne Rooney.

In that month, Rooney won the Carling Premiership Player of the Month award – at a time when he had played more games in the season than any member of the United squad other than Edwin van der Saar and Rio Ferdinand. It was then that Ferguson felt it appropriate to comment – making it clear he felt Wayne could cope whereas other youngsters would have struggled. He said, 'Over the years, there has been a pattern we have followed for players who are not physically developed. Ryan Giggs was only a scrawny little lad when he came through, and he didn't play every week. Neither did Darren Fletcher. But when you see Wayne's physique, it is completely different, and it makes it much easier. He is a fit young lad in any case, and, like any 20 year old, he thinks he can get up every morning and run 20 miles.'

The plaudits were well deserved during a season that included a string of fine performances. The best? Well, the League Cup final show was obviously a masterclass, but the game against Newcastle at Old Trafford on Sunday, 12 March 2006 arguably surpassed even that. It was a match United would win 2–0, with both goals coming from Rooney's boot. Amazingly, the brace represented his first goals in the Premiership in 2006, but they were certainly worth waiting for. The boy was in the sort of mood where he could have taken on – and probably beaten – the Toon on his own. His first goal came on eight minutes when he darted in to intercept Peter Ramage's backpass and chipped the ball superbly over keeper Shay Given. Four minutes later, he again got the better of the hapless Ramage to fire the ball home from John O'Shea's pass.

Rooney's showing at Villa Park just before Christmas also merits a mention. He executed a wonderful strike following Ruud van Nistelrooy's accomplished opener, as United made it 19 points out of a possible 21 with a 2–0 win. Van Nistelrooy set it up for Wayne with a short pass, but the shot in off the far post was simply world class. It was Rooney's tenth goal of the season and his third in two games but, even more importantly, it wiped away the clouds of gloom that had been lurking over Old Trafford for ten days since the club's depressing exit from the Champions League at the first stage.

The 2–1 defeat in Lisbon to Benfica had thrown United into meltdown and threatened Ferguson with an early exit of his own. At Villa Park he was clearly irritated by the posse of photographers out to get a picture of him that would have an accompanying caption querying whether it was his last stand. In the event, Rooney saved him from that embarrassment, and Ferguson admitted, 'After a defeat like the Benfica one, you can either wither and die or get up off your backsides, get out on the pitch and do something about it. I'm very pleased with the performance, and Ruud and Wayne are starting to combine well with each other.'

Rooney confirmed that the Champions League loss in Benfica and the FA Cup defeat at Liverpool were, along with his injury at

Stamford Bridge, the worst moments of his 2005–06 season. Paul Scholes had given United an early lead in Benfica's Stadium of Light, but the light was to go out early on the Red Devils' European campaign after goals from Geovanni and Beto. The dismal night marked the first time United had failed to emerge safely from the group stages of Europe's elite competition for 11 years. Rooney told a friend he was 'gutted' and just wanted to get home to fiancée Coleen.

The only consolation about the defeat at Liverpool in February was that at least he would have less miles to travel home than from Lisbon. Again, Wayne was 'sick to the pit of his stomach' by the loss, admitting to a friend, 'With us being out of Europe and unlikely to catch Chelsea in the league, I had set my heart on winning the FA Cup. It was a real sickener to lose at Anfield – and it was even worse that we lost to Liverpool.' No real surprise there. Wayne, born and bred in the city, had never had time for the red brigade – his heart had always belonged to the blue of his former Everton. The defeat again rammed home the folly of Ferguson's decision to ditch Keane, and Phil Neville the previous August, and not buy any central midfield replacements. With Alan Smith carried off injured, at one stage United were 'boasting' a central midfield of Fletcher, Richardson and Park up against Liverpool's powerhouse trio of Gerrard, Hamann and Sissoko. Hardly surprising United suffered, was it?

Away from the pitch, Wayne was again front-page news. There were allegations of him smoking and drinking in nightclubs. I spoke to one of Wayne's inner circle about the smoking and was told this: 'Yes, occasionally in the past he has had a fag when he has had a few beers, but, no, it is not a regular thing, and he even packed in the occasional ones because he wanted to keep his fitness up.' As for the drinking – well, show me a lad of 19–20 who does not like a drink now and again after work, and I'll show you a fibber. Then there was the gambling. It was alleged he owed £700,000 – that he had run up the debt in the five months leading up to February 2006 by betting on horses, dogs and football with Stephen Smith, a business associate of his fellow England striking partner, Michael Owen. It was even suggested Rooney and Owen had fallen out over the betting and that it had led to a bad atmosphere in the England camp ahead of the World Cup in Germany.

I was reliably informed that the duo still got on very well – indeed, that they had laughed off the suggestion that they had fallen out. A cash arrangement satisfactory to all concerned was also thrashed out between Rooney and Smith – and that was the end of the matter. Former footballer and gambler Steve Claridge perhaps summed up the 'betting scandal' best of all, pointing out that if Wayne had learned his lesson, no real harm would have been done – after all, and I know this sounds a bit of a cop-out but it is still true, £700,000 to Rooney is like £200 to the normal man in the street.

Claridge said, 'What he's got to do, though, is learn his lesson. I don't care who he is or what he does, in 20 years' time if he is still betting like that he won't have a penny to his name. I learnt my lesson. It took me a long time, but I did. I spent more than I should have – it's as simple as that. But like everybody, it gets to the point where you realise you can't win.'

Wayne's relationship with fiancée Coleen was going well, and they were excited as their £3.5 million dream house in Prestbury, Cheshire, neared completion. As this book went to print in July 2006, they had even enlisted the aid of Laura McCree, the star of the BBC's flagship lifestyle programme *Changing Rooms*, to sort out the interior design. Quite a gamble that for two traditionalists like Wayne and Coleen – Laura is best remembered for outrageous designs, including one that once left a shocked householder reduced to tears when the room transformation was revealed. She even admitted to sometimes being called 'Loony McCree' and conceded she had no time for conventional kitchens or dull living rooms. Expect the results in one of those flashy *Hello!* magazine spreads next year . . .

And how was life with Coleen, who had now, as we anticipated earlier in this book, become a star in her own right, with contracts worth around £3 million secured in the last 12 months? Wayne said, 'She's great, I love her to bits. I get told off now and again by her for kicking a ball around the house, but I have to have one near me. I'll have one in the kitchen for when I'm getting myself a drink or one on the couch to juggle when I am watching the telly. I will take one to play with my dog.'

So how would Wayne sum up his 2005–06 season? Apart, of course, from the anguish over the injury that had hit his England hopes, was he happy with life at Old Trafford and in Manchester? He said, 'Definitely. Old Trafford feels like home – I am really settled. The lads and everyone associated with United have been great to me. That means I can concentrate on my football and do my best on the pitch in every game.'

And what of the future – how would Rooney feel if, when his foot is fully recovered, his form was such that he one day won the World Player of the Year award, like his idol of the current era Ronaldinho. 'To be in the same sentence as Ronaldinho is brilliant, because, the way he is going, he could be up there alongside Maradona and Pelé as one of the best ever. I hope that in years to come people will say I was one of the best, but for now all I am trying to do is be the very best I can be.'

20

THE END OF THE WORLD

SO MIRACLES DO HAPPEN – OR WERE SOME VERY UNDERHAND tricks being played on us in the build-up to Germany 2006? How else do you explain Wayne Rooney's amazing participation – amazing in the sense that he actually *did* play – in the World Cup? Injured on 29 April, just 47 days later on 15 June he was back in the England team as they struggled to make history of a defiant Trinidad and Tobago. But was the injury actually not as bad as Manchester United had initially made out? Had Sir Alex Ferguson exaggerated in the hope that Rooney would not go to Germany? Rooney's return against the so-called Soca Warriors marked the end of one of the longest drawn-out farces in English football as the 20 year old emerged as a second-half substitute to ignite his country's stuttering show through the sheer force of his presence.

The drama had built up to a crescendo in the weeks that followed 29 April, with Sven-Göran Eriksson playing the part of a desperate Judy and Sir Alex Ferguson starring as the grumpy Mr Punch. Both sides were adamant about their positions: Eriksson was going to take his man to Germany whatever; Ferguson was determined the boy would not be risked. He was essential to the future of both men; indeed, he could determine how they would go down in history. Without Rooney, Eriksson would most likely fail on the ultimate world stage, while without his talisman to start the next season at Old Trafford, Ferguson could be looking down the barrel of a gun if Chelsea sprinted into the distance.

The pre-tournament sideshow erupted on Wednesday, 7 June, when Rooney returned to England for a scan on his broken foot. Amid TV scenes akin to those that could have accompanied the attempted assassination of a member of the royal family or the prime minister, Wayne flew into Manchester in the morning on a private jet to be taken to a private hospital for the all-important scan. After a few hours, he emerged and travelled to Liverpool to see fiancée Coleen and her family. He finally returned to the hospital late that afternoon but did not come back out until 7.45 p.m., as lawyers for the FA and United argued long and hard about the results of the scan.

Rooney was caught like piggy in the middle, but he refused to allow United to end his World Cup dream. 'He was really pissed off with it all,' a source close to Rooney told me. 'He had spent the whole day buggering about, waiting for the results, and when the results were announced, it was clear that, at worst, he could rejoin the squad and work on his fitness. But Ferguson had told the United team to go for the best deal for the club, and they were trying desperately to make sure a deal was struck that would mean he could not play until at least the second round. That made Rooney mad, and he was like a caged lion in that hospital, prowling around until things were sorted.'

Sir Alex had made a rare faux pas: he had decided not to break off his five-week holiday in the south of France to make sure he got what he wanted. That left United at a disadvantage. Without the boss's legendary temper and single-mindedness, the club did not reach an agreement to their advantage. Rooney returned to Germany and – despite a reportedly heated telephone conversation between Eriksson and Ferguson later that night – the matter of exactly where and when the star man would play would now be decided by the England manager.

When Rooney arrived back at the England base in Baden-

Baden, he was full of smiles and bear-hugged men like Stevie Gerrard and Frank Lampard, telling them, 'The big man is back in town!' Eriksson added to the upbeat mood, declaring, 'For a month I had been telling you Wayne Rooney will be fit.' In France, Sir Alex was probably cursing the Swede, and United warned the FA they could face a major compensation claim if the boy wonder was injured again.

So what to make of it all? Was the injury not as bad as first thought and certainly as initially presented by Sir Alex and United? At the end of April, Ferguson had told Wayne he probably had little chance of making the World Cup finals and should console himself with the thought that there would be many more to come. But Eriksson, for so much of his five-year tenure as England boss a weak, indecisive, negative leader, suddenly changed tact and became a high-stakes gambler.

I was told in March by one of Eriksson's few allies that he would take Theo Walcott to the World Cup, ostensibly as a fall-back for Michael Owen, a fact I reported in my *FourFourTwo* magazine column 'The Insider' to much laughter and disdain. Then the same pal of Sven's told me after Rooney's injury that the Swede would take him whatever: that Sven did not believe England could reach the latter stages of the World Cup without him. And so it proved after Wayne's whistle-stop return to Manchester for the scan on 7 June. Eriksson was apparently privately convinced that Ferguson had been trying to pull the wool over his eyes with the Rooney injury – alleging he had had made it out to be worse than it was to keep Rooney out of the World Cup – and, given Sven's new carefree approach now that he would be leaving the England job in July, it had hardened his resolve to take Rooney. He had had quite enough of Ferguson's interference over the years, thank you.

So it was that Wayne rejoined the England camp for the tournament, and he was indebted to Eriksson for standing his corner. A point for the future: if Eriksson were ever to take up a job at one of the world giants like, say, Real Madrid, he would have Rooney's ear – United fans, and Sir Alex, take note!

My sympathies, though, lay with Sir Alex over this one:

however you try to play down the impact of the injury, it was surely folly to rush Wayne back in the group stages. England had other big names, didn't they? They could surely reach the second round without him, and, even then, given that it was Ecuador they were up against, a strong argument could have been made to keep him for the quarter-finals. This would have let the foot heal completely and, just as importantly, bought some more time so that no other injury could follow on as a consequence of the initial one?

One obvious drawback to this was Wayne himself. He was born to play football and, despite the riches he was rapidly accumulating, remained to a large extent the kid who wanted to play in the back streets with his mates. Just because he had broken his foot, why should he be sidelined? My source told me, 'He was raring to go, and you have got to imagine how difficult it was for Eriksson to keep him away from the action. He was constantly nagging at him, asking him when he could play – like a kid asking a parent when he would get his ice cream.' Fair enough, but isn't it the role of a truly great coach to lay down the law?

No, I still go with Sir Alex. Rooney should have been kept back, straining on the leash. In my opinion, Eriksson gave in to the boy's constant pleas and also avoided his responsibilities by throwing the lad into the World Cup so quickly after such an awful injury. Sometimes Wayne can seem uncomfortably similar to Paul Gascoigne in that desire to play whatever. Remember when Gazza saw red in Italia 90? When he earned that booking in the semi against the Germans, the one that would have ruled him out of the final if England had got there? And how Gary Lineker pointed to the bench, with the insinuation being that Gazza's 'head had gone'? Fast forward to Germany 16 years later – Wayne was desperate to play, and only Eriksson could have delayed his return. It could be argued that it was a dereliction of duty that he did not.

Of course, Eriksson was also thinking selfishly. After the depressing 1–0 win over Paraguay, he knew England were lacking inspiration. Then, as it stood 0–0 against Trinidad and

Tobago after 58 excruciating minutes, the Swede threw Rooney on, probably as much for reasons of self-preservation as anything. This was a match he needed to win if he was to reach the semis – the yardstick by which he himself had said his reign would be judged after two disappointing surrenders in the quarter-finals of the 2002 World Cup and Euro 2004.

Gary Neville summed up the folly of throwing Rooney into the fray too early when he said, 'You have to put this into reality. He's got a broken bone in his body, and it is not just the actual break, it's the mental thing. There are other things that surround breaking a bone, such as picking up little niggles coming back.

'People are getting excited because he is training with the physiotherapists, but many players do that coming back from injury. Physiotherapists can do many things, but it is a different ball game when you're actively involved with other players. It's a different level of fitness, and when you get to matches, it's a different level of fitness again. There are many obstacles before we even think of him getting into a match situation.'

No doubt the United skipper was providing a voice for his boss Sir Alex Ferguson within the England camp, but he did have a very valid point. Neville would add, 'I want Wayne to take part . . . but, equally, I want to make sure we have 11 fit players. If Wayne is not quite right, we have to bring in Jermain [Defoe]. We need four fit strikers going into this tournament, and there can be no room for sentiment. I want Wayne to be here, but I want fit players alongside me, just as they would want a fit right-back.'

It would be ironic that Neville himself would get injured at the start of the tournament, but, even looking at it at the time, it was clearly a poor decision by Eriksson not to take Defoe to Germany. He could have stuck with his two men returning from injury – Rooney and Owen; his big target man – Crouch; and his secret weapon – Walcott; and still have taken the Spurs striker. All he needed to do was leave the extra midfielder, Jermaine Jenas, at home.

The normally cautious Alan Hansen, writing in the *Daily Telegraph*, was one of those who were following the Eriksson line

– he also advocated using Rooney in the group stages. On Monday, 12 June, he wrote:

> I watched Rooney kicking a ball around the pitch, clearly back to full fitness, if not full match fitness. His energy levels were amazing, and it was the type of moves he was making – not just running in a straight line – that showed how big a stride he has made. If his foot was right, he could play tomorrow, and certainly he could be fit to face Trinidad and Tobago on Thursday.

He was to have his wish, and Rooney's inclusion, along with that of Aaron Lennon, would transform England's performance – Peter Crouch and Steven Gerrard scoring as they beat the Caribbean nation 2–0. They were the first goals from England players in the championship, as the 1–0 win over Paraguay was secured by an own goal by the South Americans' skipper Carlos Gamarra.

After the defeat of Trinidad and Tobago, Frank Lampard made a plea to the press to end their obsession with Rooney and his fitness. He said, 'It was a lift to see Wayne back against Trinidad. It lifted the fans. So much has been said about Wayne: "Will he play, won't he play?" and that kind of thing. We always knew the moment he came on it would be a lift for the fans and the team, because he is a very important player for us, a great player even at his age. We all know that. It was a good lift for us, but we have become obsessed with the Wayne Rooney situation. Now he is fit, it is about the team – and Wayne is a very important member of the team.'

Of course, it was a vain plea. Rooney was the star of the side, the fulcrum, and he made the best copy for Fleet Street's hungry hacks. After the Trinidad and Tobago match, Eriksson gave the players a day off. They visited their partners and relatives who were staying in the five-star Brenner Park hotel in Baden-Baden, close to England's base at the magnificent Buhlerhohe Schlosshotel. Again, all eyes – and camera lenses – were focused on Wayne. In the hotel, he had often fidgeted and found it difficult to stay still – he was not the kind who was easily confined to barracks. His close mate Stevie Gerrard had kept an eye on him, telling him to relax a bit more, to take it easy.

Rooney enjoyed his day off because it was a day out. He met up with fiancée Coleen for lunch at a local restaurant called the Löwenbräu Gasthaus, where they sat outside and celebrated his return to action by devouring rump steak and chips, all washed down with a glass of Stich den Buben Riesling.

He laughed and held Coleen's hand but grimaced when people approached him for his autograph. The boy needed a bit of sanctuary, a bit of peace and quiet to come to terms with what would be a growing involvement in the tournament. A source told me, 'He is usually top man when it comes to giving out autographs and talking to the public, but he had had the press on his back for weeks and after finally returning from the broken foot really just wanted to just relax with Coleen.' Eventually, Wayne gave up, realising he would not be left alone, and he and Coleen went back to the Buhlerhohe Schlosshotel, where they spent the afternoon relaxing on a veranda at the back with Joe Cole and his girlfriend Carly Zucker.

Next stop was Cologne and the match with Sweden – and the Scandinavian journalists were as anxious as the Swedish team when Eriksson announced well in advance of the match that Wayne would face them. Peter Wennman, a columnist for *Aftonbladet*, admitted they feared his impact and made a glorious comparison between Rooney and Michael Owen, whom Wayne had replaced against Trinidad and Tobago. Wennman said:

> To remove Michael Owen and put on Rooney was like taking out a moped from the garage and replacing it with a Harley Davidson. It was like an electrical shock through the entire squad. Suddenly someone collected the ball and played it on the ground.

Dagens Nyheter's columnist Jan Lewenhagen was also impressed with Rooney's impact. He said: 'England with Rooney are a different team – a lot less predictable.'

The match itself, however, summed up England's continuing failings under Eriksson – epitomising the 'good first half, not so good second half' mantra that he repeated throughout his tenure. For the first 45 minutes, England, with Rooney back on board, were steaming. Joe Cole was the star of their night – opening the scoring with a fabulous 35-yard volley in the first half that looped over the hapless Andreas Isaksson into the top corner.

Yet after the break, England reverted to type, struggling to keep their rhythm, and panting in the humidity of the Cologne night. They looked knackered, and it was no surprise when Marcus Allbäck headed the Swedes level. Cole saved the day again, crossing late on for Steven Gerrard to head home, but Sweden equalised in the last minute when Henrik Larsson slotted the ball into the goal after some dreadful defending to make it 2–2.

It meant the Swedish hoodoo over England continued – it was now 38 years since the English had last beaten them, a dismal record dating back to 22 May 1968. That along with the knee injury that put Michael Owen out of the competition added to the feeling that all was not as it should be in the England camp, despite the fact they had finished at the top of Group B and secured the fairly easy, at least on paper, second-round clash with Ecuador.

Rooney, starting his first ever World Cup match, had looked much sharper than against Trinidad and Tobago. Inevitably, however, he faded after the break as his lack of fitness took its toll, and Gerrard replaced him after 69 minutes. That did not please our Wayne. He kicked a water bottle, punched the dugout and threw his boots away. It was the tantrum of a spoilt child – and one England could have done without in the light of the more serious agony suffered by Michael Owen at the start of the match.

Eriksson was sympathetic towards Rooney, saying, 'It's not a problem. He was more disappointed with himself. We cannot risk him to be injured. He had played thirty minutes five days before, and it was not right professionally that he played ninety minutes. I think he was more upset at himself that he didn't play as well as he wanted in the second half. He will get better and better. We can't risk to get him injured playing too much too early.'

Gary Neville, Rooney's skipper at United and on the England bench himself because of injury, was not as easygoing. He grabbed hold of Rooney and told him to calm down, to get a grip of his temper. A source told me, 'Wayne felt he should have stayed on the pitch longer and was annoyed that Eriksson had hauled him off. But he did calm down when Gary had a word with him. He likes Neville and respects him – he knows from their United experiences that he is a man worth listening to and learning from.'

England had played poorly for much of their three group games, yet had finished top and were now on their way to Stuttgart for the clash with the South Americans. As often happens in World Cup history, the English side was evolving by accident. The injury to Owen had shown that they might be best served by a five-man midfield for the rest of the competition – with Owen Hargreaves or the more talented Michael Carrick in a holding role, and one lone striker . . . surely Rooney. That would enable Joe Cole, Steven Gerrard and Frank Lampard to break forward as they did in the Premiership and hopefully net the goals that would take the nation onwards.

It was the formation they employed for the second-round clash against Ecuador, but it did not function effectively. Carrick, in the holding role, was not a total success. Amazingly, Rooney was the man of the match, unofficially at least. Thrown into a one-man centre-forward role, he excelled, giving the Ecuadorian centre-backs a nightmare day at the office. There was much talk in the press that Wayne did not like to play this way, that he did not enjoy leading the line. That was a load of bollocks – he had told me it was a role he loved; indeed, he often pestered Sir Alex Ferguson to let him loose in it at United.

For the record, David Beckham's wonder goal – a free kick from 30 yards – settled the result. It had been another anaemic performance but resulted in a vital 1–0 victory. England were through to the quarter-finals and another showdown with Portugal and Eriksson's nemesis, Luis Felipe Scolari.

After the Ecuador match, Wayne admitted his joy at taking part in the tournament. He said, 'It is good to be here and back with the lads. We have done well, and I hope that can continue – I want to just try my best and try to help us win this competition. I have always been positive from the day I got injured. My aim was to take part, and I am really happy. I was always confident I would make it. I am doing good and it [his foot] is improving every day in training and with each game, and hopefully that can keep going.

'I will play anywhere the manager wants me to play, and if that is up front on my own or in a two, I am happy to do that. As long as we keep winning, that is the main thing, and I would gladly go the whole tournament without scoring if we won it.

'It [the system] gives the midfield a lot more chances, and as long as they're scoring I am not concerned. You have got to be more disciplined, stay up there and stretch it; it is a lot harder work, but I try and do it the best I can. I was quite pleased with my performance in the last game and I was delighted with the result, and if we get the same again, I would snatch your hand off.'

Was he looking for revenge against the Portuguese after that Euro 2004 defeat? 'I think we want to put the game from two years ago behind us and just get on with this tournament and try and progress to the semi-final,' he said. 'The previous games we haven't played to our best, but we have still managed to get the result we wanted, and hopefully that can continue. I think we have got a good chance and think we can win. We have got a lot of match winners. Joe Cole, Steven Gerrard, Frank Lampard – there are a lot of players who can take the game by the scruff of the neck and win the game for us.

'We don't take any notice of criticism, and as long as we keep winning I don't see any problem; the fans seem happy, and it is just the press bullying us up – when most countries get to the quarter-finals they are happy apart from ours.'

And what about the prospect of facing his Manchester United

teammate, the dazzling Cristiano Ronaldo, who had been injured in a bruising second-round encounter with the Dutch. Wayne said, 'Although I want him fit, it would be nice if he could just miss our game because he is a great player. If he plays, it will be a tough job for us. I have played with him week-in, week-out for the last three years, and he is a handful for any team and hopefully we can keep him quiet on the day.'

Rooney and England then headed for Gelsenkirchen and the Portuguese – and Wayne made it clear he wanted to score his first World Cup goal against them. He admitted his dream was to begin a challenge on Ronaldo's fabulous record – the Brazilian had just beaten German Gerd Müller's World Cup tally when he scored his 15th goal in the 3–0 second-round win against Ghana. Wayne said, 'I hope I can do what Ronaldo has done for Brazil in my career. He has been one of the best players over the last ten years. It would be nice to get that first World Cup goal, but as long as the team wins that is the main thing. There was a time when I thought I wouldn't be here. It was a bad time to get an injury. I just wanted to get myself fit, and I've managed to do that. I'm happy with the way things are going now. I don't know how I would feel if I scored after so long out. I couldn't tell you. But hopefully I will score soon. I'm hungry.'

Well, after what turned out to be a disastrous quarter-final, that aim to overhaul Ronaldo's record tally looked a trifle ambitious to say the least. By the time Wayne was sent off on 62 minutes, his total World Cup goals haul was *zero*. His tournament ended the way it had started in that sense – he had not scored in any of the qualifiers or any of the championship matches. But he *had* been sent off once. It made depressing reading, but, if we are honest, wasn't it maybe the inevitable outcome of an ill-conceived campaign by Eriksson to rush the boy back? There had been too much pressure piled on him, too many great expectations. Eriksson had even admitted that without the genius of Rooney success in the competition was almost impossible. The boy was carrying the whole world (cup) on his shoulders for England, and that was too much. It was unfair.

Ferguson had said a month earlier that men like Beckham should have been stepping forward to ease the burden. In the event, the sight of Beckham crying over his own misfortune – after he had been forced off with an injury ten minutes before Rooney was sent off – summed up much of what was wrong with England under Eriksson. Here he was, the captain of England, sobbing like a Gazza because he thought the injury meant he would play no further part should the nation advance. It made me cringe, and at best it was pathetic. Can you seriously imagine John Terry doing that? Or would he have been urging his men on, putting his own misfortune to one side? Eriksson's 'vision' had meant Beckham could never be dropped and that England was forced to play at a slower pace, relying all the time on a Beckham free-kick to salvage their campaign. Beckham was a 'star': he himself would probably have gone crazy if he had been dropped or subbed for reasons of form. And now he lay there on the bench, sobbing tears of self-pity.

Deprived of any support up front – couldn't Eriksson have played Aaron Lennon central up there with Rooney; after all, he had initially been a central striker before being converted to the wing – Rooney suffered against the Portuguese. He was dining on scraps here and there, and he was feeling the pace of it all. At the end of April, he had suffered a broken foot; on 1 July, he was expected to take on the most demanding role in football – leading the line alone. Inevitably, he became frustrated and, again sadly inevitably, he blew up. He was dismissed after stamping on Chelsea's Ricardo Carvalho and pushing away his Manchester United teammate Cristiano Ronaldo.

There can be no excuses for his lunge, studs first on the leg of Carvalho, nor can there be any excuse for the Ronaldo episode. Both incidents merited a red card for serious violent conduct. And, of course, you cannot simply brush away Rooney's tantrum as that of a young lad seeing red. He was 20 now and a veteran of big matches; he knew the opposition were aware of his short fuse and would try to get him sent off. All we can say in his defence is that he was carrying an awful lot of pressure for a 20 year old – carrying his country's hopes on those big shoulders. It was a classic example of the man–boy syndrome: he looked like a man but acted like a boy.

On the way to the dressing-room, he appeared to shout at Carvalho and Ronaldo, calling them 'fuckin' cheats'. Ronaldo had shamefully rushed to referee Horacio Elizondo after Rooney's lunge on Carvalho, apparently demanding a red card. He then winked at Luis Felipe Scolari as Rooney made his way to the dressing-room. My source said, 'Wayne was crying with rage in the dressing-room, throwing off his boots and shouting that they were all fuckin' cheats. He was particularly pissed off with Ronaldo, whom he had thought a friend at United. He was cursing him. If Real Madrid had really made a big offer for Ronaldo, United might be better off taking it, as it's hard to see how Rooney will play with Ronaldo for years to come now. He's not the sort who easily lets go of something like this.'

The source also told me that Rooney had tried to gain entry to the Portuguese dressing-room after the match to confront Ronaldo, but he was thwarted by the other Portuguese players.

Ronaldo would later try to defuse the situation, saying, 'The English press say the referee gave a red card because I spoke, but this is not true. I said, "Ref, this is foul", but I did not say "red card" because Wayne is my friend and I play at the same team.' TV pundit Alan Shearer summed up what Wayne was probably thinking at the time when he said, 'I think there's every chance that Wayne Rooney could go back to the Manchester United training ground and stick one on Ronaldo, because he hasn't helped him there. We all know he's frustrated, but he can't do that. He's lost his temper, he can't do that, and Ronaldo hasn't helped.'

Ronaldo's cause would not be helped by words emerging from the Portuguese camp directly after the game. It did seem that they had apparently worked on the idea of getting Rooney sent off, or at least rattling him, given his hot temper. That would explain Ronaldo's wink to 'Big Phil' – mission accomplished, boss. Whatever, Ferguson would have his work cut out if the two of them were to work together again. It was common knowledge at Old Trafford that Ronaldo was jealous of Rooney. Ronaldo was the prettier one, the one with the tricks, and yet the fans adored and idolised Rooney much more than him. He was their favourite and would remain so, especially now.

England deserved credit for the way they defended at 0–0 for almost another hour after Rooney was sent off – heroics that made it all the harder to understand how they continually bottle it when it comes to a penalty shootout. Frank Lampard ended his disappointing tournament with a miss, while Steven Gerrard and Jamie Carragher also failed. A final question: just why was Carragher sent on as a sub by Eriksson to take a penalty when he had only taken a couple in his career? Why not Michael Carrick – a much more accomplished hitter of the ball? The biggest irony of the night was still to come, as Ronaldo, the man who had contributed to Rooney's dismissal, stepped up to win it for Portugal with a perfect spot-kick.

By the Monday after the match, Rooney and Ronaldo were trying to take the sting out of their very public disagreement. Ronaldo would say, 'At the end [of the match] we texted each other and between us everything's been cleared. The things that have been said regarding me and my teammate and friend Rooney are incredible. He wished me the best of luck in the World Cup. He told me we had a great team and that if we continued to play like this, we would go far.

'He wasn't angry with me, and, moreover, he told me to completely ignore what the English press has said, that all they wanted was to create confusion, but we are already used to that.'

Ronaldo added that he was not to blame for Rooney's dismissal, saying: 'I am not a referee and I don't have the power to send off a player. I had nothing to do with the fact that the referee showed the red card.'

And Rooney issued a statement on the same day in which he said, 'I want to say absolutely categorically that I did not intentionally put my foot down on Carvalho. I bear no ill-feeling to Cristiano but am disappointed he chose to get involved. When the referee produced the red card, I was amazed – gobsmacked.' He added, 'Obviously I'm bitterly disappointed to have been sent off in a World Cup finals match for England. I remember the incident clearly and have seen it several times since on TV. I am of the same opinion now as I was at the time that what happened didn't warrant a red card. If anything, I feel we should have had a free-kick for the fouls committed on me during the same incident.

'If you ask any player – and indeed almost any fan – they will tell you that I am straight and honest in the way I play. From what I've seen in the World Cup, most players would have gone to ground at the slightest contact, but my only thought then was to keep possession for England.'

Then referee Horacio Elizondo got in on the act, saying Ronaldo did not influence his decision to send off Rooney. Elizondo told *The Times*: 'It was violent play and therefore he got a red card. People can say what they want [about Ronaldo] but this had absolutely no influence. For me it was a clear red card.'

Sky TV pundit Andy Gray summed up what most people felt about Rooney's statement when he said, 'I think it has Sir Alex Ferguson's hand behind it. He probably wanted to put a lid on this as quickly as possible before it all got really out of hand.'

It had been a familiar end to World Cup 2006 for England – and just as much so, unfortunately, for Wayne Rooney. In his final news conference as England head coach, Sven-Göran Eriksson emerged with some credit, making a plea for the nation to look after Rooney and forgive him. Eriksson said, 'Wayne Rooney is the golden boy of English football. Don't kill him, because you will need him. He's a fantastic player and he has his temperament, but you can't hold that against him.'

It was a good rallying point. The likes of David Beckham would probably never play in another World Cup, but, all things being fair and equal, Rooney would have maybe another three ahead of him. He would also surely be the key man for England in Euro 2008 – a tournament they could conceivably win if new head coach Steve McClaren and his back-up men build the team around Rooney. Germany 2006 had been another learning curve for the precocious Rooney. He had not been the star of the show, but he would be the player everyone would be talking about long after the tournament ended. He had suffered a setback in Germany but would surely return wiser and stronger. At just 20, Rooney had experienced and achieved more than some players would in an entire career – and the real beauty of it all was that if he could learn from his red rage, not go off the rails and stay fit, the best was surely still to come . . .